Constructing a Powerful Approach to Teaching and Learning in Elementary Social Studies

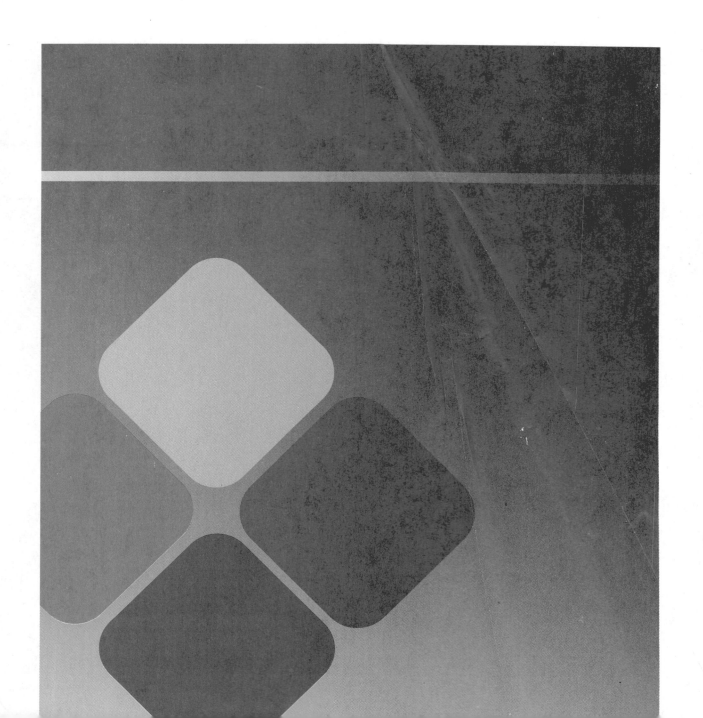

Constructing a Powerful Approach to Teaching and Learning in Elementary Social Studies

S. G. Grant
State University of New York at Buffalo

Bruce VanSledright
University of Maryland at College Park

Houghton Mifflin Company Boston • New York

Senior sponsoring editor: Loretta Wolozin
Development editor: Lisa Mafrici
Senior editorial production coordinator: Carla Thompson
Editorial assistant: Magdalena Carpenter
Senior production/design coordinator: Sarah Ambrose
Senior cover design coordinator: Deborah Azerrad Savona
Senior manufacturing coordinator: Priscilla Bailey
Marketing manager: Jay Hu
Marketing associate: Caroline Guy

Cover design and image: Diana Coe / ko Design Studio
Line art: Jessyca Broekman

Text credit: Passages by Linda Levstik are from J. Brophy (ed.), *Advances in Research on Teaching,* Vol. 4, Copyright © 1993 JAI Press. Reprinted with permission.
Photo credits: **Chapter 1** p. 19: © Conklin/Monkmeyer; p. 21: © Richard Hutchings/PhotoEdit; p. 24: © Bob Daemmrich; p. 28: © Elizabeth Crews; p. 29: © Elizabeth Crews; p. 30: © Spencer Grant/PhotoEdit; **Chapter 2** p. 46: © Myrleen Ferguson/PhotoEdit; p. 50: © Elizabeth Crews; p. 54: © Elizabeth Crews; p. 63: Everett Collection, Inc.; **Chapter 3** p. 85: © Mimi Forsyth/Monkmeyer Press; p. 87: © Laura Dwight; p. 102: © Elizabeth Crews; **Chapter 4** p. 117: © Elizabeth Crews; p. 126: © Jeff Dunn/Stock Boston; p. 128: © Bettmann/CORBIS; **Chapter 5** p. 145: © Michael Newman/PhotoEdit; p. 164: © Bob Daemmrich; **Chapter 6** p. 185: © Bettmann/CORBIS; p. 192: © Paul S. Conklin; p. 201: © Elizabeth Crews; p. 203: © Michael Newman/PhotoEdit; **Chapter 7** p. 219: © Elizabeth Crews; p. 221: © Bob Daemmrich; p. 223: © Paul S. Conklin; p. 224: © Bob Daemmrich; **Chapter 8** p. 241: © Jonathan Nourok/PhotoEdit; p. 250: © Paul S. Conklin; p. 258: © Elizabeth Crews; **Chapter 9** p. 267: © Elizabeth Crews; p. 269: © Elizabeth Crews; p. 273: © Elizabeth Crews; p. 281: © Tommy Hultgren/Daemmrich Photography Associates.

Printed in the U.S.A.

Library of Congress Catalog Card Number: 00-133858

ISBN: 0-395-81121-X

1 2 3 4 5 6 7 8 9 - DOC - 04 03 02 01 00

Contents

Preface

We wrote *Constructing a Powerful Approach to Teaching and Learning in Elementary Social Studies* largely because we were dissatisfied with the elementary social studies methods books we reviewed for our courses. In our eyes, these books failed to capture the vibrancy and power we see in school classrooms where the subject of social studies is well taught. So we built our respective methods courses around articles, book chapters, and conference papers that spoke to the issues we thought important. In this book, we have built a text that explicitly frames and develops a coherent and practical approach to teaching and learning elementary social studies. We encourage our colleagues to supplement and extend their use of the text with additional materials designed to further enrich their students' course experiences.

Students of all ages routinely describe social studies as "lifeless." We think that part of the problem is an unmanageable, neutralized curriculum, one that lists every person, place, and event of note, but makes them all seem of equal importance. Another part of the problem is the overwhelming pressure to give more and more time to the teaching of reading and mathematics to the exclusion of subjects like science and social studies. One last part of the problem is standardized testing, which typically promotes a "just the facts" approach to social studies.

These are all serious issues, yet we know that the potential for powerful teaching and learning exists. This book—through the in-text features and the accompanying instructor's resource manual—strives to help all teachers achieve that potential.

A Commonplaces Approach

Central to powerful teaching are thoughtful and reflective teachers who understand the learners they work with, who know their subject matter well, who hold a wide instructional repertoire, and who work to create powerful learning environments. This view of teaching reflects the *commonplaces of education,* a framework for classroom decision making that we adapted from the work of Joseph Schwab. The individual commonplace elements—*learners and learning, subject matter, teachers and teaching,* and *classroom environment*—are useful ways for teachers to think about dimensions of their classroom practice. Taken together, however, the commonplaces are even more powerful. In interaction, the commonplaces indeed offer a means of understanding classroom problems and situations and of planning effective units of study. They also insure that all areas of teaching practice are examined in the process of learning to teach.

Organization of the Text

We use the commonplaces to orient our own instructional practices and to shape our course syllabi. The value of that approach led us to use the commonplaces as the organizational framework for this book. Part One consists of an introductory chapter explaining the commonplaces followed by chapters devoted to each of the commonplaces in turn. Part Two examines the commonplaces in action, with chapters on purposes and goals, planning, and reflection.

The Commonplaces of Education In Chapter 1, "The Commonplaces of Education: Creating a Framework for the Social Studies Classroom," we present an overview of the commonplaces, both individually and in interaction. To do so, we dissect a case study of a first-grade social studies lesson, pointing out how each commonplace element comes into play. We also use this chapter as an opportunity to introduce other ideas that figure prominently throughout the book. Those ideas include a constructivist view of learning, the integrative "threads" that connect subject matters, big ideas as a way of framing teaching units, and the development of genuine classroom communities.

Learners and Learning Chapter 2, "Learners and Learning: Understanding What Students Know About Social Studies and How They Come to Know It," is devoted to the first commonplace—*learners and learning.* There has been considerable recent research on what children know about social studies ideas, particularly in terms of historical understanding. We draw heavily on this research and on cases of classroom learning to explore what elementary-age students know about social studies concepts, where their knowledge comes from, and how they learn new ideas. In each instance, we contrast constructivist and behaviorist theories of learning. We conclude that, while constructivist approaches are not problem-free, they provide a more powerful lens on how learners learn than behaviorist theories do.

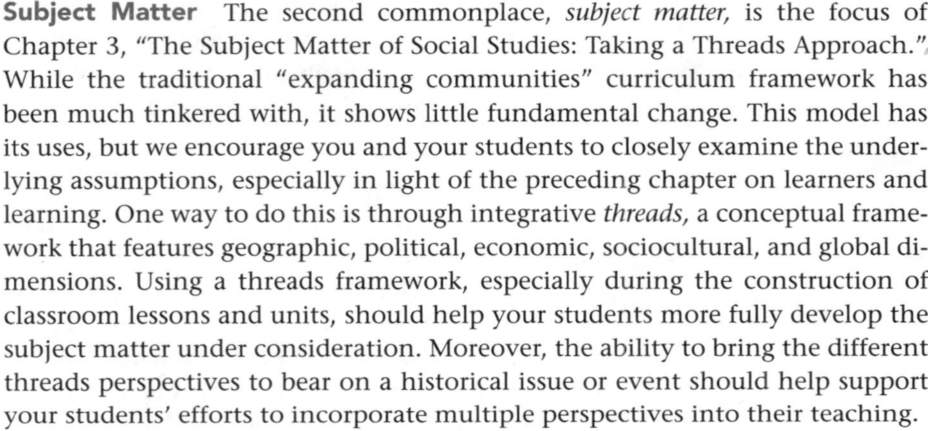

Subject Matter The second commonplace, *subject matter,* is the focus of Chapter 3, "The Subject Matter of Social Studies: Taking a Threads Approach." While the traditional "expanding communities" curriculum framework has been much tinkered with, it shows little fundamental change. This model has its uses, but we encourage you and your students to closely examine the underlying assumptions, especially in light of the preceding chapter on learners and learning. One way to do this is through integrative *threads,* a conceptual framework that features geographic, political, economic, sociocultural, and global dimensions. Using a threads framework, especially during the construction of classroom lessons and units, should help your students more fully develop the subject matter under consideration. Moreover, the ability to bring the different threads perspectives to bear on a historical issue or event should help support your students' efforts to incorporate multiple perspectives into their teaching.

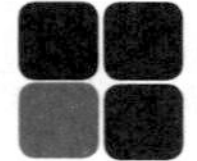

Teachers and Teaching While all of the commonplaces are important, this is a social studies teaching methods book. Consequently, we dedicate two chapters to the third commonplace, *teachers and teaching.* As in each of the preceding chapters, we draw from rich classroom examples to illustrate the point that teaching social studies is more than just having a grab bag filled with interesting strategies and fun activities.

In Chapter 4, "Teaching Social Studies I: Working with Big Ideas," we introduce the notion of a *big idea.* Neither fact, topic, nor concept, a big idea is instead a question or generalization that facilitates unit planning by helping both prospective and practicing teachers decide what to teach, what instructional approaches to use and when, and how to engage learners' thinking. We find that our students initially struggle with the construct of a big idea, so we outline several paths to "big idealand." To conclude this first teaching chapter, we discuss the use of big ideas within Lee Shulman's "Phases of Pedagogical Reasoning," a framework that we find particularly valuable as a way of thinking about teaching.

In Chapter 5, "Teaching Social Studies II: Choosing Teaching Strategies, Curriculum Materials, and Assessment Techniques," we look closely at three major elements of instruction: *teaching strategies, curriculum materials,* and *assessments.* The teaching strategies section features descriptions of a wide range of methods associated with individual, small group, and whole class instruction. The curriculum materials section is similarly wide ranging as we describe the various textual, representational, and computer resources on which teachers and students can draw. The assessment section begins with a distinction between assessment and evaluation, where the former aims at understanding what students know and can do and the latter aims at judging student products. We then discuss the differences among authentic, test-based, informal, and portfolio assessments. We conclude the teacher and teaching chapters with a discussion of the influences on teachers' content and pedagogical decisions. Using a case study, we explore and categorize those influences as personal, organizational, and policy factors, and we demonstrate how they interact.

Classroom Environment The fourth commonplace—*classroom environment*—is the focus of Chapter 6, "The Classroom Environment: Creating a Genuine Community." Teaching, learning, and subject matter are all important, but so too is the environment in which these activities occur. The notion of classroom environment or climate can be fuzzy, though, so we talk about it in terms of *discourse, classroom organization,* and *dispositions*. By discourse we mean the kind of classroom talk that occurs between teachers and students. Classroom organization refers to the ways that teachers organize students for classroom activities. And dispositions are those values and attitudes that teachers hope to foster in class. To ground these ideas, we draw a contrast between a traditional classroom environment and what we call a *genuine classroom community.* In our view, traditional classrooms reflect a factory model of schooling where the norms of quiet, efficient, individual work are valued. Genuine classrooms, we argue, focus on ideas, inquiry, and active participation. We conclude the chapter with a discussion of how teachers can negotiate the construction of a genuine community in their classrooms.

Purposes and Goals In Chapter 7, "Purposes, Goals, and Objectives for Teaching and Learning," we take up the purposes, goals, and objectives of social studies. While most methods books begin with this chapter, we believe that it makes more sense to examine the purposes of social studies *after* students have thought through some of the more practical issues of teaching and learning. The central issue of this chapter is the idea that, even if there is something of a consensus that social studies aims at citizenship education, there is neither consensus on how to define "good" citizenship nor is there consensus on how to reach that goal. We illustrate this situation through cases of four teachers and the goal frameworks they employ. To help readers construct their own goal frameworks, we discuss resources to which they might turn, such as curriculum standards and definitions of social studies, and we suggest issues to be mindful of as they make their decisions.

Unit Planning Chapter 8, "Unit Planning and the Commonplaces," provides the site in which to pull together two big themes of the book—the commonplaces and unit planning. We first demonstrate the usefulness of the commonplaces as a means of analyzing classroom situations and as a means of understanding common classroom problems. Then we discuss the nuts and bolts of unit planning through examples of unit plans developed by three of our students. We offer suggestions about the components of a good unit plan, an example of how to create a shorthand approach to unit planning, and a discussion of the purposes for developing unit plans.

Reflection Chapter 9, "Becoming a Reflective Social Studies Teacher," serves as a capstone to the book. Reflectivity, we believe, is the core of good teaching, for without it, teachers are little more than instructional robots. Thus, the ideas developed to this point—the commonplaces, threads, big ideas, and the like—will only be meaningful if teachers adopt a reflective stance. We discuss reflection in three ways. First, we describe the importance of personal and professional growth. We argue that teachers who grow personally are also growing professionally, and the reverse. Second, we discuss the nature of reflection. To do so, we use an e-mail exchange between us to demonstrate what reflection can look like and to serve as a background for a discussion of teacher educator Linda Valli's useful categories of reflective practice. Finally, we talk about "breaking the silences." The sociologist Dan Lortie decried the "egg-crate" design of school buildings for its tendency to undermine teachers' interactions with other adults. This silence tends to be destructive because, while self-reflection is essential, so too is reflective conversation with others. To that end, we strongly encourage teachers to break out of their classrooms and to find colleagues who will listen to, challenge, and respect them.

Special Practical Features

To supplement the substantive ideas just described, we built a number of practical features into the text. These features appear regularly, and they are often signaled by the appearance of unique icons. These features include the following:

CLASSROOM EXAMPLE

Vibrant Classroom Illustrations Examples of actual social studies teaching episodes are a key feature of this book. The kind of ambitious and powerful teaching and learning we advocate is no easy task. Looking deeply at the practices of real elementary school teachers, however, provides a powerful opportunity to explore the many issues classroom teachers face.

RELEVANT RESEARCH

Relevant Research Teachers who know what research says about teaching and learning social studies are in a better position to make and enact sound pedagogical decisions. Through listening to social studies teachers talk about their teaching and through our experiences as social studies teachers ourselves, we have become convinced that a working knowledge of the social studies research fosters higher levels of reflectiveness about teaching than would otherwise be the case.

TEACHING RESOURCES

Teaching Resources Good social studies teachers have good resources. This simple truth spurred us to include as many resources for teaching elementary social studies (e.g., Internet sites, trade books, articles, and multimedia resources) as possible. Long lists of resources can be off-putting, however, so we offer these resources in the context of how they might be integrated into social studies learning opportunities.

CLASSROOM MANAGEMENT

Classroom Management We firmly believe that good teaching is less about managing children's behavior and more about managing ideas in classrooms of children. To that end, we see the commonplace elements as integral to an expanded vision of classroom management. Issues of classroom management appear, then, not in a separate, isolated chapter, but rather throughout the book and in real contexts of teaching and learning.

TEACHER REFLECTION

Teacher Reflection Part of ambitious social studies teaching is constructing powerful teaching lessons and units that push both teachers and learners to greater understandings. Good teachers are able to step back and reflect on ideas, issues, and situations that arise both in their classrooms and in the nature of schooling writ large. To this end, we include a number of stopping places in the text where we use the issue at hand to pose questions for further thought.

CHOOSING GOALS

Choosing Goals As we noted, while many books like this one begin with a rather dry talk of the "proper" goals and aims of social studies teaching and learning, we postpone the formal discussion of goals until readers have had an opportunity to examine a range of teaching and learning issues. This is not to say that choosing goals is unimportant. It is, but we believe that thinking about and choosing goals becomes more meaningful in the context of real teaching and learning situations.

In Your Classroom Having a wide instructional repertoire is invaluable, so we include a range of practical teaching suggestions through our "In Your Classroom" feature. In these boxes, we describe teaching strategies such as jigsaws, book talks, mini-lessons, learning centers, and the like.

Glossary While we strove to write a jargon-free book and to define those terms that we employ in the text, we nevertheless recognize the usefulness of a glossary of key concepts.

Appendix of Children's Literature Resources The recent growth of trade books provides a powerful tool for teaching and learning social studies. An arbitrary listing made little sense to us, however, so we have appended a specific list of titles that correspond to the various unit ideas we present throughout the book.

Instructor's Resource Manual As an additional supplement to the text, we provide an *Instructor's Resource Manual.* Part One lays out a sample syllabus illustrating both ten- and fifteen-week schedules. Part Two presents a sampler of readings, activities, and assessments designed around the chapter sequence in the book. This listing is not meant to be exhaustive, but rather to suggest some of the elements we have found useful in engaging our students' thinking. Part Three offers our view of assessment keyed to the assignments described in Part Two. Part Four of the manual is an appendix of overhead transparencies, classroom handouts, and copies of two suggested readings that are no longer in print. We have secured permission for instructors to reproduce them for classroom use.

Acknowledgments

Teaching and learning are among the most human of activities. We are who we are in large part because we have taught and learned from others. Acknowledging all those who have taught us would be as exhaustive as it would be humbling, for it would include both those whose ostensible role was *teacher,* as well as those whom outsiders would define as our *learners.* The simple truth is that the soil from which we have grown as teachers has been as enriched by our interactions with our students as it has by our interactions with our teachers. A hearty "thank you" goes out to those who put up with our "studently" fumblings in their classes and to those who put up with nascent "teacherly" fumblings in ours.

While we can't possibly thank all those who helped us to this point, we can express our appreciation to those who were directly responsible for making this book as good as we hope it is. First, we thank the teachers whose lesson and unit plans figure prominently in the text of this book: Jill Korse, Katie Salisbury, Kristen Stricker, and Darlene Swannie. Second, we thank those once anonymous reviewers whose comments on earlier drafts helped us think through issues big and small: Margaret A. Laughlin, University of Wisconsin, Green Bay; Lani M. Martin, California State University, Fullerton; Saundra J. McKee, Clarion University of Pennsylvania; and Patrick G. Mullins, University of South Florida at Sarasota. Third, we thank those folks who were willing to read and respond to individual chapters along the way: Sandra Cimbricz, Lynn Pullano, Valerie Scibelli, and Michael Tinney. Fourth, we offer our thanks to the many teachers who have invited us into their classrooms to observe and to interview them about their classroom practices. Several of these teachers figure prominently in the classroom examples that appear in this book and without them the text would suffer greatly. And fifth, we thank the folks at Houghton Mifflin whose patience and expertise we surely (and sorely) tried: Loretta Wolozin, Lisa Mafrici, Elaine Silverstein, Sarah Rodriguez, Janet Young, and Carla Thompson.

Finally, we thank our families who put up with our doubts, whining, and long hours away at the computer. Bruce wishes to thank his partner, Joan, for her gracious understanding of his neglect of her while writing this book, and for listening to his complaints about the work involved. He also wishes to thank several of his colleagues at the University of Maryland who offered moral support when the going was tough and who provided helpful suggestions based on their own book-writing experiences. S. G. would like to thank Anne, Alexander, and Claire. He's indebted to Anne for her patience, good humor, and encouraging words, and he's indebted to Alexander and Claire for their tolerance of dad "playing" on his computer instead of playing with them.

S. G. G.
B. A. V.

To the Student

Constructing a Powerful Approach to Teaching Social Studies

So you want to be an elementary school teacher? That's a superb vocational choice. Elementary school teachers bring to children a fascinating world that can help them understand their lives in ways that expand their minds, enhance their curiosity, and transform them into people who are poised to enter the world of democratic citizenship, with all the rights and responsibilities that entails. This is both a rich and satisfying calling and a significant challenge. At various points you will function simultaneously as an educational generalist (someone who knows about and teaches all the elementary school subjects) and as a subject-matter specialist (someone who can focus in and teach a specific subject in depth). In this book we will help you attend to the latter, especially in the broad area called social studies. Social studies plays a crucial role in bringing the world to youngsters, but you wouldn't necessarily know that by looking into what goes on in most elementary classrooms.

Think for a minute about some of your most memorable learning experiences. Briefly describe one of them on a piece of paper. Simply note its general contours. Now think about why you picked this experience. We suspect that the learning experience you remembered was powerful because someone, most likely a teacher, challenged you to care about what you were learning. You felt compelled to accept the challenge; your curiosity to learn more was piqued; you were deeply engaged. We often ask our prospective teachers to do this short exercise. The responses they provide are interesting. Many note powerful learning experiences in mathematics or science. Some mention the wonder of learning to read. Few, however, say anything about social studies. We write this book because we believe the ideas we present in it can help change this. We want your students to remember the absorbing, curiosity-provoking, wholly-engaging social studies you provide as some of their most powerful learning experiences. In short, we are asking you to become a thoughtful, reflective, and, above all, ambitious elementary school social studies teacher, a teacher who challenges his or her students to meet the highest expectations.[1]

Although some debate surrounds the definition of social studies education, a debate we discuss in more detail beginning in Chapter 3, we define social studies in elementary school as the teaching and learning of how human beings interact with other human beings and with the world around them. Much of this interaction takes place in social contexts, thus the term *social studies,* or in other words, "the study of the social." For example, humans attempt to adapt to their physical surroundings not only by finding ways to use the land to feed themselves, but by building shelters against the elements, by designing systems of exchange for goods and services, and by creating rules and norms that guide and protect these exchange interactions. Because these activities and practices change over time, knowing something about how change occurs is also important. Elementary social studies focuses on these types of ideas and helps children learn about and understand them.

Social studies must rely on a variety of social science disciplines and the arts and humanities for its subject matter. As a result, the social studies draw their fundamental ideas and concepts from academic disciplines such as geography, economics, sociology, history, and literature. To illustrate, examine how the National Council for the Social Studies (or NCSS), a large teacher organization, defines the social studies. Notice the wide array of these disciplines and how they link to the goal of educating informed citizens:

> Social studies is the integrated study of the social sciences and humanities to promote civic competence. Within the school program, social studies provides coordinated, systematic study drawing upon such disciplines as anthropology, archeology, economics, geography, history, law, philosophy, political science, psychology, religion, and sociology. The primary purpose of social studies is to help young people develop the ability to make informed and reasoned decisions for the public good as citizens of a culturally diverse, democratic society in an interdependent world. (National Council for the Social Studies, 1993, p. 7)

For more on the nature of social studies and the academic disciplines it draws from, visit the NCSS web site at http://www.ncss.org.

The Role and Importance of Social Studies

As the NCSS definition suggests, social studies is the curriculum area devoted to preparing students to become democratic citizens. Some might even go so far as to say that social studies should be the only part of the curriculum to prepare students to become citizens of our democracy. We disagree; every subject in elementary school should help prepare democratic citizens, and social studies must play a crucial role in that effort. At least in the United States, education has long been expected to prepare children to assume the mantle of active, involved citizens who become immersed in their local communities, exercise their voting rights thoughtfully and intelligently, and pursue the common good. It's hard for us to imagine how we could neglect the social studies—the social education of children—and accomplish this goal.

In teaching children social studies, you will open their minds and hearts to a bigger, more expansive understanding of how the social world they inhabit hangs together, how the pieces fit. You will teach children where they come from as human beings, where they are, and where, with a little imagination, they might possibly go. Your task will be to open up and share this wonderful world with children by teaching them connections among and between

- How people interact with each other,
- How they interact with the natural world around them,
- How they have done so in the past, and
- How they might do so in the future.

Teaching and learning these connections is a process. It involves understanding where we as a democratic society have been in a world where some have shared our democratic sentiments and ideals and others have not. It's also a process of teaching children about where we still might go as we try to move away from our collective shortcomings and closer to our democratic ideals. We attempt to learn from our national and cultural faults as well as our successes, so that, as students learn to take on their local and global citizenship rights and responsibilities, they can dream and imagine possibilities worth striving for and achieving.

This is the world of social studies and its relationship to democratic citizenship. As a teacher of elementary school children, you may consider it a daunting responsibility to undertake, but that responsibility is paired by the thrilling ride on which good social studies teaching will take you and your learners. That ride will begin on these pages.

Key Themes and Concepts

Here is a brief overview of the key themes or concepts that we develop in this book.

- The commonplaces of education
- Constructivist learning theory
- The big ideas of social studies
- The threads approach
- Ambitious teaching
- Genuine classroom community
- Goal-mindedness and reflection

The Commonplaces of Education

We structured this book around what a leading educational theorist named Joseph Schwab (1978) called the *commonplaces of education*. Schwab maintained that we can hardly address the educational process without considering four sites in which actions and interactions occur. The four sites, or commonplaces include (1) learners and learning, (2) subject matter, (3) teachers and teaching, and (4) milieu, or classroom environment. Schwab argued that each commonplace is important in its own right, but just as importantly, each is also connected to and depends on the other commonplaces. Figure I.1 illustrates the four commonplaces and indicates their interrelationships. We use this structure to make sure that we touch upon all those important elements that go into the educational process, all those matters that ambitious social studies teachers think about as they learn and prepare to teach. We explore these commonplaces in more detail in Chapter 1 in order to give you a better sense of how we use them to provide the book's structure.

Figure I.1 • The Commonplaces of Education

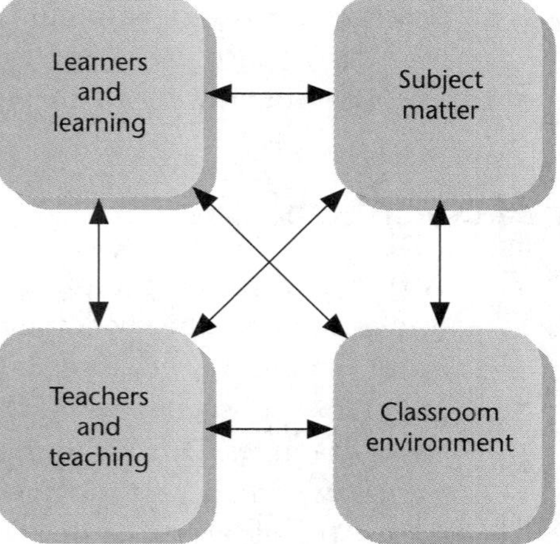

Constructivist Learning Theory

Our efforts in this book are underwritten by what some call a *constructivist* theory of learning. We argue that children are hardly passive creatures that sit silently while you pour ideas and concepts and facts into their heads, a view largely derived from the psychological theory of *behaviorism* and B. F. Skinner. We are convinced by loads of recent research that, by the time that you see them in elementary school, children have already developed all sorts of interesting ideas about their social worlds and that they will continue to construct new meanings and understandings around these ideas. Although by adult standards these ideas may appear alternately well-founded or naive, they are the raw materials you have to work with. You will need to ferret out your students' preexisting ideas and understandings, build on them, challenge them, and expand them. We argue that you, the teacher, can shape and influence the new ideas your students construct by carefully designing the learning opportunities they encounter and monitoring the meaning-making process. In this way, you will clearly affect how they come to understand their social world—never quite completely, but in significant ways nonetheless. We stress this perspective regarding constructivist theory both implicitly and explicitly all the way through this book. We discuss constructivism in much more detail in Chapter 2.

Constructivist theory also applies to you as a prospective social studies teacher. Throughout the book, we encourage you to interact with the ideas we propose to use your prior knowledge and understanding to explore those ideas not only in your mind as you read, but also with your teachers and your peers. However, consistent with our approach to constructivist theory, we must point out that we also are trying to shape your ideas about being a social studies teacher through what we present.

The Big Ideas of Social Studies

With regard to the commonplace that deals with the *subject matter* of social studies, we place heavy emphasis on working from what we call *big ideas,* and the questions they provoke. By big ideas, we mean the powerful and compelling questions and statements that run throughout the social studies. Here are a couple of examples. One big idea useful in teaching upper-elementary-grade social studies would address the question of revolution, as in the American Revolution, a struggle waged by British colonists against England in the late eighteenth century. Questions that could be asked include:

- Why were the colonists interested in separating from England?
- What did they perceive as the costs and benefits in doing so?
- What did the English think of the willfulness of the colonists and how did they react?
- Was the American Revolution necessary?

For the lower elementary grades, a big idea could hinge on questions of citizenship. Here, the questions might include:

- What makes a good citizen?

- What responsibilities do citizens have to the society in which they live?
- What rights do citizens deserve as members of that society?

These are just two examples that emerge when you consider teaching with a big idea such as the notion of revolution or citizenship.

We will stress how structuring your teaching around these big ideas is essential to bringing powerful social studies learning opportunities to your students. We will demonstrate how to work with these big ideas, how to generate questions around them to fuel the lesson-planning process. We also attempt to engage you in some mental conversation regarding these ideas.

The Threads Approach

We use the concept of subject matter *threads* to illustrate how you might draw from many of the social studies subject matters (for example, history, sociology, psychology, geography, economics) to structure the kinds of questions you generate and to build the learning opportunities you invite your students to engage in. To illustrate, take the "American Revolution" example we noted above. In choosing to break from England, the North American colonists believed they had clear *economic* reasons for doing so (for example, avoid paying taxes to England, more free trade). But they also had powerful *political* reasons (for example, desire to govern themselves, feeling unrepresented in England, desire for a more democratic—less monarchical—rule). In addition to these reasons, they had *sociocultural* reasons (Americans had formed their own separate culture and way of life in America and they sought to protect it), and *geographic* concerns (Americans possessed many natural resources that they wished to exploit without interference from England). Finally, the conflict between the colonies and England took place in a *global* context.

As Figure I.2 illustrates, each of the threads relates to a traditional academic discipline. For our purposes, these geographic, political, economic, sociocultural, and global elements are the subject matter threads you can use to build understandings around constructs, such as revolution. You can use them to generate integrative questions that allow comparisons across ideas separated by time and space. The threads pull together the sort of compelling questions people want to explore. Working with them enriches social studies learning by framing out the big ideas and giving them power to entice the imaginations of children.

Ambitious Teaching

We have high expectations of ourselves and of you. We sincerely hope to inspire you to engage your students in *ambitious* social studies teaching that motivates them to embrace powerful ideas and concepts. As noted, because much social

Figure I.2 • The Threads, Both Individually and In Interaction

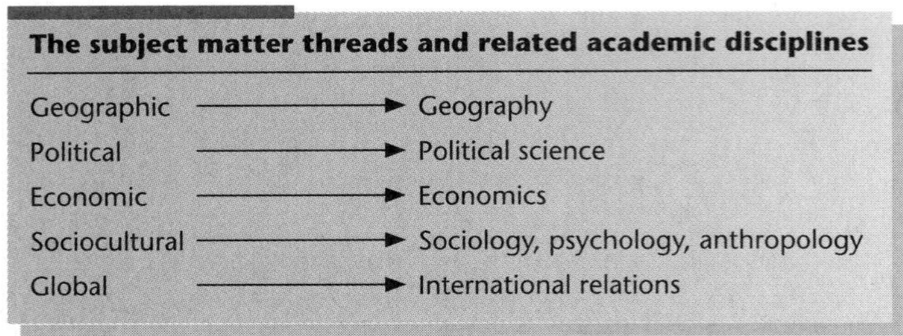

The subject matter threads and related academic disciplines

Geographic	Geography
Political	Political science
Economic	Economics
Sociocultural	Sociology, psychology, anthropology
Global	International relations

studies teaching is banal, kids end up disliking social studies. You can change this by being ambitious with what you do with your students. We have tried to make this book a straightforward learning tool, but one that challenges you. If you are inspired by the power of big social studies ideas and threads and the thrill that comes from teaching about them, you will learn to make them integral to the way you construct your classroom learning environment. This brings us to the sixth key theme.

Genuine Classroom Community

Rather than leaving the whole idea of classroom management and organization to those who write separate books about the subject, we devote a chapter to how you might go about constructing what we call a *genuine classroom community* with your students. If you work from big ideas, employ the subject matter threads and intriguing questions, and invite and challenge your students with these powerful and ambitious approaches, you will need a special type of learning environment. This genuine classroom community will have unique characteristics not easily found or described in generic books on classroom management. We'd be remiss if we didn't talk about the sort of learning community we think is necessary to pull off ambitious social studies teaching and learning, not to mention the fact that leaving it out would mean we were neglecting one of the commonplaces—the classroom environment.

Goal-Mindedness and Reflection

And finally, we think it is critical to emphasize the importance of being *goal-minded and reflective* about your social studies teaching practice. Goal-mindedness refers to the desire to develop and work from a set of educational goals for teaching social studies that pivot around a conception of "good citizenship." Now, having said that, we are quite aware of the many definitions of good citizenship. In developing a set of goals around good citizenship, your perspectives will shift and change over time. This leads us to stress the power of engaging in continual reflection about the nature of your teaching practice and the goals from which you work.

These seven themes—The Commonplaces of Education, Constructivist Learning Theory, Big Ideas, The Threads Approach, Ambitious Teaching, Genuine Classroom Community, and Goal-Mindedness and Reflection—form the substance of our ideas about becoming a successful elementary social studies teacher. The commonplaces serve as the overall structuring component, ensuring that we include all of the important aspects of education as Schwab (1978) described them. Constructivist learning theory, as its name implies, frames the key element of commonplace learners and learning. Big ideas and the threads approach anchor our treatment of the subject matter commonplace. Ambitious teaching is the central theme of teachers and teaching. And for the commonplace classroom environment, the theme of building a genuine classroom community takes center stage. Goal-mindedness and reflection themes invite you to step back from the four commonplaces as we describe them and ask yourself about your own beliefs and educational philosophies and how they influence both what we are saying about learning to teach social studies and the sort of social studies teacher you wish to become.

Features of This Book

We have built into this book practical and unique features that we hope make it a useful learning aid. These features appear regularly throughout the book and are marked by special icons, one for each feature. Here we list and briefly describe these features and introduce you to the icons.

CLASSROOM EXAMPLE

Vibrant Classroom Examples

Throughout the book, we take you into the elementary social studies classroom for examples of actual teaching episodes. We want you, the reader and prospective teacher, to dig deeply into classroom life and see real-life illustrations of the points we make. In such classroom examples, we'll show you what ambitious social studies teaching looks like. We want you to come away from reading these vignettes knowing that real social studies teachers are out there inviting and challenging their students to seize on the power and excitement of learning about social studies big ideas. We hope that these sorts of examples provide encouragement for you to become a similarly ambitious social studies teacher.

Relevant Research

We include recent relevant research about teaching and learning social studies wherever possible. We believe that a teacher who knows something about what the research says is in a much better position to reason soundly and effectively about the many, many teaching choices to be made. Listening to social studies teachers talk about their teaching—and our experiences as social studies teachers—convince us that a healthy working knowledge of the social studies research fosters higher levels of reflectiveness about teaching. In other words, the more ideas about classrooms, teaching, and learning you acquire, the better off you are.

Teaching Resources

We attempt to include as many resources for teaching elementary social studies as possible (Internet sites and tools, trade books, articles, multimedia, the like). In doing this, we illustrate these resources in the context of how they might be integrated into social studies learning opportunities.

Classroom Management

We discuss classroom management in the context of building a classroom learning community that illustrates and supports thoughtful and ambitious social studies teaching, the type we describe throughout the book.

Teacher Reflection

Part of ambitious teaching is constructing powerful teaching lessons and units that push both you and your students to greater understandings. To this end, "In Your Classroom" boxes offer practical suggestions for ratcheting up your teaching. Just as central to ambitious teaching, however, is the ability to step back and reflect on ideas, issues, and situations that arise both in your classroom and in the nature of schooling writ large. In short, good teaching is as much a mental process as it is a physical one. To encourage your thinking, we include a range of questions to ponder.

Choosing Goals

Finally, we discuss the importance of being a reflective social studies teacher. That means thinking about what you are doing in relationship to the goals you have for your students. Rather than begin with the traditional talk about the "proper" goals and aims of social studies teaching and learning, we postpone this discussion until near the end, so that we can provide beforehand some important context regarding learning, classroom organization, subject matter, and teaching. From this context, we offer a more meaningful discussion of goals, for it is within the actual classroom, and in the messages that are exchanged there, that goals have real presence. Choosing goals without supporting classroom context seems to us rather unproductive.

Content and Organization of This Book

This book is organized essentially around the four commonplaces. We begin in Chapter 1 by talking about what they are. There we provide an illustration drawn from an actual classroom to demonstrate how one identifies the four commonplaces, and to illustrate how they emerge in a teaching context. We describe the commonplaces individually, and approach the task of showing you how they intersect. Our hope is that this sets the stage for talking about them in more detail in the remaining chapters.

In Chapter 2, again using illustrations of social studies classroom life as well as evidence from recent research studies, we take up the commonplace of learners and learning. We advance the case for a "constructivist theory" of learning and show how applications of this theory work within the social studies classroom.

In Chapter 3, we discuss the social studies subject matter commonplace. It's a broad, sometimes uneven landscape, but we show you how to draw from the various social sciences and history to construct powerful learning opportunities for your students. To help you do so, we introduce and discuss both the big ideas and threads approaches. We also introduce exercises in which we invite you to build a series of powerful questions around a big idea. These questions will help you construct teaching lessons and units.

In Chapters 4 and 5, we pull the commonplaces of learners and learning and subject matter together into a two-part discussion of what it means to plan for and actually teach social studies using big ideas and subject matter threads. Again, we draw from rich classroom examples and vignettes to illustrate our points and demonstrate how this approach appears in real social studies learning environments. We try to make it clear that teaching social studies is more than just having a grab bag filled with interesting strategies and fun activities, that it requires the presence of rich, powerful social studies ideas and questions and assessments, and a learning theory that supports them, in order to have engaging consequences with your students.

Chapter 6 discusses the last of the four commonplaces—classroom environment. Here, we gather together the ideas from the preceding four chapters to describe what we believe is the type of classroom learning community that supports and sustains the pursuit of learning powerful ideas drawn from the social sciences and history. We suggest ways in which you can organize and manage this community effectively. As before, we illustrate with vivid examples drawn from actual classrooms.

As we promised, we wait until we have discussed all four commonplaces to broach the often difficult and dry subject of goals and aims for teaching and learning social studies. In Chapter 7 we lay out a set of goals consistent with the approaches we suggest. We compare and contrast them with other possible goals from school districts, educational reform documents, professional organizations, and the like. We also summon you to think about your own social studies teaching and learning goals and compare them to what we have described. Such a strategy will help you be clearer about the courses of action you can pursue and the choices you will need to make.

In Chapter 8, we offer some practical help in terms of planning and constructing social studies units. We explain what a unit plan is, how you might build one, and why it can be useful. We draw from units our students have created to illustrate the points we make.

Reflectivity is in many ways the core of good teaching. Without it, teachers are little more than instructional robots who do the same things over and over again without knowing why, and who experience dubious results in the classroom. Chapter 9 stresses the importance of being reflective and demonstrates how good social studies teachers develop opportunities for healthy professional reflection. Chapter 9, and the book, conclude with key summaries of the main ideas we have presented and some parting thoughts, observations, and challenges.

An Invitation

We believe that you will find your reading of this book interesting and exciting, primarily because we have anchored it in real classroom life and because the commonplaces frame the approach we are suggesting and hold it together in a coherent and helpful way. We don't expect that you'll always agree with the positions we stake out. We don't always agree with one another! We would enjoy conversing with you about the substance of our ideas. Our contact information and e-mail addresses are included on page 00.

Much remains to be done if elementary social studies is to excite the imaginations of children, and it won't always be easy. We hope, however, that the ideas expressed in the following pages stimulate and support your diligent and persistent thinking about what powerful, ambitious social studies teaching and learning can look like. We wish you the best with your efforts as you embark on this journey in learning to teach social studies.

NOTE

1. Before going any further, please notice that throughout this book we use the terms social studies and social education interchangeably. It is fairly common in classroom materials and other written materials to see the terms so used. If any difference does exist between the two terms, perhaps it is that social studies refers to the subject matter inherent in the social education of children.

Part ONE

The Commonplaces: A Framework for Powerful Social Studies Teaching

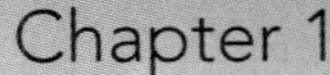

Chapter 1

The Commonplaces of Education

Creating a Framework for the Social Studies Classroom

It is 10:00 a.m. on a blustery March morning as the first grade begins social studies. "Right now we're doing some traveling," the teacher says, and the class calls out, "to China?" "to Ethiopia?" "to Africa!" A child whispers to a visitor, "We cooked chicken from Nigeria!"

Two months later, the first grade has "traveled" all the way from China and Nigeria to Australia. They gather in a semi-circle on the floor as their teacher reads a story that introduces some of the history of the Australian rain forest. As she reads, the bell rings, and several students sigh. A boy says, "I'd just like to stay and stay." (Levstik, 1993, p. 1)

Linda Levstik's snapshot description of this first-grade classroom is revealing. Teachers dream of students saying, "I'd just like to stay and stay." Why does this first-grader feel this way? Several important factors contribute:

- *Teachers* who excite children's imagination and curiosity through a range of instructional experiences that include reading stories, asking questions, and even cooking.
- *Learners* who are consistently encouraged to actively participate in their own learning.
- *Subject matter* that goes well beyond the traditional emphasis on self and family and beyond the limits of the children's neighborhood, state, and country.
- A *classroom environment* where teacher and learners talk to and with one another, where children learn in a variety of contexts, and where all hold values that support active engagement in powerful ideas.

Classes that exhibit these factors make strong impressions on children's hearts and minds and become the stuff that future generations of teachers will recall as meaningful. And that is why social studies matters—it can and should be the site of powerful teaching and learning experiences, a place where children want to "stay and stay."

In this chapter, we present an adaptation of the **commonplaces of education** described by Joseph Schwab (1974).[1] Understanding and using the commonplaces—*teachers and teaching, learners and learning, subject matter,* and *classroom environment*—will help you begin building a powerful framework for teaching and learning. When you have completed this chapter, you should be able to answer these questions:

1. ***What are the key elements of each commonplace?***
2. ***How do the commonplaces work in interaction?***
3. ***How does an understanding of the commonplaces help me think about teaching and learning?***

This photograph depicts a first-grade teacher reading a book about trains to her students. What clues about teaching, learning, subject matter, and classroom environment can you infer?

Introducing the Commonplaces of Education

Classrooms are busy, complex places. Children bring a range of physical, emotional, social, and academic strengths and needs; parents ask many questions and express many concerns; administrators hold various expectations of teachers and learners; the several subject matters elementary school teachers are responsible for threaten to overwhelm them. In addition, district and state-level standardized tests, local, state, and national curriculum standards, and the like all compete for teachers' attention. In and around this swirl, it is easy for teachers, even veteran teachers, to lose focus.

Our experience tells us that good teachers are those who are thoughtful and reflective, who can adjust to changing circumstances, and who can see both the big picture and the details. That is a lot to ask, especially of novice teachers. How will you focus your time, attention, and energy? How can you become the best kind of teacher you can imagine?

Part of the answer lies in constructing a dynamic approach to teaching and learning. Central to that approach is a guiding framework. The one we advocate features the commonplaces of education: learners and learning, teachers and teaching, subject matter, and classroom environment. Taken separately, these constructs allow teachers to focus on key elements of classroom life. For example, teachers can dig deeply into questions of what it means to learn social studies, what content is appropriate to teach, what teaching approaches they might use, and what kinds of classroom environments foster engaged and thoughtful teaching and learning. These are useful questions, and we will have more to say about them as this book unfolds.

The commonplaces are even more useful when teachers consider them in interaction—that is, when teachers plan, teach, and assess in ways that reflect attention to all four elements. In classrooms such as the one profiled at the beginning of this chapter, we see a seamless merging of the four commonplaces: The *classroom environment* reflects the *teacher's* sense that *learning* is a social and active process, which is abetted by dynamic instruction and powerful *subject matter* ideas. Firing on all four commonplace cylinders is no small feat, and even good teachers flop sometimes. But those same teachers will tell you that much of what keeps them fresh is the sense that they are always encountering new situations and learning new aspects of how they think about and do their work. The commonplaces are neither a substitute for experience nor a substitute for the passion and thoughtfulness good teachers bring to their craft. Understanding the commonplaces can, however, help you to make sense of the complexity that surrounds teaching and learning and to begin thinking your way into your role as a social studies teacher.

Figure 1.1 is a diagram of the commonplaces. The arrows indicate the interaction among the commonplaces as they operate in educational settings.

Figure 1.1 • **The Commonplaces in Interaction**

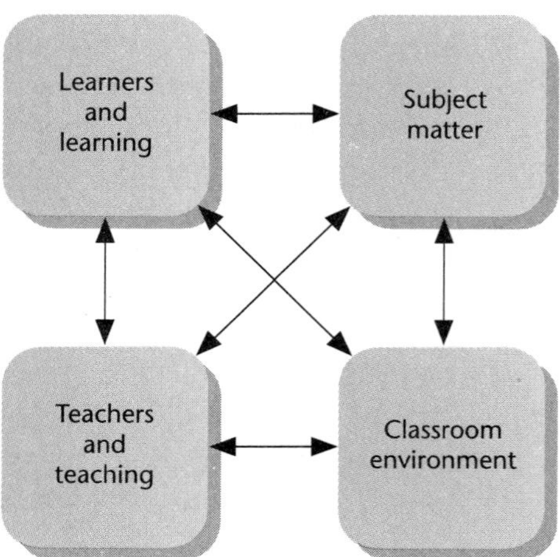

Before we talk about the commonplaces in interaction, let's look at each of them in turn and how they play out in actions of the teacher, Ruby, whose classroom is described in the opening vignette.

Learners and Learning

When you see yourself teaching, who are the learners sitting in front of you? How are they similar? How are they different? What do they know and care about? How do they learn, and where do their ideas come from? How do they feel about learning social studies, especially as it compares to learning other school subjects?

Although we address these questions in Chapter 2, our purpose here is to prime your thinking about one of the key elements or commonplaces in education—learners and learning. As odd as it may seem, teachers sometimes become so focused on what they are teaching and how they are teaching it that they almost forget that teaching is not the same as learning. Think about it: How many times have you sat in a class where the teacher is clearly teaching, and yet you were not learning anything? Now, it may have been your fault—perhaps you were not prepared for the class or maybe you were not paying attention. But it's also possible that the teacher forgot about or misunderstood those whom she or he was teaching.

These students are working on a mapping project. Group projects allow students to take advantage of their various strengths.

Part of remembering and understanding the students in front of you is thinking about the kinds of questions we listed above. There is no such thing as a generic kid. Each shares some commonalities with others, such as race, ethnicity, and gender. But these factors don't always matter, because every child also is an individual. Girls may generally act in a certain way compared to boys, but that does not mean Kara, Shaneeka, and Lucy will always think and act in the same ways. Similarly, African American, Chinese American, and Native American children exhibit traits indigenous to their cultural roots. Yet, to see those children only in terms of their ethnicity is to misunderstand the many influences on their behavior and the power kids have to define themselves.

Teachers face a tough task: They need to understand the cultural backgrounds of their students at the same time that they honor the individuality of each student. In doing so, however, they come to know how their learners are similar and different and what they know and care about. Teachers who prepare social studies units and lessons that truly help students think and learn find this kind of information invaluable.

But there is more to it. Understanding the learners in front of you is key. So too is understanding the learning process. How students learn, where their ideas come from, and how they learn different school subjects is a prime area of educational research. Some important findings are emerging, which we will discuss in more detail in Chapter 2. Here, we preview two of the most salient.

One finding relates to the distinction between **behaviorism** and **constructivism**. If you remember Psych 101, you'll recall that behaviorism is a theory about why people do the things they do. In brief, behaviorists argue that all behavior can be explained as a series of stimulus–response actions: Sunlight (stimulus) hits your eye and you blink (response). Rewards and punishments figure into the mix in that responses that are rewarded tend to persist, whereas those that are punished tend to fade. Applied to schooling, behaviorist theory surfaces in myriad ways: the division of knowledge into discrete, easily digestible bits; direct instruction of those bits; lots of student practice on those bits; lots of testing to ensure that those bits are memorized; and lots of praise when students recall the bits quickly and accurately.

Current thinking about learning challenges much of behavioral theory. Constructivism assumes that people play a much more active role in their lives: What people know and do is an active construction rather than a passive response to an external stimulus. This theory does not discount the importance of environmental stimuli: constructivists blink when the sun is in their eyes, too! Constructivists differ from their behaviorist colleagues in defining a stimulus and in understanding how people make sense of that stimulus. Put simply, constructivists believe that a wide range of stimuli, both external and internal, influence our behavior *and* that different people may make very different sense of and respond in very different ways to similar stimuli. These ideas have pro-

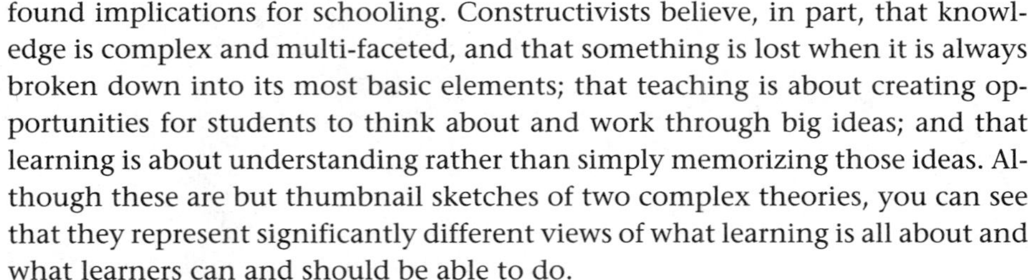

found implications for schooling. Constructivists believe, in part, that knowledge is complex and multi-faceted, and that something is lost when it is always broken down into its most basic elements; that teaching is about creating opportunities for students to think about and work through big ideas; and that learning is about understanding rather than simply memorizing those ideas. Although these are but thumbnail sketches of two complex theories, you can see that they represent significantly different views of what learning is all about and what learners can and should be able to do.

RELEVANT RESEARCH

A second finding that concerns learners and learning revolves around how learners respond to social studies as a school subject. The fact is, most don't. Surveys of students' attitudes toward social studies consistently report the same dismal finding: Most students dislike social studies (Haladyna & Shaughnessy, 1985; McGowan, Sutton, & Smith, 1990). Several factors figure into this conclusion. Students often report disliking the dull nature of many of the social studies ideas presented, most of which they already know. They resist the boring textbooks and worksheets they are handed. They object to teachers who give them no opportunities to talk about their nascent ideas. In short, few students find much of value in the traditional approach to social studies, an approach that attempts to pour discrete bits of content into their heads and then simply asks them to recall those bits at a later date. Can we blame them?

That is why teachers like Ruby represent the possibilities for social studies. Think about what Ruby knows about learning and the learners in her classroom. First, she knows that although her children have had little experience outside their own community, they are deeply interested in how other people live. Ruby understands that by helping her students look into the lives of others, they will be better able to understand their own. Second, Ruby knows that although these children need opportunities to learn some specific ideas, they also need opportunities to play with ideas, to have direct experiences, to ask lots of questions, and to try out their emerging understandings. Finally, Ruby knows that first-graders make few distinctions between "social studies," "language arts," and the like, so her units invariably take an integrated tack. Students study key social studies ideas such as geography, exploration, and culture using the tools of language (reading, writing, speaking, listening) and science (for example, understanding that differences in climate and terrain influence where and how people live their lives).

IN YOUR CLASSROOM: Probing Student Attitudes

To develop a sense of your students' feelings about social studies, construct a survey that asks them

- What they remember about their social studies class last year
- What activities they learned the most from

If you listen carefully and probe gently, students' responses to these simple questions not only will tell you a lot, but will demonstrate to your students that you care about what they think.

Subject Matter

The learners and learning commonplace is an important one, but just as important is the notion of subject matter or the ideas you want learners to learn. Several questions help frame the subject-matter commonplace:

- What is the content of the social studies?
- What content is appropriate to teach children?
- How is social studies content typically organized and what modifications can teachers make?

We discuss these questions in some detail in Chapter 3. Here, we want to preview some issues that underlie these questions.

One of the first issues teachers confront when teaching social studies is the impossibility of the task. Think about it: Social studies includes the geographic, political, economic, and cultural history of all humankind. That's a lot of terri-

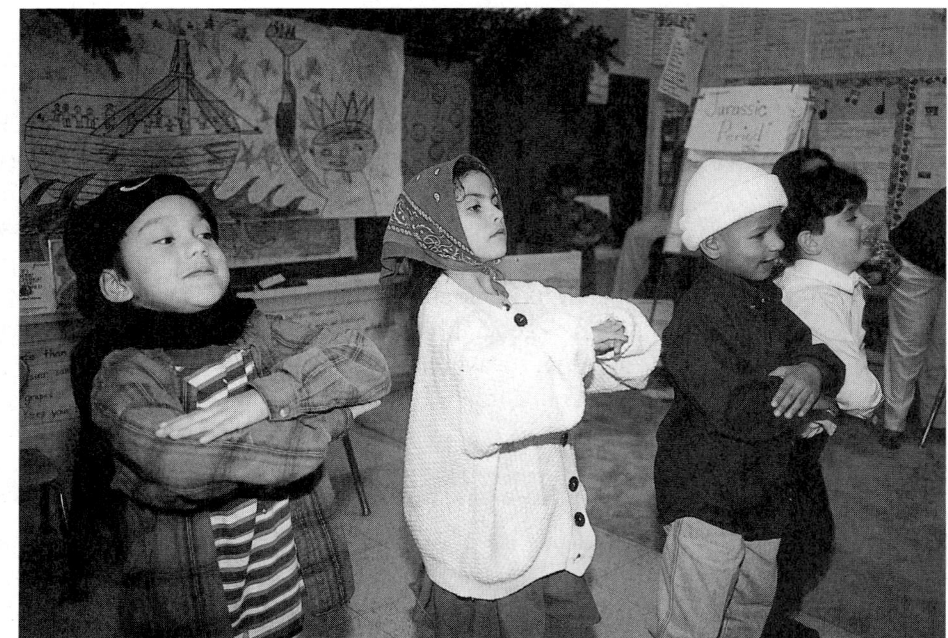

The second-graders in this picture are performing a play about immigration as part of a unit on family heritages. Notice that not only are the children dressed in ethnic costumes, but they have done large-scale drawings. Providing students with multiple opportunities to show you what they know is key to powerful teaching and learning.

tory to cover! Of course no one teacher can teach it all. (However, S. G. once taught a high school course entitled "World History." His approach: "Buckle your seat belts, kids. We've got five hundred years to cover today!" Needless to say, this wasn't the most successful social studies teaching.) Even so, most teachers feel overwhelmed by the content assigned to their grade level.

While curriculum guides, textbooks, and other teachers offer suggestions, in the end, you, the teacher, must decide what to teach, how long to teach it, and in what detail. Along with this real responsibility is a real opportunity to choose content that will build on what your students know and that will push them to greater understandings.

How to do that? Two ideas will help. One is considering the **threads of social studies.** With so much content to teach, it is easy either to give up or to simply start marching through a textbook page-by-page. Good teachers, however, use a framework to think about and organize the content at hand. The framework we propose divides the social studies into geographic, political, economic, sociocultural, and global threads.[2]

Taken separately, teachers can use these threads to help their learners to look deeply at an important element of social life. Taken together, the threads help learners to look broadly at how a social group operates and to compare and contrast one social or cultural group with another. Figure 1.2 shows the threads as both individual and interacting categories of ideas.

To see the threads in action, let's return to Ruby's classroom where attention to several threads is immediately obvious. First, Ruby encourages attention to the geographic, cultural, and global threads as she and her learners explore a range of world cultures. Second, she promotes the economic and geographic

THE THREADS OF SOCIAL STUDIES

- *geographic:* ideas related to where and how people live
- *political:* ideas about how people make decisions that affect themselves and others
- *economic:* ideas about how people use the land and resources to meet their needs
- *sociocultural:* ideas about how people communicate, learn, relax, and find meaning in their lives
- *global:* ideas about how people interact across cultures

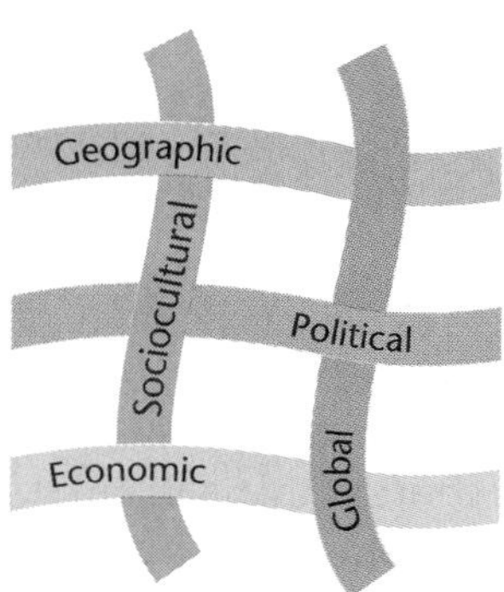

Figure 1.2 • The Threads, Both Individually and in Interaction

threads when she turns students' attention to the resources present in the Australian rain forest. Finally, although it is not apparent in the vignette above, Ruby and her learners attend to the political thread when later they discuss government decisions made about the rain forest.

Using these threads to frame and organize the subject matter of social studies makes a lot of sense. Another approach that makes sense is the construction and use of big ideas. A **big idea** is a question or generalization that helps you, the teacher, decide what to focus on in a curriculum unit. Big ideas engage learners' interests by being meaty, complex, and open to multiple perspectives and interpretations. The questions "What is freedom?" (for a unit on American slavery) and "How do we know what we know?" (for a unit on the nature of history) function as powerful big ideas because they force learners to wrestle with real and important issues. They are also powerful because they help frame the unit at hand. Slavery and the nature of history are huge topics, ones that could take most of a year to explore. Using big ideas like "What is freedom?" and "How do we know what we know?" provides a focus for the respective units. Teachers and learners can explore a range of issues in these areas, but if they keep returning to the big idea they are more likely to find deeper meaning in their explorations. Often the social studies teaching that kids complain about is aimless; they do activities every day, but they cannot see what those activities add up to. Creating and using big ideas will help eliminate such complaints.

Turning back to Ruby's classroom, we see how big ideas can play out even in first grade. For example, in the unit on cultures outside the United States, Ruby uses the statement "We all live in a neighborhood" to frame class discussions. Ruby knows that students make sense of ideas through personal connections. She also knows that, at first, foreign cultures can seem remote and unintelligible to her first-graders. So she uses the notion of a "neighborhood" to help her students connect their lives to those distant others. She and the children explore dimensions of other cultures found in their local neighborhood—family life, language, traditions, celebrations, and the like. In so doing, Ruby provides both opportunities for her learners to explore their interests and a framework to help them make sense of what they learn.

TEACHER REFLECTION

What *Don't* You Know?

Think of an interesting event in history that you know something about (for example, the Salem witch trials, the Renaissance, the 1960s). On a sheet of paper, list all that you know by thread category. That is, what do you know about the religious situation in seventeenth-century Salem (sociocultural)? the forms of government found during the Renaissance (political)? the growth of the consumer culture during the 1960s (economic)?

As you work through the five threads, you may be surprised to remember more than you might have thought. You may also discover what you don't know or don't remember well. This is important, because you will want to help your students understand that (a) no one knows everything and (b) a framework like the threads can help you figure out what you don't know. Understanding what we *don't know* is key to understanding what we *can learn*.

Teachers and Teaching

The third commonplace is teachers and teaching. Because this book is primarily for prospective and practicing teachers, we spend a lot of time talking about what teaching social studies is all about. In fact, we devote two chapters—4 and 5—to that task. In this section, however, we foreshadow some of the relevant questions and issues.

Among the key questions are these:

- What elements make up the act of teaching?
- What is the array of teaching methods available and how do teachers decide among them?
- How do teachers know what their students are learning?
- What materials might teachers use?
- What factors influence teachers' instructional decisions? What does powerful teaching look like?

As this list suggests, teaching is a richly complex activity that goes far beyond the act of delivering instruction. Unit and lesson planning, organizing students

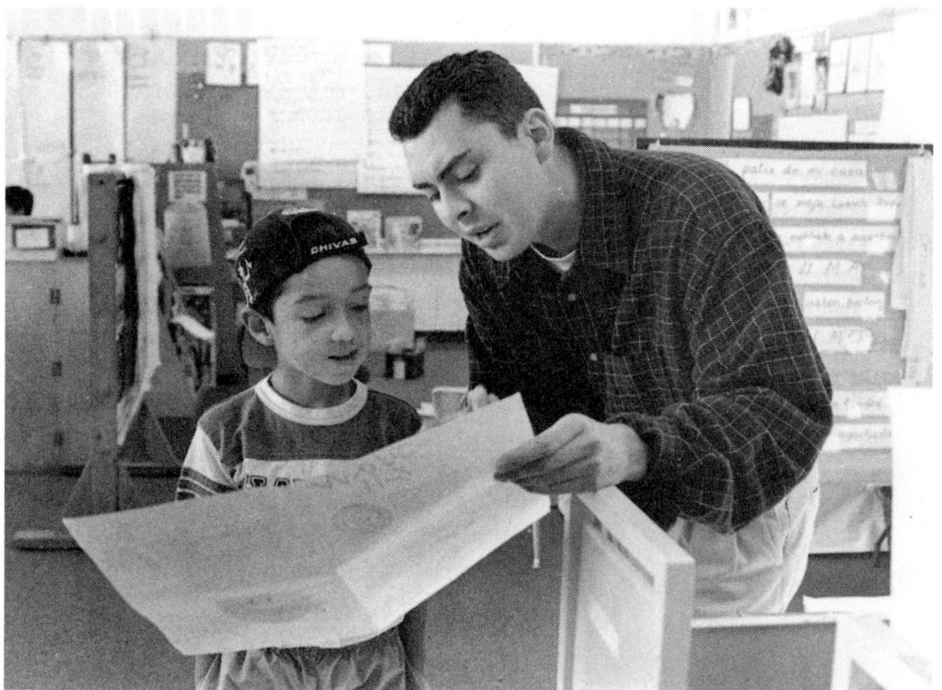

At the right, a first-grade teacher works individually with one of his students. While many believe that teaching consists largely of whole-class instruction, good teachers know that much of their work involves one-on-one interactions with their students.

for learning, choosing curriculum materials, and creating forms of assessment are big chunks of the teaching process. The instructional phase alone is complicated by choice. Recitation and seatwork, individual reading and note taking, small-group and whole-class discussion, role playing and simulation, individual and small-group projects, report and essay writing, journal keeping, learning centers, lectures . . . the list of possible instructional approaches is endless.

As we have suggested above, good teachers take into account their learners and the subject matter at hand. But other influences are at work as well. Parents' and administrators' expectations, state and local curriculum guides, school and district policies, and state and local tests may all affect teachers' practices.

Yet influences are not the same as controls. Teachers can feel buffeted by the various winds that blow through their classrooms, and they can feel frustrated when those winds blow in contradictory directions. Consider a quick example: Many of the new standards in social studies call for meatier content, higher-level thinking, and greater expectations of students. And yet, most of the state and local standardized tests still reflect basic content, low-level thinking, and little effort by students. Such mixed messages may confuse teachers. Looked at

Survey the right photograph of a first-grade classroom. What visual cues tell you how this teacher knows what her students are learning, and what kinds of classroom materials she uses?

differently, however, they may liberate teachers because they mean that teachers will be held to no single criterion. In other words, with multiple (and often conflicting) influences in the air, teachers have considerable **autonomy** to carve out their own instructional paths. Admittedly, the downside here is that some teachers will find the uncertainty paralyzing, and others will use their autonomy to do little more than the barest minimum. Thoughtful, committed, and energetic teachers, however, will find few real drags on their instructional creativity. The choices teachers must make are not easy, but those choices are theirs.

Consider how Ruby uses her classroom autonomy to make good instructional choices for her learners. For example, she faces the same state and local curriculum guides that most teachers face, yet these guides are expressed in such general terms that she can tailor her teaching around goals that seem much more important—the development of empathy for others, students' interests, and future learnings. Now, it's true that Ruby might feel she has fewer choices if her students had to take a standardized test in social studies. As we will see in the case of Don Kite (Chapter 5), however, standardized tests have no particular influence on teachers' work.

TEACHER REFLECTION

Talking with Teachers

Talk with a currently practicing teacher about how she or he decides what to teach and how to teach it. Expect to hear references to tests, textbooks, curriculum guides, past experience, and the like. Encourage the teacher to talk about how she or he weighs each of these factors and what tradeoffs result. Reflect on what these influences might mean for your teaching.

Classroom Environment

Teachers and teaching, subject matter, learners and learning—it's hard to believe a teacher's job can encompass much more than that. And yet, good teachers also pay attention to the fourth commonplace, one which goes by many names—milieu, climate, atmosphere, environment. All refer, however, to the sense or feeling one has while in a classroom. In some ways, this is the hardest commonplace to talk about because it seems so diffuse. And yet, certain features of classrooms provide ways to examine the nature of a classroom setting.

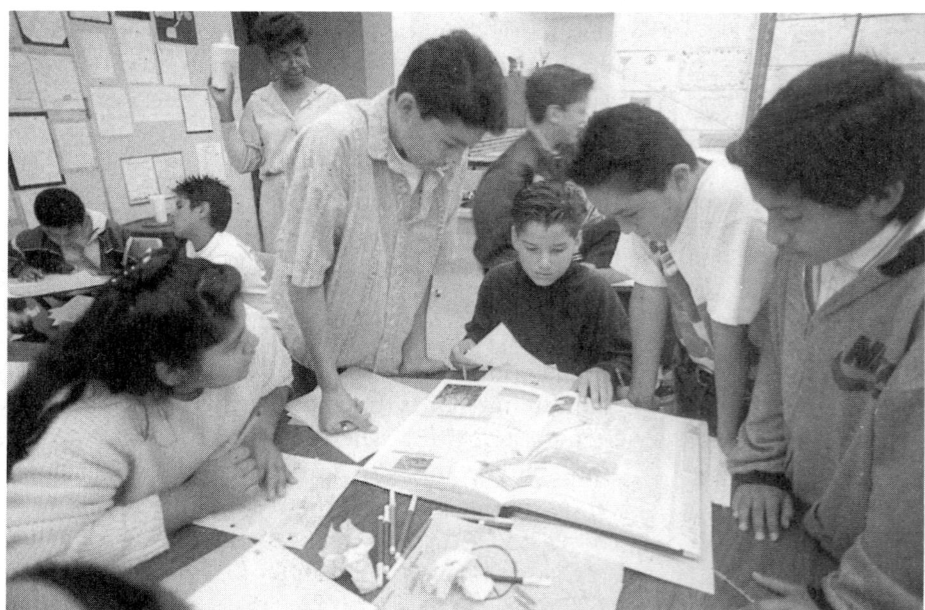

After reading about the elements of classroom environment, come back to this scene of fifth-graders working in small groups. What kind of discourse, classroom organization, and dispositions seem apparent?

First, a few questions to think about:

- What does a good classroom environment look like?
- What goes into creating a good classroom climate?
- How does a teacher know if it's achieved?

You have undoubtedly had many experiences in **traditional classroom settings.** You probably worked under a set of classroom rules that emphasized laboring silently and individually on simplistic tasks with lots of teacher rewards and punishments. Conversely, you probably have had far fewer experiences in classrooms that emphasize working together on complex assignments that carry both internal and external rewards. When asked, most teachers will say that they want to promote this second kind of classroom environment. But, with little personal experience in such settings, it makes some sense that most teachers replicate the kinds of traditional classrooms in which they were schooled.

It doesn't have to be that way, however. Creating the kind of **genuine classroom community** that we envision as the second classroom described above is no mean feat—in large part because both you and your students are so used to the traditional. We suspect, though, that making clear distinctions between traditional and genuine classroom environments will make it easier for teachers to work toward the latter.

We have a lot more to say on this point in Chapter 6. For now, however, let us highlight some key components of classroom environment. Three elements of classroom life seem most appropriate: discourse, classroom organization, and dispositions.

ELEMENTS OF CLASSROOM LIFE

- **Discourse** refers to the nature of the talk that goes on in a classroom, that is, who talks in the classroom and what do they talk about?
- **Classroom organization** concerns the ways in which learning activities are structured. For example, how are learners organized for teaching and learning, and who decides? What classroom rules are evident, and who chooses them?
- **Dispositions** are those values and attitudes a teacher and his or her learners create and practice during classroom activity. For example, is there an honest respect for and commitment to inquiry? open respect for and commitment to ideas and people? patient respect for and commitment to argument and evidence?

Comparing these elements across traditional and genuine classrooms reveals some startling differences. In traditional classrooms, much of the discourse follows two predictable patterns: the teacher talks and the students listen or the teacher asks a question, a student answers, and the teacher evaluates the answer as right or wrong. Classroom organization in traditional settings is also fairly predictable in that students do most of their work quietly and individually at their seats. Finally, the values or dispositions evident in a traditional classroom emphasize hard work, efficiency, deference to authority, and external rewards. Each of these elements contributes to a **"factory" model** of schooling, in which teachers are plant managers and students are workers whose job it is to produce, that is, learn, quickly, quietly, individually, and only in response to rewards.

Genuine classroom communities offer a sharp contrast. Although they are not as easily characterized, genuine classrooms tend to feature a greater balance between teacher talk and student talk and a greater balance in terms of who controls the conversation. This latter point is important because not only do we want to increase the opportunities children have to air their views, but we also want to increase the possibility that talk in the classroom will focus more on their ideas and interests. Genuine classrooms also emphasize more balance among activities. Rather than rely on either whole-class instruction and individual seatwork, teachers in genuine classrooms use a wide variety of instructional settings depending on the task at hand. Finally, genuine classrooms reflect values that promote respect for and commitment to ideas and people, inquiry and argument, and evidence. Because genuine classrooms emphasize student learning and understanding rather than the amount of work students produce, it makes sense that the discourse, classroom organization, and dispositions differ greatly from those found in traditional classrooms.

Table 1.1 A Comparison of Traditional and Genuine Classrooms

	Traditional Classrooms	*Genuine Classrooms*
Discourse	Teachers do most of the talking; students listen or answer direct questions	Greater balance between teacher talk and student talk
Classroom Organization	Whole-group recitation and individual seatwork	Wide variety of whole-group, small-group, partner, and individual activities
Dispositions	Emphasis on hard work, efficiency, deference to authority, and external rewards	Emphasis on ideas, people, inquiry, argument, and evidence

One reason students dislike social studies is that they tend to study it in traditional settings. In fact, we have too often seen teachers do brilliant and exciting work in reading or mathematics only to become "Traditional Teacher" when it is time for social studies. Whatever the reason for this transformation, if we don't want to simply replicate the kind of classrooms we all disliked, we need to rework the discourse, organization, and dispositions evident in them.

And that is yet one more reason why we are so impressed with Ruby, for here is a teacher who clearly is pushing beyond the traditional. First, she encourages student talk rather than monopolizing the classroom conversation. For example, students in Ruby's class who have discovered new information or have a special expertise can become class "experts" who share their knowledge and skills with others. Second, Ruby organizes students' work in a variety of ways rather than emphasizing individual seatwork. Depending on the activity, students may work in pairs, small groups, or as part of the whole class. Finally, Ruby promotes the values of sharing, cooperation, consideration, and participation rather than competition. She also takes seriously what she calls her students' "hunger to learn" (Levstik, 1993, p. 19). To that end, three dispositions are key: The first is inquiry—building on the children's expressed "need to know"; the second is providing multiple ways to "find out"; the third is providing opportunities to share discoveries, understandings, or misunderstandings (Levstik, 1993, p. 20). In these several ways, then, we see a teacher working toward the kind of genuine classroom community that will serve all her students well.

TEACHER REFLECTION

Classrooms You Have Known

Reflect on some of the classrooms you have been in. What were they like? Were some more conducive to active learning than others? What factors might have contributed to that sense? Conversely, what factors do you think were at play in classrooms where it was more difficult to learn? What kind of classroom environment will you try to foster?

Now think back to the memorable learning experience we asked you to recall in the introduction to this book, and analyze it through the four commonplaces: learners and learning, subject matter, teachers and teaching, and environment.

- What did the teacher know about you as a learner (and if it was a class situation, what did she or he know about the other learners)? What assumptions did she or he make about learning the task at hand?
- What did the teacher know about the subject matter? What big ideas did the teacher want you to think about?
- How did the teacher "teach" you? How did she or he represent ideas? How did she or he know when you had learned what they could teach you?

- What did it feel like to learn in this situation? How did you and the teacher interact?

Although thinking about your own experience in this way might have seemed new and awkward at first, we bet that the ideas fairly tumbled out once you got started. With practice, analyzing classroom situations using the commonplaces framework will become easier. We also expect that this framework will prove useful as you begin to prepare units and lessons.

With so much to think about, how can anyone manage to teach? We weren't kidding when we warned you that classrooms are complex places. The simple fact is that there is way too much is going on in the typical classroom for any teacher to attend to it all, all the time. If we had to always give individual attention to each commonplace, the job would be too big indeed. But using the commonplaces actually gets easier when you look at them together.

SECTION SUMMARY **The Four Commonplaces**

- The individual commonplaces provide a useful framework for analyzing and understanding classroom situations
- The *learners and learning* commonplace focuses on how students are similar and different, what they know and care about, and how they learn (behaviorism and constructivism)
- The *subject matter* commonplace focuses on the content of social studies and how to make it appropriate for students (threads)
- The *teachers and teaching* commonplace focuses on how teachers plan their instruction (big ideas) and the factors that play into their decisions
- The *classroom environment* commonplace focuses on classroom "feel" in terms of discourse, organization, and dispositions (traditional and genuine classrooms)

Looking at the Commonplaces in Interaction

If the commonplaces help us focus on individual elements of teaching and learning, they are even more useful in helping us understand the complex dynamics of classroom life. Teachers, no less than children, can get lost in the swirl of the classroom. We see the commonplaces in interaction as an anchor, a way of making sense, of holding strong, and of seeing new possibilities.

For example, consider the question of what learners know and care about. The most obvious connection here is to subject matter. As a school subject, social studies emphasizes people, places, and events the world over from the beginning of time until today. Wise teachers know well their students' particular interests and the subject matter content they are responsible for, and they are able to highlight instances where those interests and that content intersect.

Asking what learners know and care about raises questions about the classroom environment. Kids know and care about many things, only some of which are academic. They also care about concepts such as fairness and justice, and about having opportunities to talk about their developing ideas. If learners are to thrive, the environment in which they learn matters as much as the subject matter taught. Good teachers know that they cannot simply tell students about ideas. Instead, they create classroom environments where learners feel comfortable expressing their emerging understandings of those ideas. Those understandings will rarely sound "right" to adult ears, so good teachers are careful not to quash young thinkers' spirits and participation by judging their contributions too quickly and too harshly.

Finally, if thinking about what learners know and care about raises issues of subject matter and environment, it also raises issues related to teaching. "Knowing" and "caring" are related, but they are not the same. Many teachers home in on what students need to know, and consequently their teaching tends to emphasize direct instruction—telling students what they need to know, assigning worksheets to reinforce that knowledge, and using objective-style tests to evaluate what students know. There is nothing inherently wrong with such an approach, but in our view, it seems thin. Knowing is important, but so too is caring about what one learns. For example, it is important to know the particulars about Columbus's encounters with New World natives. At the same time, however, it seems important to encourage students to empathize with the historical characters and to understand what motivated them, how those motivations played out, and the implications of these events for children entering a new millennium. Teachers who want their students to know *and* care about history think and act differently from their colleagues who are interested in knowledge alone. They are more likely to offer learners multiple and varied opportunities for learning new ideas, to encourage learners' multiple interpretations of events, and to use a range of assessments for understanding what learners know.

To demonstrate the power of the commonplaces in interaction, let's return one more time to Ruby's classroom. In the following vignette, the researcher, Linda Levstik, describes the classroom activities that develop around some artifacts she brought back from a trip through Scotland and England. As you read, think about instances in which each of the commonplaces surfaces and how they interact.

CLASSROOM EXAMPLE

The class is putting the finishing touches on a story about things to see in Scotland and England. They are anxious to see if I have brought anything back with me, so Ruby suggests we share pictures, books, and some artifacts (hats, brass rubbing kits, coins).

Darren: What is this book about?
Linda: Vikings. It comes from an excavation of a Viking village.

The teacher allows several students to work with English money. Jake and Angel try counting out money:

Angel: Did you buy these things with this money?
Linda: Yes. You can't use American money in English stores.
Mitchell: Could you use this here? *(He joins Jake and Angel as they continue to try to count the money, reminding themselves of what each coin represents: "That's like a dime.")*

Six other children have gone to the back of the room to work on brass rubbings, and Erin wants to know if he can show Ms. Jones's class the bobby's hat he is wearing. Another group gathers around a pile of books, pictures, and magazines the teacher had been sharing. She adds the new brochures, and the group begins to discuss the age of some of the buildings:

Darren: Some of those are real new, they just make them look like real castles.
Linda: Well, we do that in this country, don't we. The one you're looking at is pretty new. It's only one hundred fifty years old.
Catrina: One hundred fifty years! That's old!
Mitchell: The Vikings are older than that.
Ruby: How long ago were the Vikings? Does anyone remember? *(No one can recall. They think it was "long, long ago, back when they had those ships.")*

Darren is working on his own, again, reading the Viking activity book and carefully copying something on a large sheet of manila paper.

Darren: Look what I've done. *(He shows how he has written his name using the Viking alphabet.)*
Roger: Let me see that. *(He tries his name, too.)*

Others gather around to see the writing. Within minutes, about half the class is trying to write in the Viking script. Darren has moved on to discover a plan for building a Viking village.

Darren: Mrs. Y., you should run this off.
Ruby: All right, we'll see if we can get copies. *(The Viking writing group decides it would also like copies.)*
Ruby: Would everyone like to do this? We'll run enough copies.
(Levstik, 1993, pp. 11–12)

Reflect on the following questions about this vignette.

- What does Ruby seem to understand about the children in her class?
- How does she approach the subject matter of Viking life?
- What teaching approaches and materials does she use to teach the class?
- What do the classroom discourse, organization, and dispositions look like?
- How do these instances of learners and learning, subject matter, teachers and teaching, and environment interact?

SECTION SUMMARY **The Commonplaces in Interaction**

- Classrooms are bustling places, with much for teachers to think about and do.
- Considering the commonplaces in interaction provides a more comprehensive means of analyzing and understanding classroom activity.

Elementary school children contribute so much in their enthusiasm to think, learn, and grow that teaching them is truly rewarding. What other profession offers so many opportunities to touch the lives of others on a regular basis? At the same time, the hustle and bustle of an elementary school classroom offers teachers plenty of opportunities for confusion, frustration, and anxiety. With so much to think about and react to, it is easy to feel lost. Time and experience help, but approaching the classroom with a framework like the commonplaces in mind also will help as you fashion and refashion yourself as a teacher.

CHAPTER SUMMARY

1. What are the key elements of each commonplace?

- *Learners and learning* highlights similarities and differences among students, what they know and care about, and theories about how they learn, such as behaviorism and constructivism.
- *Subject matter* highlights the concepts and ideas of social studies and ways, such as the threads, to transform them for instruction.
- *Teachers and teaching* highlights the big ideas teachers use to develop their instruction and the influences on their teaching decisions.

- *Classroom environment* highlights the differences between traditional and genuine classrooms in terms of discourse, organization, and dispositions.

2. ***How do the commonplaces work in interaction?***

Classrooms are complex places. Elements such as the individual commonplaces are prominent, but none truly exists independently of the others. Thus, for example, a teacher's view of learners and learning has implications for the subject matter she or he teaches, the instructional strategies she or he chooses, and the classroom environment that develops.

3. ***How does an understanding of the commonplaces help me think about teaching and learning?***

Good teachers see connections. A framework like the commonplaces helps teachers plan their instruction and analyze and work to remedy problems.

TEACHING RESOURCES

Print Resources

Barr, R., Barth, J., & Shermis, S. (1977). *Defining the social studies.* Arlington, VA: National Council for the Social Studies. This classic work is a good place to begin understanding the teaching and learning of social studies.

Jenness, D. (1990). *Making sense of social studies.* New York: Macmillan. A short history of the field, this book offers a grounding in the founding ideas and ideals of social studies education.

Good sources for current articles on teaching and learning social studies are the National Council for the Social Studies journals, *Theory and Research in Social Education, Social Education,* and *Social Studies for the Young Learner.* Another good source, particularly for practical classroom articles, is the Heldrof publication, *The Social Studies.* All of these journals are available for subscription and most libraries carry them.

Technology Resources

- **http://www.ncss.org**

The National Council for the Social Studies is the leading professional organization for teachers of social studies. Their website offers a range of useful information and resources both to beginning and practicing teachers.

NOTES

1. This list represents an adaptation of Schwab's conception of the commonplaces, which were learners, teachers, subject matter, and milieu. Schwab's conception focuses on the "translat[ion] of scholarly material into curriculum" (Schwab, 1978, p. 365). We are interested in process, but we believe Schwab's ideas can be expanded to encompass a way of thinking about all that goes on in a classroom.
2. The idea of using social science constructs to provide a conceptual framework is an old one. Our presentation of the threads is adapted from that developed by Dr. Patricia Ames. Her version consisted of five elements: physical, political, economic, socio-cultural, and international. We develop the rationale for our version in Chapter 3.

Chapter 2

Learners and Learning

Understanding What Students Know About Social Studies and How They Come to Know It

CLASSROOM EXAMPLE

Ten-year-old Helen has spent the social studies portion of fourth grade studying the history of the state of Michigan. From this purview, she has constructed a window from which to view the broader landscape of American history. Here, at the end of fourth grade, standing on the precipice of fifth-grade American history, she excitedly offers her version of how the United States came to be:

The British and the Americans, they fought. The United States was really poor and it didn't have that much, but the British had fabulous stuff and they weren't poor. They had clothes and stuff like that. Then, America was just a poor country. There were people there but they weren't the richest part of the world. The British agreed never to fight the Americans again, and America agreed to that. They never fought again, but the British—I'm not sure about this part—but I think the British went against their promise, and the British left and they had to do something like sign a paper or something to get it together, a promise, and the British left and they never got a chance to sign or do whatever they had to do to make the promise. But this time, America was rich and had a lot of soldiers and the Americans won over the British and that's how we got our country. The British won three or four times, and America won only once. The Americans won so the British—there was only one or two people left.

What does Helen know? What does she do with what she knows? Here, Helen weaves her version of the birth of the United States. She has read about the French and Indian War and the battles fought in Michigan by the British against the French and their Native-American allies. She has some knowledge of the Revolutionary War, waged only a decade or so later between the American colonists and the British. In her tapestry, she weaves these elements together in a rather fanciful, elaborated account (VanSledright & Brophy, 1992). In short, she creates new cloth from old thread.

However, Helen's version of these affairs bears only slim resemblance to the accounts historians have researched and written. Her historical tapestry, compellingly arranged and highly imaginative, places ideas from different histories, different wars, and different combatants, into one fabric. Helen's storytelling fails to separate these wars and define the chronological space dividing them. Why? What's going on here? Why has she failed to learn her history lessons?

Helen's account demonstrates the active knowledge construction characteristic of young learners. But fourth grade is Helen's first encounter with chronologically arranged history taught systematically across a school year (a common social studies curriculum pattern in the United States: state history in fourth grade and survey U.S. history in fifth grade; see Brophy, VanSledright, & Bredin, 1993; Naylor & Diem, 1987). She is only beginning to think historically and to develop a larger sense of historical understanding. Her account indicates how her thinking about the history she learned, coupled with whatever **prior knowledge** she has picked up from casual reading, television, film, mass culture, and earlier grades in school, coalesces around the idea of war in America. She is beginning to form an active set of ideas about this larger concept of war. However, as young learners often are apt to do, she over-generalizes the idea of wars fought for American independence to include more than simply the American Revolutionary War. She weaves the Revolutionary War together with threads of the French and Indian War, not surprisingly, since this war played a much larger role in the history of Michigan than did the Revolutionary War.

What has Helen learned? Is she constructing the sort of knowledge that a teacher might want her to construct? Helen's interesting though conflated and naive retelling of the birth of a nation might be reason for concern, particularly if one of your goals is to get Helen to develop a more valid accounting of the American past.

At this point, however, our concern is less with the factual accuracy of Helen's knowledge than with the active, imaginative intellectual process she is demonstrating. When elementary-grade learners read about and study dynamic social studies topics such as the French and Indian and Revolutionary Wars, they are constantly busy creating new ideas in their heads and rearranging old ones as you present new topics and social studies concepts. This is the active, though sometimes bumpy, cognitive terrain on which you will teach social studies to your students. The process of creating new ideas, knowledge, and meaning from the residue of prior conceptions and experiences in a learning context is what educational theorists call "constructivism."

We will come back to the idea of constructivism and its rich implications for teaching social studies later in this chapter. For the moment, consider a second story by Rita, another student who also has studied Michigan history in fourth grade. With relish and animation, she talks about why Europeans called the Western Hemisphere the "New World."

CLASSROOM EXAMPLE

> They used to live in England, the British, and . . . they wanted to get to China 'cause China had some stuff they wanted. They had some cups, or whatever—no, they had furs. They had fur and stuff like that and they wanted to have a shorter way to get to China, so they took it, and they landed in Michigan, but it wasn't called Michigan. I think it was the British that landed in Michigan, and they were there first so they tried to claim that land, but it didn't work out for some reason so they took some furs and brought them back to Britain and they sold them. But they mostly wanted it for the furs. So then the English landed there and they claimed the land and wanted to make it a state, and so they got it signed by the government or whoever, the big boss [laughs], then they were just starting to make it a state, so the British just went up to the Upper Peninsula [in Michigan] and they thought they could stay there a little while. Then they had to fight a war, then the farmers, they were just volunteers, so the farmers went right back to try to put their families back together again.

What does Rita know, and what does she do with it? Rita, like Helen, conflates pieces of territorial Michigan history with European efforts at finding a shorter, more economical trading route to the far east. That exploration resulted in the fur trade—well, at least in Michigan—but Rita over-generalizes this trade a bit. The British play a central role. The French are not mentioned, yet the war to which she alludes (unless she is speaking of the Revolutionary War—we don't know for sure) pitted the British against the French in a seven-year war over control, not only of the Michigan territory, but over these two European powers' dominance of trade around the world. Does Rita understand all this? It's difficult to tell; what she says reads a bit like "fact stew." However, if we realize that she is a novice, we begin to see the active, constructive capacity of her mind to combine new learning opportunities with prior knowledge and conceptions of the past.

Also notice how her allusions to the French and Indian War differ from Helen's. Could you tell that both had the same social studies teacher in fourth grade, were taught the same curriculum, and read many of the same books? Their overall experiences were much alike, yet their ideas and the way they build new conceptions differ. Why?

Constructivist theorists believe that learning can be highly idiosyncratic, as different minds with various degrees of prior knowledge about a topic or concept engage new ideas in various ways. The result is often mysterious, making teaching problematic and uncertain, but endlessly interesting and engaging nonetheless. One thing is clear: the old notion that children's minds are like **blank slates** on which the teacher simply writes the appropriate knowledge, and later tests to check for its presence, is seriously misleading. Using prior ideas and understandings, Helen and Rita are busy constructing their own views of things, however idiosyncratic. The notion of the mind as a blank slate simply will no longer do, and Rita and Helen present us with crystallized illustrations that show us why not.

So how do we make sense of the vignettes above? Helen and Rita may not have all their facts right, but their responses are animated, interesting, and deeply engaging. Are these two girls the exception? In one sense, they are. Most children report being bored by the dull parade of facts and worksheet instruction they experience in their social studies classrooms. Helen and Rita, however, seem alive with ideas and naive assumptions about what they are learning. We believe Helen and Rita really are like most other grade-school students: They like to think and talk about provocative, meaty ideas. It's not that students cannot or refuse to like social studies, but that much of what passes for social studies in their classrooms seems rather lifeless. Creative teachers can change all that, as we will see.

In this chapter, we want to focus attention on the commonplace called Learners and Learning. When you have completed this chapter, you should be able to answer the following questions:

1. ***What do elementary-age children know about social studies?***
2. ***How do children learn about social studies?***
3. ***Where do they learn about social studies?***
4. ***What is constructivism as a learning theory and what are its assumptions?***
5. ***What are the problems and promises of constructivism for social studies teachers?***

Knowing and Learning About Social Studies

What Do Children Know About Social Studies?

What do students know about social studies, where do they learn it, and how? These questions seem simple enough to answer, but as it turns out, we have much yet to learn about what students know concerning subjects such as history, geography, economics, and the like. We know even less about how they acquire knowledge, and less yet about where they learn their social studies ideas.[1] These questions have been researched extensively in language arts and mathematics, and to some degree in science.

IN YOUR CLASSROOM: Understanding How Children Construct Meaning

The following will help you gain a sense of the active, meaning-construction process young learners engage in.

- Choose a social studies topic that children in elementary school might know something about (for example, Native Americans, school or classroom rules, the Civil War, how people use shelters, where natural resources come from).
- Choose two or three students and find a quiet spot where you can talk to them.
- Begin with two questions: What do you know about [the topic you chose]? And where do your ideas come from?
- Probe the ideas they suggest by asking them to say more, as appropriate.
- Tape-record their answers.
- Listen carefully to the tape-recordings and compare and contrast the children's responses.

Social studies educators, by contrast, traditionally have focused more on theoretical issues of curriculum selection, history of the social studies profession, and social education goals than on issues of what and how students learn. Those researchers who have examined children's knowledge about social studies subjects and topics through surveys have yielded some limited information about what children know. Recently, more detailed studies using interviewing techniques indicate that young children hold little deep knowledge about major social studies topics and subjects, that what they learn develops rapidly and incrementally and is influenced by prior experience and understanding but remains wide open to change.

RELEVANT RESEARCH

The latter is particularly true when it comes to how they deal with economic concerns such as banks, money, exchange, and consumer goods (see Berti & Bombi, 1988; Jahoda, 1984); political ideas such as governing processes, political leadership, the role and influence of the President of the United States (see Coles, 1980; Moore, et al., 1985); and about how society works in general (see Furth, 1980; Turiel, 1983). Information is emerging, too, on what children know about history.

To explore what your elementary students might know we'll begin by exploring the research on children's ideas about economics, politics and government, and geography. We'll then look at some studies from a fairly large and growing body of work on children's historical understandings.

RELEVANT RESEARCH

Children's ideas about economics In a detailed and wide-ranging study conducted in the late 1980s, two Italian researchers (Berti & Bombi, 1988) interviewed small groups of working- and middle-class Italian children ages four to fourteen to see what they knew about work, work roles, payment for work, ideas about a "boss," where money comes from, views of rich and poor people, understandings of banks and production and distribution, the value of money in buying and selling, and other general economic topics. Here are three examples of what the researchers found.

- *How do people get paid for working?* Children about age five believe that workers are paid directly by consumers for their work. They also know little about the range of occupations. As they get older, their knowledge of the range of occupations grows rapidly. They begin to differentiate occupations clearly, and a notion of a "boss" emerges around age eight. At this age, the children still struggle with how a boss gets money to pay workers, but by age twelve or so, the children begin to understand that goods and services are exchanged for money used to pay workers and that money "circulates" through an economy.
- *"Who's the "boss"?* The youngest children are fully aware of bosses or owners, but do not differentiate them. A boss is anyone these children think to be in charge. By age seven, children can verbally differentiate a

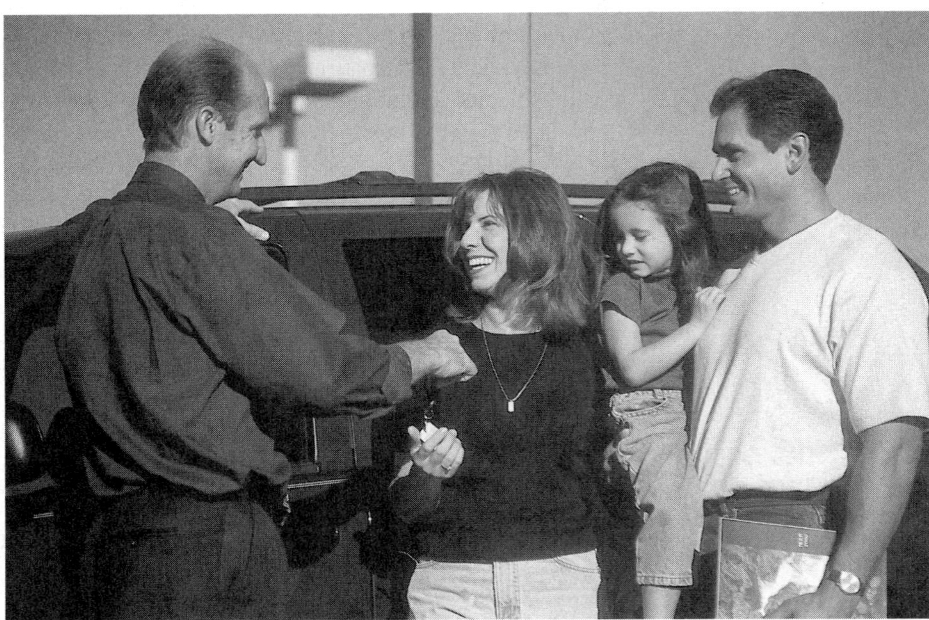

Economics lessons can occur in many venues, both inside and outside the classroom. What might this child be learning as her parents take the keys to their new car?

boss from an owner, and by age ten, they can explain how a boss directs workers based on orders given by an owner. These older children also are quite adept at constructing "pyramids of authority"; that is, they can explain who reports to whom in the organization.

- *Who are the rich and the poor?* The youngest children have little understanding of *rich and poor,* thinking that being poor is odd since anyone can get money by simply going to the bank. These ideas change rapidly as children come to realize that people obtain money as a result of working. By ages six and seven, the children think that people who work are rich and that being poor is a result of being unable or unwilling to work. These children also tend to think of their own families as rich. By age eight, the children construct a fairly complex three-tiered hierarchy, placing what they call "normal people" in the middle (middle class). They also develop "degrees of richness" related to how hard one works. By ages eleven and twelve, the children begin explaining that intensity of work does not necessarily translate into greater or lesser "richness." Their views begin to show more sophisticated analyses of richness and poorness with greater levels and degrees of differentiation between them.

TEACHING RESOURCES

Teaching Economics

A good source of teaching lessons, activities, and curriculum standards related to economics is the National Council on Economic Education. Their home page is at

- http://www.nationalcouncil.org

"Virtual Economics," a free CD offered by EconomicsAmerica, is loaded with neat instructional activities. The information on ordering the CD is at

- http://www.economicsamerica.org/catalog/cat3.html

RELEVANT RESEARCH

Children's ideas about politics and government Children know about more than the economic world. They are also forming ideas about their political worlds. In the U.S., two researchers were curious about young children's political knowledge (see Adelson & O'Neil, 1966). Based on interviews, they report that six- and seven-year-olds could name favorite politicians they knew, but could not describe much about how the political process works. These youngsters also have difficulty imagining consequences of political choices. They conceptualize government in terms of services it offers (for example, trash pickup), see it as a justified authority, and tend to be insensitive to individual liberties.

RELEVANT RESEARCH

In Australia, a similar study on political ideas draws from a much wider range of elementary-age students (Connell, 1971). The study's results suggest that, although younger students do not see politics as a matter of making choices, they later learn that it involves selecting from alternatives. Once this shift occurs, the children quickly begin to take political positions and to develop consistent political preferences. However, notable variation appears in how quickly students make the shift to the new ideas. By the pre-adolescent years, many of the Australian children begin to see themselves as political actors in their own right, capable of making choices with real consequences for themselves (for example, making personal choices about ecological matters such as recycling and understanding how those decisions influence their environment). But again, not all children move to these understandings at the same speed. Some are thinking with more cognitive complexity when others are still having some difficulty with personalizing choices and preferences.

RELEVANT RESEARCH

Robert Coles (1980), a noted child psychiatrist, spent years traveling around the United States in the 1960s and 1970s, talking to young children about their views of politics and government. He interviewed black children and white children, Hispanic and Native-American children, and middle-class, working-class, and poor children. He finds that kids' views of politics and government vary considerably. For example, relatively wealthy middle- and upper-middle-class kids give government leaders far more favorable reviews than do poor children. Poor children, even as young as six and seven, can be quite cynical about politicians, noting that they believe that politicians support whatever rich people want. Black children, too, tend to be more cynical about politics than white children. Some black children Coles spoke with in the deep South think that it is a white world, ruled by and for white people. African Americans, they believe, have little hope of changing that. By contrast, white children, especially those from suburban and upper-middle-class backgrounds have mostly positive and supportive things to say about country, politicians, and government, thinking of themselves as inheritors of that positive heritage.

TEACHING RESOURCES

Teaching Politics and Government

The Center for Civic Education offers a variety of classroom-based materials for teachers. Their home page is at

- http://www.civiced.org

Coles (1980) also finds that, contrary to general public perception, children, even young ones, are astute in their observations about political life and the workings of authority in inter-relationships. Often, children resort to platitudes when describing inter-relationships, power, and politics in school or casual conversations with adults, but in private, when pressed "children [are] constantly noticing who gets along with whom, and why" (p. 40). In summarizing some of his findings on children's views of political authority, Coles notes, "Children ingeniously use every scrap of emotional life available to them in their . . . development, and they do likewise as they try to figure out how (and for whom) the world works" (p. 41).

RELEVANT RESEARCH

Children's ideas about maps Much of the research that deals with children's ideas in geography centers on maps and how children develop the necessary reasoning to understand them. The studies focus on three areas: perspective taking, maps as models of the world, and navigation (Gregg & Leinhardt, 1994).

Much of the early research conducted in the 1950s to mid-1970s with regard to perspective taking—how one uses maps to understand what they show—describes children as going through **developmental stages.** For example, children pass first through a stage where they hold a simplistic perspective, then at a certain age, move to a slightly more complex perspective, and so on, with clear age boundaries marking each stage. However, by the 1980s, other studies successfully challenged these developmental-stage approaches. This later work on what children know about perspective suggests that, initially, they have difficulty with the idea that a map represents a perspective of an actual space (the world, a country, a state). Researchers claim that this is because children construct understandings of space and perspectives of space gradually. Greater levels of exposure to maps as perspectives on actual space speed up the process of attaining the idea, often regardless of age. Children also initially have difficulty with conventions such as north, south, east, and west. Again, repeated exposure speeds up how quickly even younger children learn the conventions. This is especially true with north and south, because educators can assist by using north-as-up and south-as-down conventions, something even young children know. East and west are more difficult because their orientations on a map are always relative to where the child is positioned.

RELEVANT RESEARCH

To understand maps as models of the world, children need to know what the different symbol markers on the maps represent. Children who have not been exposed to maps struggle with the symbol system. For example, Liben and Downs (1989) find that children variously describe urban centers on maps—frequently shown as yellow dots—as eggs or firecrackers going off. But again, with repeated exposure to the map symbols, children at young ages can master their meaning. It does take them longer, though, to obtain the idea that the symbols stand for some actual real-life objects. The speed at which they attain the latter understanding depends largely on the amount of detail found on the map; simpler maps help them grasp the idea more quickly (Bluestein & Acredolo, 1979).

While researchers tell us that young children have difficulty learning some geographic concepts, good teachers know the power of providing a variety of physical world representations for children to explore.

Symbols such as latitude and longitude lines can pose problems for young children if they are presented on a rounded surface, such as a globe. However, children as young as six and seven do learn quickly the idea of latitude and longitude if they are presented on a flat surface. Scale is a another symbol that can confuse children. However, one study demonstrates that children with exposure to model three-dimensional objects that represent larger objects (such as a toy truck model of the real thing) quickly understand scale.

RELEVANT RESEARCH

The work on children's knowledge of navigation using maps is relatively sparse. Navigation refers to using a map to plan a route or trace where one is going. As you can imagine, young children who have had experiences with parents and relatives using maps to navigate on, say, a vacation trip, learn rather quickly to interpret navigation aids on maps. These children can have some fairly good map-reading and navigation skills by the time you see them in second or third grade, when maps and map skills are often taught. Research documents that children as young as three years-old, know how to navigate a room using a map to find a hidden object, provided the map is simple, is accurately oriented to the room from the child's viewpoint, and includes clear landmarks, such as doors, furniture, windows (Bluestein & Acredolo, 1979). Other studies confirm similar results, noting that the presence of clear landmarks is a key to navigation for the younger students. The studies also indicate that as children grow older, their sophistication in map use grows quickly with extended exposure.

TEACHING RESOURCES

Teaching Maps

You can find many classroom lessons and activities around using maps through TeacherNet at

- http://www.teacher.net/curriculum/socialstudies.html

Drawing Conclusions About What Children Know

In just these few research-based illustrations we've seen that children know a surprising amount about varied aspects of their social worlds. They also display sometimes startling growth in their ideas about sociocultural, economic, and political topics. We can conclude that elementary-aged children's ideas change and expand, almost overnight it seems, highlighting the capacity and desire kids have to actively build and modify their knowledge. After reading studies like the above, we wonder what elementary teachers mean when we hear them say "kids can't do or can't learn" when it comes to social studies. Even young children can learn many things in fairly quick order, if teachers take time to assess the ideas they hold and help them construct ideas built upon what they already know.

From these preceding studies we can draw a second conclusion. It appears that children's ideas quickly become more sophisticated and differentiated as they actively construct new meaning from concepts and experiences they encounter in school. As the studies of the Italian, U.S., and Australian children suggest, children also pick up a host of ideas about their social, economic, and political worlds independent of school, from their parents, friends, popular culture, television, and their own personal experiences.

We also can draw a third conclusion. Even young children show almost unlimited capacity to learn ideas, concepts, and principles about their present world and that of the past. Sometimes educators are tempted to think that children are moving through some sequential, fairly rigid developmental-stage process. You may have heard about **Piagetian theory** used to describe children as "being in a certain stage." We want to argue that making this claim is shortsighted. We know of no neat, agreed-upon method of labeling students by developmental learning "stage," or of any method on the immediate horizon. Yes, children do appear to move in some type of progression from understanding simple ideas to having much greater command of complex concepts and questions. However, children appear to move along at different speeds, and most seem to be willing to grapple with almost anything that's interesting, even if it's a difficult idea. The variation in children's development defies any simple method of categorizing them by age-specific stages. And we have no clear sense yet, based on social studies research, how challenging them with complex ideas in classroom contexts can speed along what they learn.

And one last conclusion: Children do have difficulty understanding and retaining the new ideas they encounter if they are not connected to their prior knowledge, if they lack coherence, and if they are not embedded within a meaningful context. Take for example the *National Assessments of Educational Progress* (NAEP) done by the United States government. These assessments are administered every five years or so in the social studies areas of history and geography, as well as in reading, the sciences, and in mathematics. To get a look at some of these results, consult this web site: *http://www.ets.org*.

In the late 1980s, Diane Ravitch and Chester Finn (1987) published a book that analyzed results of the history portion of the NAEP. They note that students do poorly, are unable to remember many key historical events and important figures, and even have difficulty placing an event as memorable as the Civil War in the correct part of the nineteenth century.

If we take a closer look at the analysis, however, and couple it with what we know about how history is typically taught in U.S. classrooms, the poor results make our point. In the typical approach to teaching history, students read a standard, often difficult to understand textbook, answer questions at the end of the chapters, listen to a teacher lecture about the facts in the textbook, and take a multiple-choice test on Friday (Goodlad, 1984; Shaver, et al., 1980). Students receive little help in connecting new historical ideas to their prior knowledge and usually receive little historical context in which to situate what they're supposed to learn. Rather, they are asked simply to memorize "the facts" and spit them back out on the tests. Nothing much sticks, and this comes as no surprise. Learning about social studies turns out to be much more than simple memorization. We discuss how to teach social studies as more than memorizing facts in Chapters 4 and 5.

Generally speaking, the results of these studies suggest that, though young children can possess underdeveloped and naive ideas about societies and their economies, the situation changes dramatically in a few short years, from the time the children are about five and six to the time they leave elementary school. As we have said about Helen and Rita, children are active meaning makers, busy constructing an understanding of their worlds. The richer the ideas they have to work with and the more tightly connected ideas are to what children already know, the more robust children's understandings and the quicker their development. This is especially true in the area of history, where a spate of studies have emerged recently. But before we explore where children acquire their historical knowledge and how they learn it, let's review the research-based ideas we've touched on so far. We devote a separate section to the topic of ideas about history because so much recent research has emerged.

SECTION SUMMARY What Children Know About Economics, Politics and Government, and Geography

- By the time children enter elementary school, they know a surprising amount about their social worlds. Not all their ideas are entirely accurate, but children have formed some fairly sophisticated models of social life already.
- Children's ideas about economics and politics and government change and expand almost overnight, indicating their capacity and desire to actively build and modify their knowledge.
- Children's thoughts on these subjects quickly become more sophisticated and differentiated as they actively construct new meaning through the process of being challenged with interesting ideas.
- Children's capacity to learn ideas, concepts, and principles about their present world and that of the past appears almost unlimited, even though some "age-specific developmental stage theories" claim the young children cannot manage complex ideas that have abstract elements.
- Children have difficulty understanding new ideas they encounter if they are not connected to prior knowledge, if they lack coherence, and if they are not embedded within a meaningful context.

RELEVANT RESEARCH

Children's ideas about history Perhaps one of the most systematic studies of what elementary students know and learn about American history was a yearlong project that followed ten middle-class white students across their fifth-grade year (Brophy & VanSledright, 1997). The researchers interviewed the students in depth before and after seven different commonly taught history curriculum topics. Here is a quick summary of the results.

Students' knowledge of the history content of each unit before studying it is relatively sparse. Students often report that they know nothing. When they claim to know something, their ideas are often loosely structured and underdeveloped. This is not surprising, because they have not studied American history

Children learn in many ways. As these third graders try on 19th-century women's garments, they are experiencing history firsthand. Think about how you might extend the power of this learning opportunity when the children return to their classroom.

in any systematic way before. However, after studying the material in class using textbooks and **trade books,** and listening to the history stories their teacher told, they report significant gains in what they know. In short, across the span of one school year, their knowledge of history increases significantly. Several of the ten children interviewed persist in retaining certain naive conceptions (for example, that Native Americans had completely disappeared, that Johnny Tremain signed the Declaration of Independence), but overall, their knowledge growth is rather remarkable, thanks in part to a skillful, dynamic history teacher. Helen and Rita were both involved in this study.

RELEVANT RESEARCH

A study done with six U.S. eighth-graders about to embark on a lengthy exploration of British colonization in North America, further underscores what is likely happening for kids who take the history NAEP referred to earlier, namely that historical facts, shorn of a compelling explanatory context such as a story or narrative, make little sense to learners. The researcher finds that, even though the students covered this same material in fifth grade, they have difficulty remembering much of what they studied (VanSledright, 1995). In interviews, five of six students recalled the name Jamestown from fifth grade, but can say little more about it. This is the case with most of the questions regarding what they remembered from their fifth-grade study of colonization. The one exception concerns Plymouth Rock and the early Plymouth colony. Students are able to tell the common, celebratory story about the colonists' arrival there and the first Thanksgiving. They claim they remember this so well because they have heard the *story* in several elementary grades as a part of the Thanksgiving holiday celebration. The other historical material get "all jumbled in my head," said one of the students, because it seems like all he did in class is memorize facts that make little sense because they lack a meaningful context.

RELEVANT RESEARCH

For years, researchers and teachers thought that history was too abstract and complex a subject for young children to understand. They often cited children's trouble with dates and historical chronology as evidence for this conclusion and cited the Piagetian developmental stage theory to claim that youngsters could not understand the abstract concepts inherent in historical study. To further examine the basis for this idea, two researchers explored how fifty-eight U.S. elementary students (approximately eight students in each of grades K–6) constructed understandings of historical time (in contrast to clock time or contemporary calendar time) (see Barton & Levstik, 1996). They were interested in testing further the claims that children below ages seven or eight often can not make reliable distinctions about events in the past. What they found is intriguing.

The fifty-eight students were asked to place nine pictures taken from a variety of historical time periods (for example, colonial era, the late nineteenth century, the 1950s) in the order they occurred chronologically. Not surprisingly, the responses vary by age. The youngest children, five- and six-year-olds, are able to make quite clear distinctions in historical time, but placing the pictures by actual dates has little meaning for them. They use picture context clues such as clothing and hairstyle and their background knowledge of such cultural artifacts to base their choices. For example, "Kindergartner Mickey . . . explained that the colonial picture was the oldest because 'they don't got nothing to wear 'cept those clothes,' " and first-grader Mindy "noted that the colonial picture was the oldest 'cause there isn't anything to move and they walked all the time' " (Barton & Levstik, 1996, p. 431). Not until about third grade do dates begin to make sense, and not until fifth and sixth grades do children begin to link dates with their background knowledge about event periods, such as colonization of the Atlantic seaboard by the British. For instance, fifth-grade Rodney "compared the 1920s and 1950s pictures by observing that 'in the thirties and twenties, that's when the cars like these start coming out, and these cars come out in the '60s . . .' " (Barton & Levstik, 1996, p. 433).

The authors conclude that such sizable agreement across grade levels in placement of the pictures indicates that children have a large body of chronological history knowledge at their disposal. They use this outcome to dispute earlier claims that young children are not ready for historical study. Elementary school teachers, they contend, can help to enhance young learners' ideas of the past and historical chronology by building on their existing knowledge of changes in popular culture such as clothing, technology, and hairstyles, and avoid relying exclusively on dates as organizers.

IN YOUR CLASSROOM: Establishing Historical Context

If you teach a unit on the English Pilgrim settlers who arrived in North America on the Mayflower, you might begin to establish historical context by using pictures of

- current forms of water transportation compared to ships such as the Mayflower
- supplies present-day explorers might take with them compared to pictures of tools and such materials the Pilgrims had taken along
- pilgrim clothing compared to present day attire.

Engage students in a discussion of the differences, helping them to explain why such differences have developed.

Many of these studies suggest that young children have a tendency to oversimplify aspects of both the past and present, especially if the ideas they develop are heavily influenced by popular culture and not offset by other more balanced learning experiences. Although their ideas become more differentiated and less simplistic over time, children may continue to hold over-generalized conceptions that can be difficult to dispel. Nonetheless, children appear game for almost any big, rich idea—known or unknown—that can engage their minds, regardless of age. Yes, some students will struggle more than others with powerful ideas, but how teachers present these ideas, not student age, seems to be the most important factor.

All of the conclusions we have drawn so far underscore our point about curious, active children's minds busily constructing meaning from almost everything they see, hear, and read as they build understandings from them. They also suggest that children can persist in retaining naïve or misconceived ideas that make sense to them, ones not countered with different conceptions. We will return momentarily to these points and what they might mean for you as a social studies teacher.

SECTION SUMMARY **What Children Know About History**

- Children tend to oversimplify aspects of the past (and also the present) if the ideas they develop about history are heavily influenced by present-day popular culture.
- Children can hold and retain over-generalized conceptions about history that may be difficult to change.
- Children, regardless of age, appear game for almost any big, rich idea—known or unknown—that can engage their minds.
- Some children will struggle more with historically complex ideas, but how teachers present these ideas seems to be the most important factor, not age level.

How Do Children Learn About Social Studies Ideas?

Despite a fairly sizable pool of research studies on what children know about social studies, *how* children learn it remains somewhat of a mystery. Current learning theories, such as constructivism, show promise in helping us understand how learning occurs, but much more research must be done. For now, constructivism suggests that children, as we have noted, are active, meaning-making creatures, who build understandings from their experiences and then continually use those understandings to refine and construct new ones. In the area of social studies, research has focused on how children learn from text material, especially in history, because children's access to the past is so heavily mediated by books. Let's examine a sample of this research.

RELEVANT RESEARCH

Two researchers explored what fifth-graders learn from commonly used U.S. history textbooks (McKeown & Beck, 1990). They interviewed the fifth-graders before and after a unit on the American Revolution in which a textbook was the major source of information. They also interviewed sixth-graders who had taken the same fifth-grade history course the year before to see how well they retained what they had learned. The interviews indicate that many of the fifth-graders have serious trouble making sense of the textbooks they read, and the sixth-graders have trouble recalling what they learned in fifth grade. Again, this should come as no surprise—try remembering what you learned from your history textbooks.

The researchers point out that textbook authors often assume too much background knowledge on the part of students. Textbook authors also use an impersonal "language of objectivity" that dehumanizes the content and distances the students from the information. In addition, textbook authors frequently write passages that lack coherence (that is, they leave out key connecting words such as "meanwhile," "and then," "in order to," and so on). As a result, these problems encourage youngsters who lack prior knowledge to overcome them to back away from the history textbooks, and possibly from the study of history altogether, setting the stage for the dislike of history and social studies we mentioned earlier. To illustrate, compare the differences between the two text passages in Figure 2.1. Notice the blandness of the textbook account compared to the trade book version.

The same two researchers use what they call "**repair strategies**" to fix the textbook passages to see if they help students better learn the information (McKeown & Beck, 1994). The repair strategies include (a) providing more background historical context information in the passages to help overcome students' limited prior knowledge and (b) actually rewriting sections of the textbooks to make them more coherent. Both repair strategies are helpful. The researchers conclude that students would benefit by studying a curriculum with fewer historical topics, covering those topics in greater depth, and encountering more of the added contextual information that enhances coherence.[2]

Figure 2.1 • Comparing Textbook and Trade Book Accounts (adapted from McKeown & Beck, 1994, p. 16)

Two text accounts of British taxes passed following the French and Indian War

History textbook passage (from Silver Burdett, 1984, p. 106)

The British lawmaking body was and still is called Parliament. The colonists were not members. The British started passing laws to tax the colonies. Britain thought the colonies should pay their share of the cost of the French and Indian War.

History trade book passage (from Fritz, 1977, p. 30)

England had been fighting a long and expensive war, and when it was over, the question was now how to pay the bills. Finally a government offical suggested that one way to raise money was to tax Americans. "What a good idea!" King George said. After all, the French and Indian part of the war had been fought on American soil for the benefit of Americans, so why shouldn't they help pay for it?

TEACHER REFLECTION

Choosing Classroom Resources

These studies and others like them suggest caution in selecting and using textbooks because of their often adverse influences on learning. You probably will need to augment your use of textbooks with narrative accounts and perhaps fictional trade books, of which the classroom book market offers many (see the list of children's literature titles in the Appendix). However, switching away from textbooks and embracing these alternative books, although it carries distinct advantages, requires you to remain vigilantly reflective and thoughtful about your choice of texts and teaching practices. To illustrate, let's consider several studies that explore the influence of alternative history texts on students' understanding of the past.

RELEVANT RESEARCH

In one study, researchers investigated the relationship of children's responses to textual narratives about the past—the sort of storytelling style found frequently in **historical fiction** and trade books—and their understanding of the history they read about (Levstik & Pappas, 1987). The study looks at small groups of U.S. students in grades two, four, and six. The authors conclude that (a) young learners are quite capable of constructing their own historical narratives, (b) even the youngest children were open to and interested in historical information and find aspects of social history appealing, (c) ample historical context and style of presentation in the texts are both key elements with respect to what students learned, and (d) researchers and teachers consistently underestimate young children's capacity to make sense of the past and think intelligently about it.

RELEVANT RESEARCH

As a case in point, consider the story of Jennifer, a fifth-grader from Kentucky. Linda Levstik (1989), a researcher at the University of Kentucky, examines the relationship between Jennifer's learning of history and the **narratives** or stories (for example, historical fiction) she read in class. Jennifer finds narratives more appealing than textbooks because they provide a sense of wholeness and moral resolution and emphasize the humanness of history. Jennifer's embrace of historical narratives causes her to use them as a reference point from which to judge the quality of the history textbook:

> The social studies [text]book is old and doesn't have as much information in it like [fictional] books do . . . and they give you a lot of information that no social studies book ever tells you. . . . The social studies book doesn't give you a lot of detail. You don't imagine yourself there because they're not doing it as if it were a person. That would be a very interesting social studies book if they told a few things about the people as if it were from their own eyes. . . . But the textbooks don't like to be interesting, especially. (Levstik 1989, p. 114)

Levstik concludes that it is important to provide students with more than just textbooks as sources of historical information. She recommends integrating language arts with historical study as a means of joining the learning of history with the art of interpretation and the creation of narratives, two processes taught more commonly in language arts, yet closely linked to history. However, Levstik does say that reliance on the fictional narratives to teach history can lead to distorted understandings if students are not clear about the distinctions between historical accounts and fictional recreations, or if they were exposed to fictional selections depicting events that were not historically valid.

RELEVANT RESEARCH

Another study yields some evidence to support Levstik's concerns (VanSledright & Brophy, 1992). Interviews with ten fourth-graders who had read historical fiction accounts during their exploration of state history that year, indicate that some of them, particularly the lower achievers, produce stories and fancifully elaborated accounts as responses to questions about what they learned. The students appear to equate storytelling with history, so that if an account is based in the past, is dramatic, contains action, is personalized, and is constructed around a **story grammar** framework (conventional beginning, middle, and end), then, to them, it constitutes history. These students seem unaware that historians and novelists often have different goals in mind when they write.

For these fourth-graders, the use of narrative or storytelling, especially in fictionalized accounts of history, operates in two opposing directions. It motivates the students to read and engage with the past because the students find the fiction interesting. But it also fosters beliefs about history and historical evidence that are at odds with how historians do their work.

RELEVANT RESEARCH

In a more recent study, investigators further explore how kids make sense of history when they read from textbooks and alternative trade-book accounts (VanSledright & Kelly, 1998). Researchers conducted several detailed interviews with six fifth-graders about what they were learning from the texts and a **think-aloud protocol,** where students talk out aloud as they read. The six students read two accounts of the Boston Massacre, one taken from a history text that contained eyewitness testimony, and a more general account taken from a text that had no eyewitness reports.

The researchers draw several conclusions from their results: First, students view history as an objective, fact-based account of the past and see their task as being to get those facts; on the other hand, the students demonstrate virtually no sense about ways to judge the viability or accuracy of the various historical representations they read. Second, the students are unsure about what to do when information from one text conflicts with another. And third, the students are unaware of the various ways that evidence from the past, such as diaries, artifacts, and letters, have been used in constructing the different types of history texts. This causes most of them to believe that any text type—textbook, fictional account, diary, letter—is equally valid in representing history. But when the students are pressed to choose a most accurate type of text, they select the textbook because its apparent objective nature fits more readily with their similar objective view of history, and because their classroom activities involve the search for historical facts and information. These fifth-graders construct a view of history as an objective retelling of past events. Despite evidence that different retellings sometimes contradict each other making the objective, retelling view suspect the kids resist giving up the idea.

Some evidence does indicate that several of the students make judgments about the history texts they read based on an author's point of view. These students assess the texts' descriptions of an event by building a mental model about the various ways an event might have occurred, depending on one's perspective. For example, one student explains how events of the Boston Massacre look different depending on whether you are a British soldier being charged by a mob of Bostonians, or a Boston citizen being threatened by British soldiers with loaded guns and bayonets. These results are encouraging, for they suggest that students, if given the opportunity to make judgments about historical accounts and coached how to do so, can make some fairly sophisticated analyses of the history they read. Again, the moral of the story seems to be that it's unwise to sell kids short; many of them are much sharper than we think.

SECTION SUMMARY **Drawing Conclusions About How Children Learn Social Studies Ideas**

- Children (like adults) are meaning-making creatures who take what they have learned from past experiences and use it to make sense of new ideas and experiences they encounter. Exactly how this works in a child's mind remains something of a mystery.
- Although how children learn is in part mysterious, we can speculate that how they learn social studies occurs in relationship to activities, such as watching TV, playing games, listening to parent talk, going to the store, going to school, and the like. From research studies, we know that how kids learn comes from interactions with social studies texts of various types.
- Textbooks have been repeatedly criticized for their inconsideration of young readers, their inability to sustain coherent ideas, their emphasis on details at the expense of overall main ideas, and their often dull expository style.
- Textbooks must be supplemented with other texts (historical fiction, trade books, letters, biographies) if learning is to occur in meaningful ways for students.

- Using a variety of texts provides an important set of learning opportunities for students, requiring that they develop an understanding of how to read different types of texts.
- Multiple accounts of historical events are essential in enabling students to understand how historians (and others) construct these accounts based on evidence and rules about how to use that evidence.
- Books used thoughtlessly, whether fact-based views presented in textbooks or those views from, for example, historical fiction, can distort students' perspectives and retard their developing critical, interpretive, and constructive-thinking capacities.

Where Do Children Get Their Ideas About Social Studies?

Where children get their social studies ideas has been less actively researched than what children know and how they learn. Before looking at a few research studies, we should note that it is easy to speculate about where children get their social studies ideas. For example, because children are busily trying to make sense of their experiences in the world (as are adults), they are curious about most everything around them. As a result, play is a rich source of learning about social organization, social norms, and hierarchies of authority and power. Popular culture, with all its messages about the values and mores of daily life, makes its way into a child's world via television, radio, film, videotapes, games, newsprint and magazines, and now the Internet. Parents and community life also are robust sources for childhood learning. We also know that the local context in which a child learns (such as the country, the social class, the community—urban or rural) makes a significant difference. For instance, what children come to understand about banks and work roles in Italy can be different from what same-aged children learn about banks and work roles in, say, a third-world country such as Cameroon. Or similarly, a child who grows up in an impoverished inner-city neighborhood likely will have different ideas about work from a child who lives ten miles away in a comfortable, wealthy suburb. Of course, the systematic experiences children encounter in school and with text material (as we noted above) also teach much about the current world, the past, what a culture values.

RELEVANT RESEARCH

One study of where children's social studies ideas come from examines how fifth-graders make sense of the arrival of English settlers at Jamestown (Afflerbach & VanSledright, 1998). In the study, seven fifth-graders are asked to read from two different texts, one a traditional textbook account of the early colonial settlement, and a second one that describes the early colonial events from

Visual media, in the form of television and movies, can send powerful messages to students about history. This scene from *Pocahontas* depicts Pocahontas imploring her father to save John Smith's life. An interesting in-class exercise might be to have your students write their own dialogue for this scene after studying a unit on Native life and then compare the students' efforts with the film version.

the perspective of how the colonists, despite having what appeared to be ample food supplies, almost died of starvation in the winter of 1609–10. Students are asked to think out loud as they read and explain how they are making sense of the texts. The textbook passage includes a brief description of John Smith's encounter with the Powhatan Indians and the role Pocahontas had in convincing her father, the chief of the Powhatans, to spare Smith's life. All seven students had seen the Disney film *Pocahontas* and used it to filter their understanding of the account in the traditional textbook. For the students, the film, despite being animated, holds greater authority for them than the textbook account. Several students take issue with the textbook description, noting that they think the book is getting some of the ideas wrong because it leaves out details they had seen in the film.

The authors dub the way the students use the film to judge the textbook (in contrast to the other way around as is often the case) the "**Disney effect**" (Afflerbach & VanSledright, 1998). This Disney effect indicates, as we have been arguing, that children create meaning from an array of sources. Children use those ideas to filter new ideas and construct new ways of thinking about concepts they encounter in the classroom. This example demonstrates the power of film in popular culture, for example, to influence this meaning construction process.

IN YOUR CLASSROOM: Assessing Children's Ideas

If you have an opportunity to teach a topic that has been the subject of a recent children's film, you might begin by assessing your students' ideas about the topic, based on what they have seen. You could start by holding a question-and-answer session in which you ask who has seen the film, what they have learned from it, and how accurate they think the film was. Listen carefully, the understandings that your students describe will be what you have to build on as far as teaching them new ways of thinking about the topic. This exercise also should help raise motivation to study the topic because many of your students likely will already know something about it and have ideas to offer. In short, the topic hooks into their existing experience. But, again, listen carefully to what they tell you so you understand how their ideas may differ from or resemble what you intend to teach. After you teach the topic, you might revisit the film and compare what the film conveys and what you studied in your classroom.

RELEVANT RESEARCH

Robert Coles's (1980) work supports some of the speculations made about where children's ideas come from. Specifically, he notes the power of the local culture to influence children's ideas about their social worlds. In one rather touching illustration, he notes:

> In the South, for years, I heard black children speak of sheriffs and policeman as "devils," without picking up the hint that they were giving attitudes long held. In 1965, in McComb, Mississippi, I asked a six-year-old child who was President. She said she didn't know, "but they killed President Kennedy and they killed Medgar Evers."[3] I asked who "they" were. She said, "the people who don't like us." (p. 28)

Coles points out the power local customs and cultural norms, such as segregation and discrimination by whites against blacks in the days before and during the Civil Rights movement, have in shaping young children's perceptions and ideas of social life. At six years of age, this African American girl from the deep South, Coles observes, already knows a "great deal about what social scientists call the subject of 'race relations,' " and " . . . is fully capable of a firm political judgment: The relatively well-off people don't *themselves* want to be reminded too pointedly how things work in their favor [because] it is a discomforting accusation" (p. 28).

If recent research is beginning to help us understand what students know, it also is helping us understand how they have come to know what they do in particular contexts and settings. We hope questions about what children know about social studies, where they learn it, and how they learn it will continue to drive research efforts. From what we do know, though, we can begin to shape some theories about how children learn social studies, and how the sources of their ideas influence the way they construct meaning.

SECTION SUMMARY Where Children Learn About Social Studies

- Clearly, children learn from text material and ideas they encounter in school, but they also learn from a variety of other sources outside of school. These include parents, film, TV, neighborhood play and community activities, church, popular mass culture, local culture, and so on.
- The power of non-school activities and sources to influence children's thinking about social studies sometimes can be stronger than in-school sources. However, classrooms are highly influential sources of learning.

A Constructivist View of Learning Social Studies

Consider for a moment how you learn and when that learning is most powerful. Are you a "blank slate" on which someone or something "writes" so that you can later reproduce that knowledge? Or do you learn best when you actively integrate new ideas with your prior knowledge, assumptions, and experiences? We suspect that your most powerful learning experiences are more akin to this latter characterization. So too for your students.

This talk of learning and knowing leads us back to exploring constructivism—a theory of how people learn. To reiterate, constructivism suggests that your sociocultural context and prior knowledge and experience interact with new ideas to influence how you create new understandings. As evidence accumulates, researchers and educators increasingly believe that learning primarily consists of ongoing sense making. Rather than simply absorbing ready-made classroom information, students need to make sense of what they learn and construct meaning for themselves if there is any hope that they will be able to remember it.

Behaviorism: Assumptions About Learning

Research about what students know and how they learn has led many educators to rethink their views of learning. Until recently, most believed in behaviorist theories. These theories trace their origins to the latter part of the

Figure 2.2 • Learning Process in Behaviorism

Stimulus ⟶ **Learner's response** + **Teacher's reinforcement** = **Learning**

nineteenth and early part of the twentieth centuries, and especially in the United States to the psychologist **B. F. Skinner.** Behaviorists such as Skinner are interested in how people learn but focus on the *measurable* aspects of that learning. They shun such unmeasurable cognitive processes as the unconscious, popularized by **Sigmund Freud.** Their concern with measurable learning activity and behavioral outcomes gives raise to the term *behaviorism.*

Skinner thought that humans learned best when they were on a **positive reinforcement** schedule. In other words, people encounter and respond in various ways to learning stimuli. The learning **stimulus** might be anything—a new book, a lecture, a film—that a teacher introduces in class. If a learner encounters the learning stimulus coupled with some sort of reinforcement—praise from the teacher, a reward of some sort, a good grade—he or she learns. Even if learners receive reinforcements only part of the time a stimulus is presented, they will still learn. Learners neither learn nor retain stimuli not followed by some reinforcement. A simplistic overview of this learning cycle is depicted in Figure 2.2.

To "undo" **responses** that are deemed inappropriate, the teacher can do one of two things: Create a situation in which the learner encounters an unpleasant result when he responds incorrectly to a stimulus, or simply ignore the incorrect behavior and thus not reinforce the response. For example, if a student encounters the unpleasant result of poor marks on a test, it would be designed to make the student stop doing poorly, change his behavior so he did better on the tests, and thereby learn what was expected. Using a reinforcement schedule comprised of rewards and unpleasant experiences, Skinner, in a much heralded experiment, taught pigeons to play ping-pong. Unfortunately for school-age children, who have much more complex mental processes than pigeons, behavioristic ideas and operations soon found their way into the classroom.

Behavioristic theories rest on certain assumptions. We center our description on several that relate specifically to how educators employ the behaviorism model for thinking about learning in schools. Behavioristic models applied in school settings assume first that learners need information broken into small, easily digestible bits of information and procedures to be learned. These manageable stimuli can be built one atop the next in a simple progression that allows the teacher to design a reinforcement schedule.

Second, those information bits and procedures are arranged in hierarchical and sequential order: simple facts first, then more complex facts, followed by these facts arrayed around concepts, and so on toward complex modes of thought such as critical thinking. Any disruption in this order causes inappropriate learning that must be undone. "Undoing" is considered an inefficient use of classroom time, so the stress is placed on establishing the proper order of learning stimuli.

Third, given similar learning stimuli or inputs, one can expect learners to produce similar outputs, or learning outcomes. Learners and outcomes can vary somewhat, but this is considered an aberrant result and one to be avoided. The teacher wants all the students on the same page at the same time, so to speak.

Fourth, because of their assumption that learning something precedes being able to think intelligently about it, behaviorists argue that a student needs to learn or memorize facts before thinking about and ordering them into more complex wholes.

Fifth, learning is considered a largely passive, or at best a reactive activity in which students have their mental slates written on in such a way that they are unaware that learning is actually occurring. Finally, reinforcement schedules using rewards or unpleasant experiences are to be arranged carefully to maximize learning outputs.

As you can see, teachers in this scheme are like learning engineers in charge of arranging learning stimuli and managing learning outputs by the rules of behaviorism. Students are relatively passive recipients of these stimuli–response arrangements and reinforcement schemes. If you think about your own school experience, especially in elementary school social studies, you will probably recognize how much of your classroom conduct was shaped by teachers who bought into these assumptions and built learning opportunities around them. When you think back, was social studies about learning an endless array of facts about which you were tested in some sort of paper and pencil manner? If you scored well, you were rewarded with praise and good marks. If you did poorly, you experienced the discomfort of thinking you were not learning effectively or at all.

Constructivism: Assumptions About Learning

As many good social studies teachers know (and educational researchers are now figuring out), these behaviorist assumptions just do not hold up very well. Go back and examine Helen and Rita's comments about the birth of the United States and the search for a trade route to the Far East. They demonstrate quite clearly that young minds are hardly passive, blank slates but rather active and cognitively busy learning systems. Because students' prior knowledge varies, sometimes significantly, teachers can hardly assume that variation is aberrant behavior. Variation is the rule, not the exception. Helen and Rita, in theory at least, experienced the same set of fourth-grade social studies learning opportunities (stimuli), taught by the same teacher, using the same set of social studies texts. Yet they developed different ideas about similar events (outputs), leading us to seriously question the viability of behaviorist learning assumptions.

As we have been saying, young learners actively use what they already know to make sense out of new ideas they encounter. Reinforcement schedules and rewards fail to work if these learners make no sense of the ideas and knowledge the classroom offers them. Teacher-as-learning-engineer, who erects knowledge on the flat, blank slate of the child's mind, seems hardly an apt metaphor either. The learning coach and facilitator appears more appropriate by constructivist lights.

Constructivist learning theorists also make certain assumptions about how young children learn. The following are several we consider central to teaching social studies.

Learners are sense makers First, young learners are sense-making creatures. From our adult perspective, they are naive in their knowledge and assumptions. This should be no big surprise; for children's experiences, although rich in many ways, lack the depth and breadth of adults' experiences. Children's accounts of ideas and events often seem fragmentary and disparate. Helen and Rita's historical reconstructions are good illustrations, as are many that emerge from the research. They take what makes historical sense to them initially and wed it with new ideas about the past that they encounter in their Michigan history course. The result is a curious admixture of accurate historical conceptions, fanciful elaborations, and odd **conflations.** However, their accounts are disparate, elaborated, and conflated not because they do not "know" enough; rather they are struggling both with making sense of ideas that they have not quite grasped yet and with the newly-found prospect of sense-making itself.

Learners construct meaning using language Second, children (and adults, for that matter) make sense by constructing meaning. Language is their most important tool here. Students use talk of facts, concepts, principles, and, yes, theories of their own to construct around them a world that has meaning and appears to hold a degree of coherence. Although Helen and Rita's remarks may seem to us somewhat incoherent, they do in their own ways make perfectly good and coherent sense to the girls.

Learners are cognitively active And third, learners actively make powerful associations among and between facts, concepts and principles. One way to think about this is in terms of *webs of meaning*. For example, Helen may approach her study of the birth of the United States with established ideas regarding the concepts of war, poor and rich, country affiliation, Michigan, Americans, and perhaps the British. She probably possesses some facts that help anchor these concepts (for example, war involves conflict and fighting, Americans live in Michigan, the British come from England), and she most likely holds some partially formed theories and principles, uniquely her own, that allow her to interconnect the facts and concepts (for example, wars are fought between rich and poor countries). In the classroom she heard stories about the birth of the United States that interacted with and modified her preliminary associations in ways represented by her response (for example, the Americans and British were once friends, but later they fought because the British broke a promise not to fight). To assess how her understanding of Michigan and U.S. history changed, we would need to have formed a picture of what her understanding looked like before her classroom study of Michigan history. Because we didn't do that, we can only speculate here about how Helen constructs meaning.

Learners' ideas vary Learners' understandings are hardly static or fixed. Each day in a variety of ways, these webs of meaning and understanding are modified and reconstructed by experiences both in school and certainly out of school, all in ways difficult to predict and anticipate. Because of this, you will need to listen closely to students' ideas and theories about their worlds. The ideas learners bring to the learning context are the raw materials—not the blank slate—you have to work with. This is a fundamental difference in assumptions about learning that demarcate the older behaviorist approach from the newer constructivist one.

We are encouraged by the implications of constructivism for teaching. Yes, it makes teaching more complex and difficult in some ways, but it also makes it more engaging and rich in many others. We're further encouraged that many constructivist learning/learner assumptions have been borne out by research results emerging, especially in the area of history education. However, some features of constructivist assumptions complicate teaching and make it problematic in actual practice. As we continue our examination, we will suggest strategies for addressing those problems.

The Problems of Constructivist Views

The constructivist view of learning social studies has far-reaching implications. Some of those implications show great promise while others are problematic. Many of your students will be able to make sense of the learning opportunities they create on their own, but experienced teachers know that others will need help. This is an important point; the constructivist story, as we have said, is not entirely rosy all the time.

First, we explore four interrelated problematic features of constructivism:

1. How do you, as their teacher, know what your children know?
2. How can you learn to "hear" what your students are saying about what they know and are learning?
3. What do you do if students have naive, misconceived, or conflated ideas about social studies?
4. How do you validate what your students know and the meanings they construct while still attempting to influence their naive, inaccurate, or conflated concepts?

How to know what your students know By now it should be clear that in order to help your students build new ideas and construct new meaning, you must first figure out what your students already know. If Helen and Rita are any indication, we can draw several conclusions. Your students' prior conceptions will be varied, most likely naive, over-generalized, and may show conflations of one cluster of ideas with other, generally unrelated ones. Some of your students will have a fairly rich array of concepts that make good sense by adult and academic disciplinary standards, and others will have little knowledge. All of this complicates planning to teach social studies and predicting what your students can and will learn.

One of the most effective methods for finding out what your students know is to ask them. But taking the time to talk individually with twenty-five or so students is a luxury few teachers can afford. Classroom discussions of what your children know about a topic as you begin its study can help create an impressionistic portrait of their prior knowledge. Yet, some students will say little in such discussions, which leaves you guessing. Other approaches are necessary.

IN YOUR CLASSROOM: Using K-W-L Exercises

One strategy we have seen successfully employed in social studies classes is the **K-W-L** exercise (Ogle, 1986). This exercise can be done in two parts, often as a paper-and-pencil activity. The letters represent each of three questions: "What do I **K**now about this topic or subject?" "What do I **W**ant to learn about it? and "What have I **L**earned?" You ask the *K* and *W* questions of students at the beginning of a topic study and the *L* question after you've finished the study. If the students can write well enough, they can write their responses in a journal, or you could prepare an activity sheet on which they could write. The many variations on this approach are limited only by your imagination.

Your work here is to help your students tell you what they already know. This will complicate your next task of structuring learning opportunities, because you will quickly discover that what students know is quite varied and can change in unpredictable ways, as we have seen with Helen and Rita. But this is much better than assuming that their minds are blank, that all you need to do is provide a carefully engineered set of learning stimuli, and that they are learning, until the test lets you know otherwise. You're better off building on and working from what your students already know, even though it might be unstable knowledge.

How to "hear" what students are saying We cannot overestimate the importance of learning to hear your students, to understand the sense they are making of the social studies they encounter with you. Learning to hear your students will take time. You must come to know them individually as well as in a group context. You must hear what they say when they tell you about the prior conceptions they hold. Reread Helen and Rita's accounts of the past. What is going on in these two fourth-graders' heads? What are they actually saying about what they know? What about Levstik's Jennifer? What is she saying? Learning to hear will require asking questions and pondering what your students reply. You can enhance your understanding of children by using several means of recording what students do with what you ask them to learn.

IN YOUR CLASSROOM: Probing Students' Ideas

Asking your students to keep **journals** could be very helpful, as well as getting them to draw pictures of their social studies ideas. Some teachers audiotape their social studies classes, while others assign group projects that allow them to sit in on discussions of ideas students exchange as they accomplish a social studies activity. Some children's language can be awkward and inarticulate. Their ideas may be ill-formed or inchoate. They will need your help to draw the ideas out, which can be difficult and time-consuming, but is essential to good social studies teaching.

We should caution, though, that learning to hear your students is an ongoing task, never perfected or complete. Why? Because you filter what others tell you through your own understanding of the world, through the assumptions you make and the knowledge you hold. **Empathy,** the ability to put yourself in your students' shoes, so to speak, is at best only an approximation. We can never walk away from our own two feet entirely. But that should not stop you from trying to hear what your students are saying. Hearing them, even if only partially, will make your planning and teaching more effective. What you hear will be the floor on which you can build the **scaffold** of social studies learning.

What if students don't have the "right" ideas? Much traditional elementary school learning in social studies can be characterized as the pursuit of facts: the correct names, dates, and events in history; the "right" ideas about how cultures function, how people buy and sell goods in the marketplace, how governments govern, and so on. In elementary school, you probably took social studies tests and filled in worksheets, and most likely, your teachers graded your efforts right or wrong. In many elementary schools, teaching students to produce correct answers is a real concern for teachers, especially in an educational climate that holds students, teachers, and schools accountable for such test results. You will face this same issue.

As we have seen, the wide variation in students' prior knowledge about a given topic, the naive conceptions they bring, and the different approaches they take to constructing meaning, all make it difficult for you to move them to a place where they can begin to construct more accurate and less naive understandings. This, after all, is a worthwhile goal. Students need to know about and draw upon the centuries of knowledge we have constructed about sociocultural, historical, political, geographic, and economic events. Much of this knowledge helps us solve social problems and make sense of our world. Jerome Bruner (1996), the educational psychologist, calls this knowledge the "**cultural toolkit.**" He argues that this toolkit provides the means by which people navigate the sociocultural world. Without it, people cannot function successfully in society.

However, as much as we might wish it were so, knowledge of a culture simply can't be reproduced in children's minds for at least two reasons. First, as we have seen, learning doesn't work that way. Second, cultural knowledge itself is constantly changing. We continuously modify our culture as we invent new ways of solving our problems (such as the changes in the way we communicate wrought by the computer and technological revolution). Also, we are forever debating what our culture ought to value, for example, the best education for all children or only some, how to protect the environment while fostering economic growth through the use of natural resources. **John Dewey** had this notion in mind when he referred to human minds, their individual and collective learning processes, and the culture they produce as "evolutionary" in nature. All of this makes teaching doubly difficult. You want kids to learn about all those important ideas the culture holds dear. But students as well as ideas evolve; if learning is to occur for them you must also ensure that your students have ample opportunities to make sense of it in their own way.

Much of our response to this problem is to suggest that it will be virtually impossible to influence all your students in the same way, to get them all on the same page at the same time, and to ensure that they are constructing the "correct" ideas. Tension will be ever present in your classroom between how your students construct knowledge and the knowledge from history and the social sciences that many of us take as given. We refer to this as a **dilemma,** one that all teachers face and do their best to manage (VanSledright & Grant, 1994). But to manage it effectively depends upon taking time to understand the ideas your students have constructed and are in the process of rebuilding. It also will depend on how you "listen" and thus "hear" what your students are saying about the way they construct an understanding of the social world they encounter in social studies and also away from it.

TEACHER REFLECTION

Considering Naive Conceptions

The following exercise is one method of examining this dilemma of what happens when "kids don't have the 'right' ideas." Although it won't necessarily tell you "what to do," it will help you better understand the different avenues available to you for managing the dilemma. This also is a great exercise in being reflective about your teaching.

Go back and reread both Helen's and Rita's comments at the beginning of this chapter. Look for naïve conceptions and jot them down on the left half of a separate piece of paper, leaving ample space between them (four or five lines). Select six to eight that you think are especially problematic. Divide the right half of the paper in two columns. In the left of these two columns, describe how you might address these naïve conceptions through your teaching. In the right of the two columns, speculate on what might happen for both girls if you did not attend to their naïve conceptions at all.

Which children's ideas do teachers validate? This, too, is a difficult question because it relates closely to the dilemma we just considered. In its more extreme form, constructivism maintains that no ideas are wrong: that, by school and test standards, wrong ideas are only alternative conceptions. These alternative conceptions are grounded in students' different levels and types of background knowledge and constructed around the way old knowledge interacts with new knowledge. As we have seen, how this works is uncertain at best. So herein lies a powerful tension. Alternative conceptions are real and legitimate, and they form the backbone of potentially new and creative ways of thinking. To invalidate them, by constructivist lights, is to invalidate the person who holds them, retard imagination and creativity, and chase away some potentially valuable and valid insights. Yet, many of your students' alternative conceptions remain inaccurate and can create learning conflicts that lead to untenable ideas. Thus, you face the same dilemma described above. And once again, part of managing the dilemma involves you getting students ideas—as fuzzy and potentially inaccurate as they are—out on the educational table and working with them.

Start by thinking of Helen. She appears to conflate the American Revolutionary War with the French and Indian War. These were historically distinct events, separated by more than ten years. Should Helen's alternative view of these wars be allowed to continue? If so, might it give her trouble later as she encounters historical texts that dispute her view? If she continues to retain it, how entrenched will her idea become? Will it grow increasingly resistant to change? We have no good answers to these questions, but some research suggests that alternative conceptions can be quite impervious to change, even to direct instruction, if held for long periods. Therefore, your task as a social studies teacher will be a delicate one.

TEACHER REFLECTION

Listening to Students

You will need to balance the competing demands of students' ideas against the knowledge adults accept as accurate (that is, Bruner's "cultural toolkit"). You will need to listen to your students. You will need to pepper them with questions in order to learn about their alternative ideas. And, if they hold untenable cultural and historical understandings, you will have to challenge them without simultaneously invalidating who they are as curious, cognitively active learners. Occasionally, you will need to fight the temptation—provoked by frustration over your students' stubbornly inaccurate conceptions—to give in and simply provide your students with the "right" answers, the ones that appear on tests or worksheets. At the beginning of Chapter 3, we provide an vignette drawn from an actual classroom, in which the teacher, Ramona Palmer, holds a discussion with her fifth-graders about the Bill of Rights. We encourage you to flip forward to that chapter for a firsthand look at how a good social studies teacher asks her students questions to lure their ideas out onto the educational table and challenge some of them without also invalidating the students.

Managing classroom dilemmas is perhaps one of the most demanding tasks that face social studies teachers who embrace a constructivist perspective. But this embrace is not all tension and dilemma management; it includes promises of great rewards for social studies teachers. Figure 2.3 lists both the problems and the promises of constructivist teaching. We've discussed the problems, now let's explore the promises.

Figure 2.3 • The Problems and Promises of Constructivist Social Studies Teaching

Problems	Promises
Knowing what your students know	Shifting control for learning to children
Hearing what students are saying	Enhancing motivation
When students lack the "right" ideas	Increasing expectations
Validating children's ideas	Increasing the joy of teaching
	Building interdisciplinary connections

CLASSROOM MANAGEMENT

The Promise of Constructivist Views

The problems of a constructivist view are real and important, but so are the promises. We already have alluded to the promises, but here we briefly sketch out five of them that we believe make a compelling case for its embrace.

Shifting control for learning First, constructivist approaches can help your students feel more in control and responsible for their education. By validating your students' ideas and allowing them expression, you send the message that their thinking is respected and important, that they too can contribute something valuable to the learning process. This allows you to create a learning climate in which students can account for why they think as they do. This, in turn, sends the message that they are accountable to you and fellow students for the nature of and the reasons behind their thinking. This shifts the onus for building understandings on to students; your responsibility is to act as a facilitator and coach of a learning process.

Enhancing motivation Second, shifting a good share of control and responsibility for learning to students can enhance motivation to learn. Your students will see that they are in charge of and must direct their own learning. They will learn to make reasoned choices about the way they construct their understandings. They will become more engaged and persistent in the learning tasks they set for themselves.

Increasing expectations Third, you can increase your expectations of what students can accomplish and so introduce earlier in a child's learning experience more complex social studies ideas and concepts. In turn, this supports a generally more powerful and robust overall curriculum that can lead to better-informed students who are more cognitively adept at earlier ages. This is crucial to a culture that continues to become more information driven and dependent.

Increasing the joy of teaching Fourth, a constructivist approach to learning can increase the joy of teaching. If students are in greater control of their learning and demonstrate stronger motivations to learn, you have before you an eager audience, waiting for you to provide resources and learning opportunities. You end up spending less time on disciplining students and generating an array of rewards in order to cajole them into the drudgery of learning facts about which they have little interest or control.

Building interdisciplinary connections And finally, a rich, robust curriculum made possible by this approach provides more opportunities to build **interdisciplinary** connections. You can connect ideas across disciplines and school subjects, such as reading and social studies or social studies and science, that might otherwise be impossible because of the time required to lay down basic facts in each area. Students get excited about these connections. Light bulbs go off in their heads in ways that stimulate the production of new ideas and enhance their desire to learn more.

You probably are entertaining all sorts of questions about another of the commonplaces—teachers and teaching. But before exploring those questions connected to teaching, let us look at a commonplace that bridges learning and teaching—subject matter—the stuff students have opportunities to learn and teachers are charged to teach.

CHAPTER SUMMARY

1. What do children know about social studies?

Elementary-age children come to school knowing a surprising amount about their social worlds. Although their ideas are not always accurate, children have formed some fairly complex notions of social life. These ideas can change, expand, and grow even more sophisticated as children construct new meanings.

Children's capacity to learn ideas, concepts, and principles appears to be almost unlimited, especially if those ideas, concepts, and principles are coherent, embedded within a meaningful context, and connected to the students' prior knowledge and experiences.

Children's prior knowledge can interfere with new learning, however: Old ideas can be hard to shake! At the same time, however, children are interested in and can comprehend complex ideas.

2. How do children learn social studies?

Children (like adults) are meaning-making creatures who take what they have learned from past experiences and use it to make sense of new ideas and experiences they encounter. We don't understand this phenomena well, but we can speculate that how they learn social studies occurs in relationship to activities, such as watching TV, playing games, listening to parent talks, going to the store, going to school, and the like.

Considerable research on the use of textbooks, particularly history texts indicates that textbooks should be supplemented with other texts (historical fiction, trade books, letters, biographies) if learning is to occur in meaningful ways for students. Using multiple texts is an especially important means of presenting varied perspectives on historical ideas and events.

3. *Where do children learn about social studies?*

Children learn from text material and ideas they encounter in school, but they also learn from a variety of sources outside school. These include parents, film, TV, neighborhood play and community activities, church, popular mass culture, local culture, and so on. The power of non-school activities and sources to influence children's thinking about social studies sometimes can be stronger than in-school sources. However, classrooms continue as influential places of learning.

4. *What is constructivism as a learning theory and what are its assumptions?*

The principal tenets of constructivism include the notions that learners are primarily sense-making creatures who construct meaning for the most part using language and are cognitively active, busy making sense of their world. Learners' ideas vary as each child uses his or her distinct prior experience, knowledge, and understanding of the world to construct new meaning.

5. *What are the problems and promises of constructivism for social studies teachers?*

The problems include knowing what your students know, hearing what students are saying, understanding when students lack the "right" ideas, and validating students' ideas. The promises of constructivism include shifting control for learning to children, enhancing motivation, increasing expectations and the joy of teaching, and building interdisciplinary connections.

TEACHING RESOURCES

Print Resources

We highly recommend that you read more on the research studies we cite both in the chapter text and in the reference section. Our summaries of these studies are limited because of space. A wealth of additional information can be gleaned by consulting the primary sources themselves.

Technology Resources

- **http://www.wam.umd.edu/H1/~bvansled/thsig/information.html**

This is the web site for the Teaching History Special Interest Group. This site contains a link to a list of references, many of which consider how children and young adolescents learn history. Many of these studies are well worth consulting.

NOTES

1. Clearly, we can speculate that children's ideas come from their everyday experiences going to the store or the post office or the bank or listening to parents tell stories of their experiences. And of course, children learn much in school. Our point is that researchers have not closely examined the "where question." For the most part we are left to our speculations.
2. To read several critiques of social studies textbooks, see Beck, McKeown, and Gromoll (1989); Larkins, Hawkins, and Gilmore (1987); and McCabe (1993).
3. Evers, an African-American civil rights leader, was assassinated.

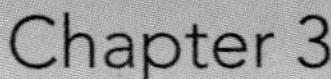

Chapter 3

The Subject Matter of Social Studies: Taking a Threads Approach

Ramona Palmer, a fifth-grade teacher, is deeply engrossed, along with her eager and active students, in considering the Bill of Rights. Palmer's twenty-eight students include eighteen girls and ten boys. Most of the children are European American, as is Palmer, but the class also includes three African-American and two Asian students. Palmer has been teaching for almost fifteen years in this suburban school in a moderately large northern midwestern city.

To better understand what her students already know, Palmer asks them to explain in their own words the meaning of each amendment in the Bill of Rights. Next, her fifth-graders take several minutes to write down one amendment they would be willing to give up if someone passed a law requiring it, and the reasons for their choice.

After several minutes, she says, "If you're willing to give up the First Amendment, stand up." Cameron, a small, wiry boy, rises. He stands alone. Palmer smiles and says, "That's all right, Cameron. There are no right or wrong answers with this; it's what you believe." Palmer repeats process for each of the next seven amendments, with small groups of students standing for each.

A discussion of Cameron's willingness to give up the first amendment ensues. Palmer asks him to read the amendment from the book. As soon as he finishes, he shrugs his shoulders, smiles, and claims he has changed his mind; he no longer wants to give this one up.

Palmer: But why were you willing to give it up in the first place? I'm really curious. This amendment protects the rights of free speech, the press, and personal opinion.

Cameron [bashfully]: Well, I just liked the other ones better.

Palmer: If you gave it up, how would this affect you?

Davey [interjecting]: You wouldn't be able to give your opinion!

Palmer: How many of you think that if we gave up this right it would infringe on some very basic American principles? [almost everyone's hand goes up immediately] What would it be like if we didn't know about this, couldn't read about it in the newspapers. I'm going to take Cameron's position for a minute. What about those papers like the *Star* or the *Enquirer?*

Several students: Yeah, they exaggerate!

Palmer: Yes. Should there be rules for supplying evidence in these papers?

Cameron: No!

Adrienne: I think there should be guidelines for what they can print.

Palmer: What about 2 Live Crew [a rap group]?

Marvyn: They're okay! If it bothers some people, they don't have to buy it. They put those labels on there that say there's obscene words and stuff on the record. I guess that's okay.

Sam: I think that the swearing and the words that they use are okay. Everyone does it.

The class erupts into a polyphony of voices. Students compete to be heard above the rapidly rising volume. Palmer tells them to stop. She asks them to raise their hands and speak one at a time.

Davey: I agree with Sam.

Jarron: You could bleep out the bad stuff.

Palmer: But then some records would be all bleep.

Davey: Well, it's okay because people are doing it. It's not really hurting anybody.

Palmer: But it's not really okay to say so just because everyone is doing it. What if everyone was murdering? Is that okay?

Students: No!! That's not okay.

Abigail: I think it's unfair to people who like their music.

Palmer: Davey, you said it doesn't hurt anybody. I disagree with you. The lyrics in some songs—I'm just arguing with you—make me out to be a bimbo. I'm offended.

Davey: But you don't need to listen to it.

Palmer: But what if people start to believe this stuff. I'm just giving you an example.

Adam: But in PG movies, they all swear. What's the difference?

Frederic: I've never heard a song about women's right to vote.

Palmer: I'm just saying, what do you do if it insults women? What about blacks? Marvyn?

Marvyn [a black student]: Well . . . well, if you want to listen to it, it's okay.

Palmer: Marvyn, are you hedging? Should we allow it if it insults blacks? Yes or no, Marvyn?

Marvyn: Well, if . . . yes.

Adam [a white student]: There's a movie out right now called "White Men Can't Jump." And some black people call each other niggers.

Palmer: Should that be allowed?

Addie: You should be allowed to do it in the privacy of your own home.

Palmer: Should we allow a parade . . . if someone was a member of the KKK and wanted to have a parade down the streets of our city, is that allowable? [five hands go up]

Barry: That's freedom of speech!

Palmer: I want you to talk this over with your parents tonight. We have to go on to number two, the right to bear arms. Lots of you are ready to give this one up; why?

The class shifts to a discussion of the second amendment: the right to keep and bear arms. This one creates as much disagreement as the first. Throughout the ebb and flow of the discussion, many students sit up in their desks on their knees. Their hands often slice the air in a frenzied effort to attract Palmer's notice. Aware of their eagerness, Palmer moves around the room calling on students. As soon as one student finishes their statement, she calls on another. At one point she asks students to address each other.

The students debate the pros and cons of owning and carrying guns. Several boys defend the practice on the grounds that people needed to protect themselves from would-be terrorists, warmongers, and burglars. Two girls attempt to counter that position by suggesting that guns are more apt to cause accidental shootings than actually serve to protect those holding them. One boy, advocating open gun ownership, has a father in the state House of Representatives fighting for more stringent gun control. Palmer asks if the class thinks it acceptable if their classmate disagrees with his father. They all agree, citing First Amendment protections.

With class time quickly running out, Palmer reminds the students that she wants to cover the additional amendments the following day. She wants them to reexamine their positions and come to class prepared to make statements. With two minutes remaining, Palmer pushes on to a brief consideration of the Fourth and Fifth Amendments (search and seizure limitations, due process), for the moment skipping over the Third. In the process of considering these amendments, several students become confused about the due-process rule, "innocent until proven guilty." Palmer tries to set the record straight by asking students to reread the actual amendment.

TEACHING RESOURCES

The next day Palmer resumes the discussion. She asks Adam to read the Third Amendment (quartering of soldiers) from his book. Four students had elected to drop this amendment in the earlier lesson segment. Palmer notes this and asks why. Several students who oppose dropping this amendment object to the possibility of soldiers entering and living in your home. Drew argues that the soldiers could be controlled. Sam raises the possibility of harm to civilians if our enemies knew soldiers were quartered in our homes. Palmer acknowledges Sam's point, then pushes on to the Fourth Amendment (search-and-seizure limitations), considering it a second time. Students discuss the nature of arrest warrants for several minutes. After that, Merry reads the Fifth Amendment from the textbook (due-process provisions).

A discussion ensues concerning the double jeopardy clause. Palmer asks several students to explain their understanding of this clause. Students appear confused about how the amendment requires the prosecution to prove guilt and how the double jeopardy clause protects the accused from being tried repeatedly for the same offense. After several analogies and direct explanations extolling the protective features of the amendment, Palmer seems convinced that students understand its rudimentary qualities. Students, many again up on their knees in their desks, protest as Palmer asks Cameron to read the Sixth (additional due-process provisions), Seventh (right to jury trial), and Eighth (prohibitions against cruel and unusual punishments) Amendments from the textbook. Eyeballing the clock, Palmer insists that they push on if they are to consider all the amendments. As Cameron finishes the Eighth Amendment, several students sing out, "Cruel and unusual punishment!"

Palmer: We could discuss this one for a long time. Some people would object that capital punishment is cruel and unusual.

Several students: So what's your opinion? Tell us!

Palmer: The [school] district says if I tell you then I run the risk of letting my values influence you. I can't. . . .

Students [objecting]: Oh, we won't tell . . . tell us anyway. . . . Just get on with it!

Another student: My mom will understand!

Palmer: Okay. [Students fall completely silent; watching Palmer.] But this is just *my* opinion. I have a lot of trouble with this. It's not black-and-white for me. I really struggle . . . it seems very cruel on the one hand, but if it was my child . . . I think then I'd want to have capital punishment.

As Palmer pauses, Adam interjects his opinion, arguing an eye-for-an-eye approach. Palmer turns to an analogy. One of her female friends was murdered in an altercation with someone being pursued by the police. Her friend's brother now frequently objects about paying taxes to keep this murderer alive in prison.

Sam: Is he in prison for life?

Palmer: Yes. And he had a record for killing others. The reason I'm telling you this is to explain how opinions about capital punishment vary a lot.

Frederic: What if it was your job to pull the lever?

Palmer: It wouldn't be! I could never do that! I'm too afraid of the possibility of executing the wrong person. That's a strong argument against capital punishment.

Adam: What if someone killed your students? Could you do it then?

Palmer: I don't know! My emotions might have the better of me. That's so hard for me to say.

As she finishes her sentence, Palmer begins passing out several review sheets for an upcoming test. Several students near the front receive the papers, groan, and say, "Oooh, worksheets! This is capital punishment!" Palmer smiles wryly.[1]

COMMONPLACE CONNECTIONS

- What does Palmer seem to think is important about the *subject matter* of the Bill of Rights?
- What view of *learners* does she seem to hold?
- How would you characterize her *teaching?*
- How would you describe the *classroom environment?*

What is going on here? A lot. This is a wonderfully rich and powerful set of lesson segments conducted by an astute social studies teacher. Look at how excited the students seem, how well behaved they appear even though the discussion is animated and threatens to explode into chaos any minute, and how skillful Palmer is in conducting this extended treatment of the Bill of Rights. In this chapter, we will use Ramona Palmer's Bill of Rights lessons as a means of exploring a second commonplace, *subject matter.*

We thought about talking of the commonplace *teachers and teaching* next. In fact, we argued ourselves into and out of that tact several times. But then we realized that, in some ways, it didn't really matter: If the commonplaces are as integrated and recursive as we believe, then we could take up subject matter, environment, or teaching and still make the points we think are important.

That made us feel better, but it didn't solve our problem. We gave the matter some more thought and concluded that it makes better sense to think about subject matter as an important bridge between learning and teaching. That is, on the way to constructing your teaching practice, you will bring together your ideas about what your students know and how they learn with your ideas about what you might teach them. We'll be exploring the subject matter of social studies and the question of "What will I teach?" When you have completed this chapter, you should be able to answer these questions:

1. ***What does the traditional social studies curriculum look like and what problems are inherent in it?***
2. ***What are the threads of social studies and how do they relate to the notion of teaching with rich ideas?***
3. ***How much latitude do teachers have in making curriculum choices?***

Social Studies Subject Matter: But There's Just Too Much Here!

How did Ramona Palmer know she should teach the Bill of Rights? How did she know in what depth to teach it? Such questions are central to understanding the subject matter of social studies. But they are not easy questions. Perhaps you have heard teachers talk about how much they are "required to cover." They sometimes complain vociferously that they have too much subject matter to deal with and not enough time. The question arises about what and how to choose.

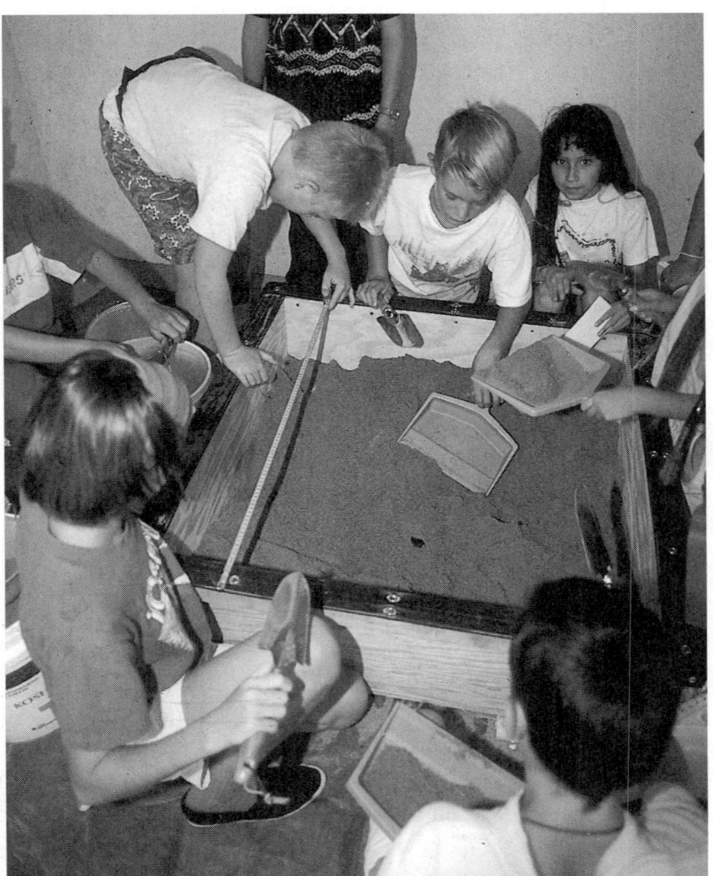

These fourth-graders are engaged in a sandbox archeology lesson. Far from the study of history and geography alone, social studies encompasses a wide range of subject matters.

Defining the Social Studies

All teachers, and especially new teachers, find that the first step to answering questions about the subject matter of social studies is a clear definition. Recall this definition of social studies offered by the National Council for the Social Studies (NCSS), a large national organization of teachers, curriculum specialists, and researchers:

> Social studies is the integrated study of the social sciences and humanities to promote civic competence. Within the school program, social studies provides coordinated, systematic study drawing upon such disciplines as anthropology, archeology, economics, geography, history, law, philosophy, political science, psychology, religion, and sociology. The primary purpose of social studies is to help young people develop the ability to make informed and reasoned decisions for the public good as citizens of a culturally diverse, democratic society in an interdependent world. (National Council for the Social Studies, 1993, p. 7)

As you can see, the conceptual range of what social studies is to include is daunting. According to NCSS, social studies embraces history and the social sciences (for example, economics, geography, political science), while including connections to religion, philosophy, literature, and so on. Broad enough to encompass about everything one might teach? It certainly appears so. How are teachers to choose what to emphasize, what's important for students to know and learn? Definitions such as this give teachers considerable latitude, but are not particularly useful for making classroom decisions.

The Traditional Social Studies Curriculum Pattern

Ramona Palmer's Bill of Rights unit clearly fits under the umbrella of the NCSS definition, but so do many topics. A second, more definitive source of ideas about the subject matter of social studies is a curriculum guide. **Curriculum guide** is a generic term for a document that expresses a set of subject matter goals and objectives. Also referred to as a **scope and sequence,** a curriculum guide tells teachers what broad content areas they are responsible for (the scope) and in what order they should be presented (the sequence). Curriculum guides may be produced by state departments of education and local school districts.

If you were to read elementary school social studies guides from around the United States, a pattern would emerge. Figure 3.1 illustrates the traditional pattern of social studies curriculum:

Figure 3.1 • **The Traditional K–6 Social Studies Curriculum Pattern**

Grade level	Focus	Examples
Kindergarten	Self	Him/herself and the most immediate environment
1	The family	Similarities and differences across families
2	The immediate neighborhood	School, post office, fire station
3	The local community	Government, services, city and rural life, geography of the community
4	The state	Its history and geography
5	The United States	Its history and geography, sometimes in connection with Canada and Mexico
6	The world	Its history and geography

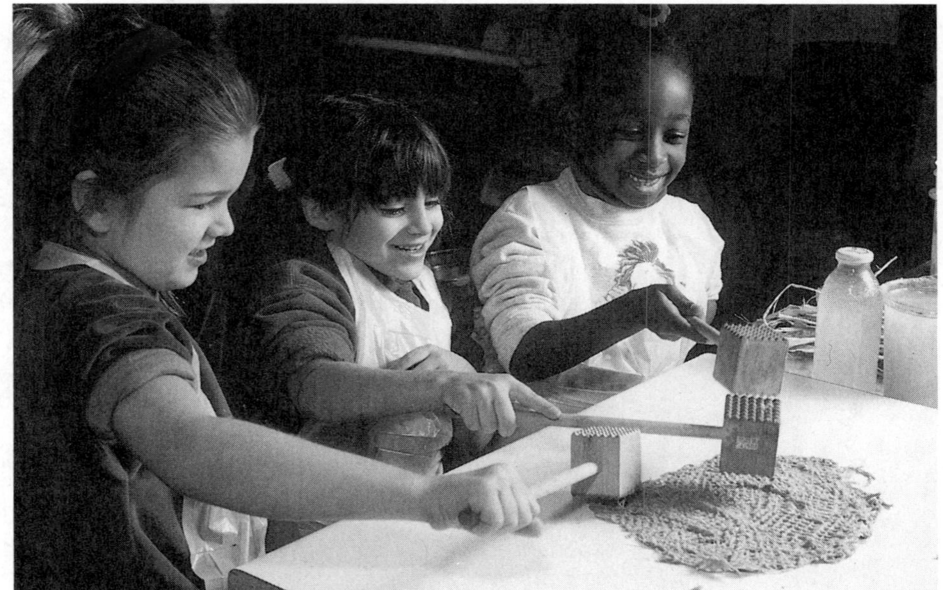

The children in this photograph are studying Japanese culture by pounding wood pulp to make paper. Judging from your understanding of the "expanding communities" scope and sequence, what grade level do you think these children represent?

During the 1940s and 1950s, a curriculum theorist named Paul Hanna (1963) advanced a curriculum sequence. He dubbed it "**expanding communities**" because the child begins learning first about herself and immediate community and gradually expands outward, considering larger and more experientially remote communities as she gets older. As Figure 3.2 suggests, you can think of this as a series of concentric circles, with the child at the center.

Figure 3.2 • A Diagram of the Expanding Communities Model

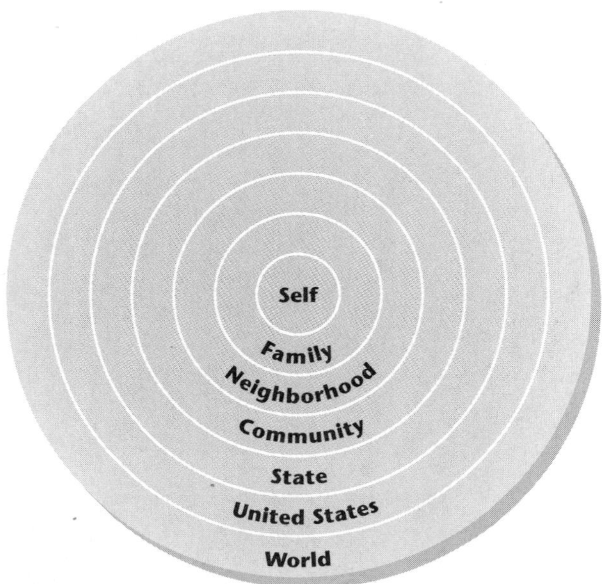

Since Hanna first advanced the expanding communities approach, it has become the standard elementary school curriculum sequence across the country. In many school districts, social studies curriculum sequences follow this expanding communities model in some form. Social studies elementary textbook series also follow this sequence.

TEACHER REFLECTION

Recalling Schooling Experiences

Recall your experiences in elementary social studies classrooms. How closely did the subject matter parallel the expanding communities model illustrated above? What do you remember about the lessons and units your teacher taught? How might your experiences as a learner inform your practice as a teacher?

Hanna bases his curriculum idea on two principles, both tied to the work of psychologist Jean Piaget. One involves the assumption that children learn best when they deal with ideas *known* to them and related to their immediate experiences (for example, themselves, their family, their neighborhood) and then gradually move to ideas that are *unknown* to them (for example, history of the country or world). Ramona Palmer's Bill of Rights unit seems to fit within the expanding communities model. The Bill of Rights is a big part of U.S. history and, as indicated above, this is a common fifth-grade curriculum area.

Hanna's second assumption involves the belief that children reason from the *concrete* to the *abstract*. This principle implies that students are more comfortable with tangible and familiar ideas and that they have difficulty dealing with conceptual matters until they reach an advanced stage of thinking. This notion has some intuitive appeal, but we have already seen a few classroom examples that challenge this premise. Recall the first-grade classroom Linda Levstik (1993) reports on in Chapter 1. Concepts such as "rain forest," "resources," and the "excavation" of Viking sites are clearly abstract notions, and yet these first-graders hardly seem confused. Similarly, Ramona Palmer's fifth-graders are handling some pretty powerful ideas: censorship, due process, and the like. Yet, although they undoubtedly have less than adult understanding of these ideas, we get no sense from the vignette that they are befuddled.

Not only does Hanna's second principle seem problematic, but as we see it, so does the first. Again, we point to the first-graders profiled in Chapter 1. According to Hanna's scheme, these youngsters should be unable to understand world cultures, a subject reserved for grade six. The point is that research results on how children make sense of social studies ideas simply contradicts Hanna's conception of their development. As we reported in Chapter 2, quite young children appear able to make some sense of both unknown and abstract ideas. Working from the known to the unknown and from the concrete to the abstract may help, but one shouldn't approach a social studies curriculum with rigid ideas about this sequence.

The expanding-communities model that forms the basis for many social studies curriculum guides may be ubiquitous, but in fact it is not especially helpful in understanding how teachers like Ramona Palmer make curricular decisions.

Other Curriculum Sources

Beyond definitions and curriculum guides, teachers can also draw on state and national curriculum standards, textbooks, and tests for curriculum ideas.

Curriculum standards "Standards" for teaching social studies have been developed by individual states (for example, California Board of Education, 1988; New York State Education Department, 1998) and by national-level curriculum groups and organizations (for example, National Council for the Social Studies, 1994; National Center for History in the Schools, 1996). Such **curriculum standards** documents typically offer little detailed information to teachers. Consider, for example, the following references to the Bill of Rights in the *Social Studies Resource Guide* (New York State Education Department, 1998) social studies standards and in the *National Standards for History* (National Center for History in the Schools, 1996).

> Legal, political, and historical documents define the values, beliefs, and principles of constitutional democracy. In the United States these documents include the Declaration of Independence, and the United States Constitution and the Bill of Rights. . . . (New York State Education Department, 1998, p. 12)
>
> Analyze the significance of the Bill of Rights and its specific guarantees. (National Center for History in the Schools, 1996, p. 89)

Neither of these references would prevent Ramona Palmer from teaching the Bill of Rights as she does, but neither do they offer much in the way of guidance. Think about all the questions a teacher might want addressed: For example, what particular "values, beliefs, and principles of constitutional democracy" and "specific guarantees" do these curriculum authors suggest teachers teach? To what level of detail should teachers and students delve? What constitutes an adequate level of student understanding? Like definitions and curriculum guides, standards documents tend to provide general rather than specific guidance.

TEACHING RESOURCES

Curriculum Standards

To get a sense of the wide array of curriculum standards available, see

- http://www.indiana.edu/\H1\~ssdc/eric_chess.htm

Standardized tests State-developed, **standardized tests** are probably even less useful for daily planning. We will have more to say about the influence of testing on teachers' practices in Chapter 6. Here, we suggest that tests are not necessarily a strong indicator of what your classroom curriculum ought to be. Two related considerations drive our thinking. One is the fact that no test can adequately cover the length and breadth of a school subject. Think about it—how many questions would you imagine necessary to get a real sense of what sixth-grade students know about world cultures? Twenty? Fifty? One hundred? Now add a second consideration: Most standardized social studies tests span multiple grades. For example, the typical fifth-grade social studies test is designed to assess not only students' understanding of the fifth-grade curriculum, but the K–4 course of study as well! Add that such tests rarely ask more than fifty questions, and that the questions generally change from year to year, and you begin to see the problem with expecting standardized tests to set your curriculum.

RELEVANT RESEARCH

Textbooks Although they are often decried as dull and banal (Brophy, McMahon, & Prawat, 1991; Fitzgerald, 1979; Loewen, 1995), social studies textbooks are a common source of classroom curriculum. And that makes sense because in this one resource teachers have a large set of information about their subject.

We take up the issue of textbook use in Chapter 5. Here, we want to emphasize the point that, although textbooks can be useful resources, they can prove limiting if they are a teacher's only resource. Just as a teacher of reading would never dream of using a single text to teach all aspects of reading, neither should a teacher of social studies ever think that a single text can define the full set of issues she or he might want to pursue with learners. A more sensible approach, then, is to use a textbook as part of a palette of resources that can help teachers make informed curriculum choices.

So how does Ramona Palmer make curriculum decisions? With the exception of a state-developed, standardized test, she reports that she draws primarily on three sources. The district curriculum guide, which features an expanding communities sequence, is one reference point. As she explains, "We have to follow those district guidelines, and if we go over and above any of those, we have to follow a policy from the Board of Education in which it has to meet certain curriculum standards." Palmer also uses a textbook as a source of curriculum ideas. Her units generally reflect the chapter sequence in her book, but she also makes liberal use of trade books both to supplement points the textbook makes and to explore ideas and issues it does not. Finally, Palmer relies on her professional judgment. Rightly, her school district refrains from prescribing all elements of the curriculum; as long as a topic meets "certain curriculum standards," she can follow her pedagogical nose. Although this is easier for veteran teachers than it is for novices, the point is the same: Although curriculum guides and standards, tests, textbooks, and the like may seem to direct teachers' curriculum choices, in fact, teachers have considerable instructional latitude.

SECTION SUMMARY **Defining the Social Studies**

- As defined by the leading professional organization, the social studies cover a wide range of ideas, topics, and issues.
- The expanding-communities curriculum model has been in place for some time, but the principles that underlie that model are open to question.
- In addition to the expanding-communities model, teachers can draw on curriculum guides and standards, standardized tests, and textbooks for curriculum ideas. None is all-inclusive and teachers must still use their professional judgment.

Social Studies Subject Matter: The Threads Approach

Curriculum guides and standards, tests, and textbooks, although they do not hold all the answers, are important factors in choosing what to teach. Teachers sign contracts to teach what school districts deem important, which may be expressed in curriculum guides or textbook series. You most likely will encounter some version of the expanding-communities approach, which will give you, as it did Ramona Palmer, some direction in terms of the subject matter that you teach. How to teach the topics, under what classroom circumstances, and with which embellishments fall under your professional discretion. In short, you have considerable instructional room in which to maneuver. We like to think of the act of converting the topics in the curriculum guide into powerful social studies ideas and teachable representations as *transforming* the curriculum.

Transforming the Social Studies Curriculum with the Threads Approach

Like the study of mathematics, literature, and science, the study of social studies gives children powerful ways to make sense of the world. As we have seen, social studies covers wide conceptual ground. In order to learn how their world works, children need to explore how and why people behave as they do (from psychology), how people operate in group settings (from sociology), how cultural groups are similar and different (from anthropology), how economic and political systems function (from economics and political science), how people interact with their physical environments (from geography), and how people make sense of the past (from history).

As this list indicates, teachers can look to the **social science disciplines** and to history for rich ideas to help them shape what we want children to understand and accomplish. Remember Ramona Palmer's Bill of Rights discussion: Her students were deeply engrossed in some powerful ideas. Students seem to love rich, weighty ideas and questions. But what ones do teachers look for?

In each discipline, key ideas and questions animate the work. These ideas and questions come from the traditional academic disciplines you probably studied in college. For pedagogical purposes, however, we have translated these disciplines and the ideas and questions they represent into a more convenient form, the *threads*. The threads are a conceptual framework by which teachers can give their students insights into social phenomena. Figure 3.3 shows the five threads and their respective ideas.

Figure 3.3 • The Threads of Social Studies

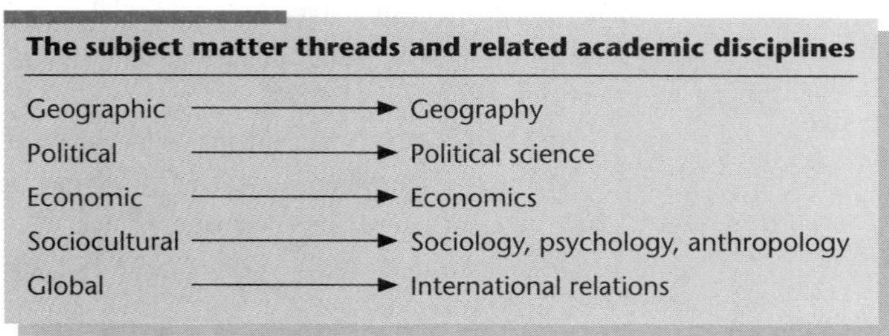

The subject matter threads and related academic disciplines

Geographic	→ Geography
Political	→ Political science
Economic	→ Economics
Sociocultural	→ Sociology, psychology, anthropology
Global	→ International relations

Now let's consider each of the five threads and their ideas individually. Remember that the key ideas and questions listed below are meant to be illustrative rather than exhaustive. In other words, we expect you will expand these lists as you work with the thread categories in the context of your curriculum.

Thread name: **Geographic**
Discipline: Geography
Key ideas/questions:

Land forms—What are the surface features of an area? Which features matter to the inhabitants and in what ways?

Location—Where are people, places, and surface features located? How does the location of one entity influence that of another?

Climate/Weather—What are the prevailing weather and climatic conditions? How do these conditions affect life in a particular area?

Resources—What natural resources are available and in what supply? Which of those resources do the inhabitants use?

Population—How are people distributed across an area and how densely are they concentrated? How do the people of an area interact with their physical surroundings?

Thread name: **Political**
Discipline: Political science
Key ideas/questions:

Decision making—How are rules made, interpreted, and enforced in a society?

Power—Who holds power in a society and who doesn't? How has this changed (if it has) over time?

Structure of government—How have people decided to organize themselves to make decisions? What benefits and drawbacks to these forms of government are apparent? How is the structure of government changed?

Thread name: **Economic**
Discipline: Economics
Key ideas/questions:

Property—What do people own? How do they come to own it?

Means of exchange—What form of exchange (for example, money) do people use to obtain what they want?

Labor/Management—Who works for whom in a society? How does that relationship work?

Scarcity/Surplus—Which goods and services are plentiful in a society and which are scarce? How does the scarcity or surplus of something influence its cost?

Thread name: **Sociocultural**
Disciplines: Psychology, Sociology, Anthropology
Key ideas/questions:

Class—How is the society organized? Which groups have more power, influence, and such than others? Is it possible to move from class to class?

Race/Ethnicity/Gender—How do these factors influence the way people are perceived throughout the society?

Education—How do people transfer the accumulating knowledge and experience from one generation to another?

Arts—How do people represent themselves and their lives in writing, art, music, and dance?

Recreation/Leisure—How do people spend time when they are not working or attending to family matters?

Thread name: **Global**
Discipline: Anthropology, International Relations
Key ideas/questions:

Competition/Cooperation—How do cultural groups interact? In what ways do they cooperate and in what ways do they compete?

Conflict—How do cultural groups handle conflicts between themselves?

Change—How do norms, values, and institutions of cultural groups change over time?

You may have wondered, as you read the above lists, what happened to history. Although it is a key academic discipline, we do not include history as a separate thread for one simple reason: We believe the threads are equally useful for understanding *both* current phenomena and past events. In other words, working through the thread categories can contribute as much to children's understandings of the Industrial Revolution as to their grasp of recent situations such as the U.S. role in Bosnia.

That said, the discipline of history contributes a key set of ideas and questions that will help push your students to even more powerful understandings.

These ideas and questions deal with *how* people go about examining what interests them: how historians gather information about the past, how they decide what happened, where they look for evidence that events occurred, and what they do with evidence when they find it. Historians make claims that events happened in certain ways. How do they know? Are their claims trustworthy? If so, on what grounds? It is essential that children learn to ask these questions if they are to become thoughtful consumers and creators of ideas in their own right.

IN YOUR CLASSROOM: Learning History by Doing It

One activity to help your students not only to learn history, but to investigate it, is to construct a unit around a local history project. A good example would be to invite your students to explore the history of their school.

Using the threads approach, assign groups to find out when the school was originally built and why on this particular location (geographic thread). Ask another group to investigate the economic and political changes in the surrounding neighborhood that necessitated the building of the school (economic and political threads). Encourage a third group to explore how the school population changed over time, examining such issues as ethnic and racial makeup and the like (sociocultural thread). Finally, assign a fourth group to survey the school and local population to determine the ethnic character of the area (global thread).

Such an approach might require using the local library, city hall, and the Internet to locate documents and records. In addition to understanding the documents, you will need to help your students learn how to interpret these documents by teaching them to pay attention to (1) who the authors were, (2) when they were written, and (3) why they might have been created in the first place.[2]

Understanding the Threads: Returning to Ramona Palmer's Classroom

The case of Ramona Palmer's teaching that opened this chapter demonstrates several of the threads. Reread the vignette that opens the chapter, asking yourself what evidence you see of the threads.

As we see it, the discussion and debate broaches serious *political* issues. The primary focus of this analysis deals with issues of governing, a central issue for those involved in political science: How do people govern themselves? How is power to make choices distributed across a society? What regulates the system?

What is the proper relationship between the governors and the governed? Much of the talk in the discussion hinges on students debating and making sense of these deep questions.

The issue of capital punishment is tied to *sociocultural* and *economic* issues. Why do people murder? Is it related to socioeconomic class? Who will act as executioner? What does it cost government to exercise the act of capital punishment allowed by the Bill of Rights? Is the cost worth the effort? If not, what are more cost-efficient alternatives? If so, why don't more states use capital punishment? These questions raise serious economic and sociological issues.

Reviewing the thread connections in Palmer's lessons raises two important points. One point concerns the inter-relatedness of the threads. As we see in the paragraph just above, discussing the practice of capital punishment leads us to consider political, sociocultural, and economic threads at the same time: The laws that govern the administration of capital punishment reflect the norms and values of our society, but they also reflect the economic costs and benefits of punishment. One might study capital punishment as a purely political, sociocultural, or economic issue. As Palmer's presentation suggests, however, the issue is enlivened when considered from multiple thread directions.

That said, the second point is that a teacher need not always address every thread category in every lesson. Did you notice, for example, that Palmer leaves aside the geographic and global threads? She does so largely because they are not directly relevant to this discussion of the Bill of Rights. However, if the class extended the capital-punishment discussion to other nations, they would be asking questions that deal with the global thread. If the class went on to consider how the practice of capital punishment is distributed across the United States, they would be dealing with geographic questions.

Palmer doesn't take the time to deal with all the possible threads, but the discussion is laced with many of them nonetheless. She could stop at any point and broach them, as she does when her students push her on her position regarding capital punishment. Ramona Palmer is making crucial decisions about how to allocate classroom time while working with the richest ideas, questions, and threads time allows.

Other Examples of the Threads Approach in Practice

Consider this common curriculum guide dictum for fourth-grade state history:

> Students are to know the Native American tribes that inhabited the state and where they lived.

We would argue that if taught as expressed, this would be impoverished instruction. What are the rich ideas and understandings your students can dig into? What evidence of the thread categories is apparent?

We don't see much power in asking students to memorize a bunch of names and locations. Simply teaching topics, lists, names, and places and events that can be counted off on work sheets and multiple-choice tests provides little incentive for your students to learn. Most importantly, research strongly suggests that your students quickly forget these lists and names and topics.

Now, what would happen if you began with the question:

> What was life like for Native Americans in this region before colonization, and how has it changed since then?

If you asked your students to consider this question, they would have much digging to do indeed. They would need to learn something about Native American social life (sociocultural thread), where they lived and why (geographic thread), how they made rules to live by (political thread), how they satisfied their basic needs (economic thread), and how they interacted with other native groups and with the Europeans (global thread). Cast this way, the question becomes a vehicle to explore both historical and contemporary circumstances and events, which in effect ties the past to the present.

The threads here are unmistakable and help weave together what students need to understand. By taking the initial topic, Native-American tribal names and locales, and reframing it around a penetrating question, you gain considerable power in what you invite students to do. By choosing topics and developing rich questions around them that focus on the threads, you are helping yourself select from the welter of teaching choices.

TEACHER REFLECTION

Making Connections

A rich social studies curriculum lies in the connections you help students make between ideas and questions. The threads conceptual framework is designed to help you think about those ideas and questions. As you look at the various curriculum resources available, push yourself to reflect on the potential thread connections you might make with learners.

Now it's your turn to try out this selecting and transforming process using the threads approach. A common social studies topic in early elementary school is "the nature of local communities." Think hard for a few minutes about this topic and make some notes. Draw on your subject matter knowledge from history and the social sciences and on the thread category descriptions above.

- What rich ideas concerning communities surface?
- How might you make these ideas engaging and suitable for, say, second- or third-graders? Generate a list of ideas and questions that make use of as many threads as possible. Write your questions in the spaces below.

IN YOUR CLASSROOM: Using the Threads Approach

Topic: ____________________

Ideas/Questions: ____________________

If you have difficulty with this exercise, you may need to read up on the topic in order to figure out the subject matter connections. This shouldn't be any big surprise; good teachers frequently read up on the subject matter they teach in order to gain depth of knowledge and to understand more about the connecting threads. You should expect to have questions about your subject matter. This is both natural and good; no one can know deeply every topic or issue. And your curiosity in pursuing your questions may turn out to be highly infectious in your classroom.

To help with the process, you also may want to include your students' questions by asking them directly to talk about their curiosities before you begin a unit (for example, using the *W* of the K-W-L exercise we mentioned earlier). Finally, the more experience you have in this, the more effective you'll become. We encourage you to be patient but persistent.

In several respects, the threads approach resembles a "thematic" or "integrated" curriculum, in which teachers chose a large theme and draw from a variety of subject matters (mathematics, social studies, reading/language arts) in order to build a "thematic and integrated unit." The difference here is that what is referred to as a thematic unit involves cross-subject-matter integration. We are talking about within-subject-matter integration. We are making a case for focusing on integrating social science and history subject matters along the threads that connect them together in a big idea, rather than integrating different subject matters, such as mathematics and social studies.

There is nothing the matter with thematic units and cross-subject integration. In fact, when you teach you may wish to expand on our thoughts about the threads approach to include other subjects beyond the social studies. However, our emphasis here is the integrative power of working *within* the social studies through the threads.

SECTION SUMMARY **The Threads Approach**

- The social sciences and history provide the disciplinary background for the social studies. For pedagogical purposes, we have translated these disciplines into *threads*.
- The threads are: geographic, political, economic, sociocultural, and global. Each thread category represents a particular set of ideas and questions.
- Social studies topics can be broken down by individual threads, but the real power of the threads approach is when a teacher and students see the interconnections among the threads.

Social Studies Subject Matter: You Must Choose

Let's begin this section by returning, once more, to Ramona Palmer's Bill of Rights unit. Palmer's choices reflect how she wants her students to confront and build understandings of the subject matter. She is constantly choosing and acting on those choices.

Why? The most immediately noticeable reason in this cascade of lessons is the relationship between time and what she knows about representing her subject matter. She could dig deeply and explore all the threads and their many rich questions, but she also must pay attention to the clock. For now, let's focus on the way she chooses to represent the subject matter.

Ramona Palmer opts to cover the first eight amendments, skipping the ninth and tenth—an important choice. These, she notes, are more complex than she wishes to deal with at the moment. She decides to concentrate her attention on the threads contained in the first eight amendments, threads rich enough to make the points she wants. We see that she avoids a strictly textbook-dominated approach. Like many social studies teachers, Palmer could have pushed on after students read and recited the textbook-inscribed amendments, but she didn't. She wants her learners to explore the ramifications of these amendments for their personal lives. She does so through a give-and-take discussion where she asks students about their implications for topics the students know about (rap music, movies, gun laws, capital punishment).

In this way she breathes life into a document that is at once both two hundred years old and of very present importance. She represents the subject matter of the Bill of Rights as having clear late-twentieth-century political, social, and economic implications. Her students see the connections and run with them in a highly engaging conversation. The point here is that Palmer is choosing how to represent the subject matter at almost every turn. That's what teachers do.

Yes, the social studies curriculum *is* in your lap, and you *must* choose. Making these choices about social studies subject matter can be daunting, and even downright frightening. But if you learn to use this threads approach, and with it the process of generating questions that your students will find intriguing, you will be well on your way. Remember, you are after the rich, meaty ideas that make social studies subject matter such an interesting area of the curriculum. And remember that avoiding the process of choosing is really still choosing. What do we mean? Consider the following.

Choosing by Default

For various reasons, some social studies teachers fall prey to the seductive temptation to slavishly follow the curriculum guide and to teach social studies as though it were a set of simple topics comprised of a vast array of facts for students to memorize. We have pointed out how such teaching lacks power and results in quick forgetfulness on the part of students. Let's examine a few reasons why teachers fall into this trap, along with some different ways to think about your teaching, that may help prevent you from being so tempted.

Substantive content knowledge in social studies History and the social sciences, from which the social studies draws much of its subject matter, is heavy on what some call **substantive** or **propositional knowledge.** We can think of social studies as a collection of facts about how the world works, objective knowledge that makes up a portion of our cultural knowledge base. And we might assume that if students merely memorize this knowledge, they will know what they need to know and that teaching has been successful. But, as the last chapter and Ramona Palmer's Bill of Rights discussion suggest, other choices exist for thinking about social studies knowledge and learning.

Think back to Helen and Rita, introduced in Chapter 2. The girls produced widely different interpretations of the American history they studied in fourth grade. You have no guarantee that, if you reduce the social studies curriculum to a set of facts students need to memorize, all students will learn the same information. Learning is much more than memorizing facts; it's about constructing understandings. Children bring different prior knowledge to the learning context, knowledge that interacts in unpredictable ways with the new ideas they encounter in your classroom. Asking children to memorize social studies facts and knowledge propositions simply ignores this important aspect of the learning process and limits student achievement. We cannot stress this point enough.

Moreover, many of the so-called social studies facts and propositions that we tend to take for granted and find piled on top of one another in social studies textbooks are really "somebody else's facts" (Holt, 1990, p. 2). Who produced the knowledge in social studies school textbooks? Mostly white men with a decidedly Western outlook on culture, history, economic systems, and so forth. What is Marvyn, an African American student in Palmer's class, supposed to think about this? What if his ideas about our culture and history—and he gives us some interesting possibilities in the discussion of the Bill of Rights—differ strongly from those he gets from the textbooks and from his teachers who ask him to memorize what it holds? Can he trust the book and his teacher and the facts each convey? Are they his "facts"? In other words, are the circumstances of his life as a black youngster, with a heritage that traces its roots to slavery, the same as the European American or Asian American children sitting around him? Do they all agree on the so-called "facts"?

RELEVANT RESEARCH

While one could argue that there should be agreement, we disagree because we know that it is simply impossible to shove these ready-made textbook facts into Marvyn's head, especially if they oppose those he already holds and run contrary to his experience (Coles, 1986). His different ideas and perspectives growing out of a different heritage must be respected and allowed to interact in an open forum with the ideas he encounters in class. Reducing the curriculum to a set of memorizable facts will sell short students of color like Marvyn, girls, Asian Americans, Latinos and Latinas, and even white, middle-class students. Chances are, you won't get away with it, either. Expect students to turn off to your teaching, act bored, act up, challenge you, or any combination of these.

The point here is that social studies knowledge is produced by human beings to help them understand their worlds. This knowledge reflects the perspectives of its authors and therefore can reflect multiple cultural experiences or purviews and biases. Historical and social science knowledge is always open to interpretation and reinterpretation, depending on one's perspective and the evidence one can muster to change an accepted view. Children must have opportunities to bring their ideas, perspectives, and evidence to this changing-knowledge table as well. As we argued in the last chapter, this doesn't mean that teachers need to accept as valid all the ideas students hold or construct. Clearly, it would be better if children jettisoned untenable ideas and replaced them with ones that are based on careful argument and evidence. This brings us to a last point.

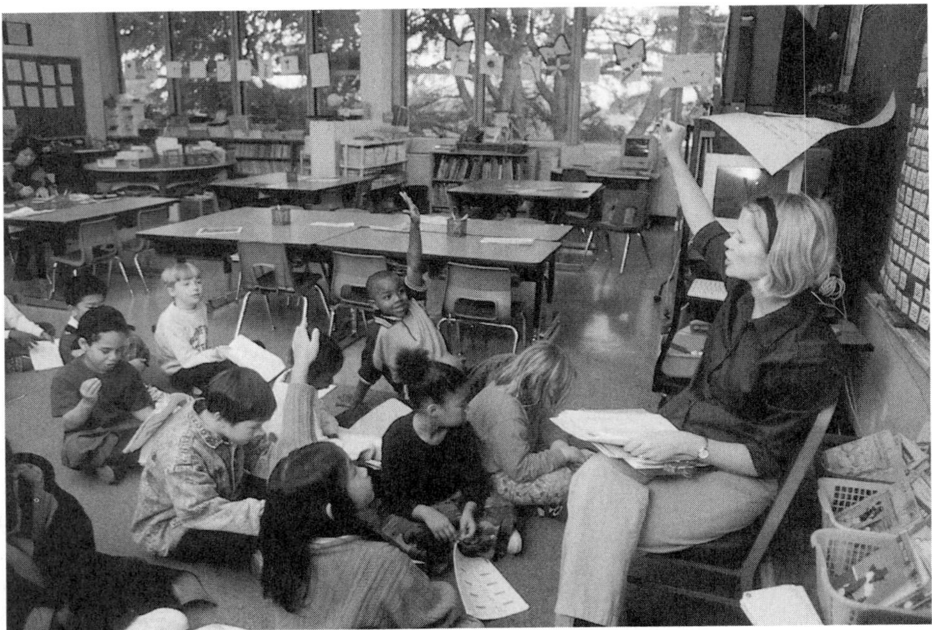

Social studies knowledge is a human construction. Adults, through their roles as historians, psychologists, political scientists, and the like, help construct knowledge. What role do children have in the construction of knowledge?

Creating social studies knowledge Equal in importance to knowledge of social studies itself is the process of creating knowledge. For example, how have historians figured out what went on during the American Revolution? How have economists figured out that capitalism, as an economic system, functions the way it does? What assumptions do we make and take for granted? In other words, how do we know what we know? Students need to learn as much about methods of creating knowledge as they do about social studies facts and propositions. They need to learn about the tenuous and problematic nature of creating knowledge. They need to learn that a problem-laden process creates problem-laden knowledge, knowledge that cannot be accepted at first blush. Social studies knowledge and its creation process requires close scrutiny. They, too, are part of the connecting threads, as you saw in the previous example of researching history with your students.

Some people refer to research methods as the **procedural** or **syntactic knowledge** of subject matter, that is, understandings of the procedures employed to create knowledge. In history and the social sciences in the Western world, we build knowledge through a process of careful research and data gathering, followed by rigorous analysis, interpretation, and argument based on the accumulated evidence. To the extent that an evidence-based argument is accepted by people, it becomes knowledge and perhaps fact. Children need to learn about this process as well. The social-studies-as-fact view ignores it, so students receive both a limited and limiting view of the social studies, which deprives young learners of the opportunity to assess and evaluate accepted knowledge. They lose the opportunity to understand that knowledge is actually multifaceted, plural, and multicultural.

Yes, you will encounter social studies curriculum guides that stipulate what is to be covered. These guides also may intimate a social-studies-as-fact view and suggest that your teaching must conform to this perspective. But, as we continue to stress, you really have enormous latitude in choosing and selecting. Most curriculum guides are vague, and schools lack the resources to hire "curriculum police" to make sure you follow the guide to the letter. Nor would they want to. School districts do more or less try to recognize that you possess some professional autonomy and attempt to create an atmosphere in which you can exercise your professional judgment. The choices are largely yours!

Embracing the Choosing Process: What to Teach

We invite you to step up and embrace this choosing process. Exercise the threads approach as a method of enhancing the quality of the subject matter choices you make. Good social studies teachers with whom we've worked show us that using these threads and engaging their professional judgment in the careful choosing process have profound influences on what and how students learn social studies. These good teachers also know that the process can be difficult and require considerable outside reading and research, but they tell us that the benefits for themselves and their students almost always far exceed the costs incurred. Ms. Palmer is a fine case in point.

But specifically, what are these benefits?

1. Knowing the social studies subject matter makes it easier to see connections and establish threads and so streamline your work.
2. In a similar vein, knowing the subject matter expands the curricular possibilities upon which you can draw, allowing you richer choices.[3]
3. Knowing social studies subject matter deeply also helps you figure out the important questions, those that people are asking in the disciplines and ones your students might be curious about.
4. Having significant knowledge of social studies helps you "hear" your students, which helps you decide how to respond when they express nascent ideas and misconceptions as you ask them questions in class.

Subject matter knowledge is the bridge between learners and learning and teachers and teaching. And the bigger, stronger, and wider the bridge, the larger, weightier, and more powerful the ideas that can traverse it.

SECTION SUMMARY Choosing Social Studies Subject Matter

- The "default" curriculum choice some social studies teachers make is to follow the content and structure of curriculum guides and textbooks and to teach as if the content is but a set of facts to be memorized. We argue, however, that this choice offers little understanding of or benefit to children.
- The benefits to avoiding the default choice include seeing connections and streamlining your work, expanding the curricular possibilities, figuring out important questions, and hearing students as they begin constructing powerful ideas.

In the next chapter we span the social studies subject matter bridge from learning across to teaching. Specifically, we put to work the threads approach as a means of framing the rich questions you choose, and introduce this fusion under the notion of teaching with *big ideas*.

CHAPTER SUMMARY

1. What does the traditional social studies curriculum look like and what problems are inherent in it?

The traditional social studies curriculum follows the *expanding-communities* model proposed by Paul Hanna in the early 1960s. The model organizes the K–6 course of study by moving progressively away from the child (for example, K—Focus on Self . . . Grade 6—Focus on the World).

Two principles underlie Hanna's approach: moving from *known* to *unknown,* and moving from the *concrete* to the *abstract.* Researchers have raised serious questions about both of these principles.

2. What are the threads of social studies and how do they relate to the notion of teaching with rich ideas?

The *threads* are a pedagogical translation of the traditional academic disciplines of the social sciences and history. The threads categories are geographic, political, economic, sociocultural, and global.

The threads, and their attendant academic disciplines, offer teachers a wide range of complex and powerful ideas and questions that can serve as the basis for unit and lesson planning.

3. How much latitude do teachers have in making curriculum choices?

A lot. Teachers can draw on various resources as they plan their classroom curriculum. None of the available resources is all-purpose, and so teachers must make a range of curriculum decisions.

Some teachers make a "default" choice to follow, for example, the structure and content of a social studies textbook, or the list of topics indicated in a curriculum guide. This default choice, however, seldom succeeds with learners, largely because of how they learn. Choosing is not easy, but the benefits to embracing the choosing process far outweigh the disadvantages.

TEACHING RESOURCES

Print Resources

Gerhke, N., Knapp, M., & Sirotnik, K. (1992). In search of the school curriculum. In G. Grant (Ed.), *Review of research in education* 18:51–110. Washington, DC: American Educational Research Association.

Hahn, C. L. (1985). The status of social studies in the public schools of the United States: Another look. *Social Education* 49, no. 3:220–23.

Thornton, S. (1994). The social studies near century's end: Reconsidering patterns of curriculum and instruction. In L. Darling-Hammond (Ed.), *Review of research in education* 20:223–54. Washington, DC: American Educational Research Association.

Each of these works presents a useful description of how the current social studies curriculum came to be.

Several professional journals regularly provide lesson, unit, and general curriculum ideas for teachers. See particularly *The History Teacher,* published by the Society for History Education, and *Social Education* and *Social Studies for the Young Learner,* published by the National Council for the Social Studies.

Technology Resources

Two good general-purpose web sites to begin exploring the thread categories are

- **http://www.yahoo.com/socialsciences**
- **http://www.yahoo.com/arts/humanities/history**

These two sites provide a wealth of information about issues percolating among social scientists and historians.

Another good site for exploring thread categories is

- **http://www.execpc.com/~dboals/boals.html**

This is one of the most comprehensive sites on the Internet for teachers interested in locating curriculum materials and resources related to the threads.

For a project designed to bring students, teachers, and subject matter experts together in an e-mail exchange, see

- **http://www.tapr.org/emissary/**

See also the April, 1999, issue of *Social Education,* for a variety of web sites on different social studies subject matter threads.

State-level Law-Related Education (LRE) programs exist across the country. They provide a wide array of curriculum resources, unit and lesson plans, and speakers, and all generally for free. For the contact people in your state, see

- **http://www.indiana.edu/~ssdc/state.html**

NOTES

1. For more on Ramona Palmer's teaching, see Chapter 5 in Brophy and VanSledright (1997).
2. For more on lessons and units like this, see *Doing History: Investigating With Children in Elementary and Middle Schools* (Levstik & Barton, 1997).
3. For more on this important benefit, see Wilson (1990).

Chapter 4

Teaching Social Studies I:
Working with Big Ideas

CLASSROOM EXAMPLE

Sandra Prosy is a fifth-grade teacher in an urban elementary school in New York state. She is a middle-aged European American; her twenty-one students are predominantly African American. She begins the first day of a new unit on American government with a recitation:

Prosy: What kind of government do you think we will talk about?

Angela: Public schools?

Rashona: City?

Prosy: Who runs the city?

Michael: The mayor?

Prosy writes *city* on the board and asks, "Who is the mayor?" A girl calls out, "Luciano." Prosy nods and writes *Luciano* on the board. "What other kinds of government are there? What other areas need to be run?" she asks.

Deion: Community.

Tina: State.

Prosy: Yes, what state?

Michelle: New York.

Prosy: Who runs our state?

Tom: The governor.

Prosy nods and writes *state, governor,* and *Pataki* (the current New York governor) on the board. As she does, a boy calls out, "What about county?" Prosy says, "Well, yes, but I'm looking for something that starts with an *F*." A girl guesses, "Federal?" Prosy responds, "Right. And who runs the federal government?" A boy offers, "Rush Limbaugh!" while the rest of the class shouts out, "Bill Clinton!"

The next day, Prosy begins class by distributing a worksheet entitled, "The Government of the United

States." She gives the children eight minutes to complete it, instructing them to write "in cursive only." The remainder of class time is spent reviewing the worksheet questions:

Prosy: The _______________ is the head of the executive branch?

Angela: The president.

Prosy: The courts are in the _______________ branch?

Whitney: Judicial.

Prosy: The president takes the oath of office on January twentieth. This is called _______________ day?

Deion: Memorial day?

Michelle: Independence day?

Prosy: It's called 'Inauguration day.' During his years in office, the President lives in the _______________?

Rachelle: The White House.

COMMONPLACE CONNECTIONS

- What does Prosy seem to consider important about the *subject matter* of U. S. government?
- What view of *learners* does she seem to hold?
- How would you characterize her *teaching?*
- How would you describe the *classroom environment?*

Janice Mead is also a white, middle-aged teacher. Unlike Prosy, Mead teaches fourth grade in a largely white, upscale, suburban elementary school. Mead is also different from Prosy in that she uses trade books in addition to a standard textbook, she often groups learners for work assignments, and she makes learners responsible for information.

On the second day of a unit on American slavery, Mead introduces the Underground Railroad. After a brief recap of the previous day's discussion, she explains, "Now we're going to learn some more facts." She distributes copies of the trade book, *If You Traveled on the Underground Railroad* (Levine & Johnson, 1993). Mead announces, "I'm going to give each person a question, and it's going to be that person's job to read the question on the appropriate page and come up with the important points." Continuing, she says, "Now, you should write your important points on a piece of paper or an index card to help you remember. When we're back together as a class, we're going to review the questions, and you're all going to give us the answers. You're going to be the expert on that question."

Although each learner is responsible for one question, Mead organizes the class so that students can work in pairs. She urges them to read the relevant information "a few times" and to "tell your partner the answer to your question, how you would explain it."

Mead allows the class twenty minutes to read the text, make notes in response to their questions, and talk with their partners. She calls the class to order and asks Larry to read his question (How did the Underground Railroad gets its name?)

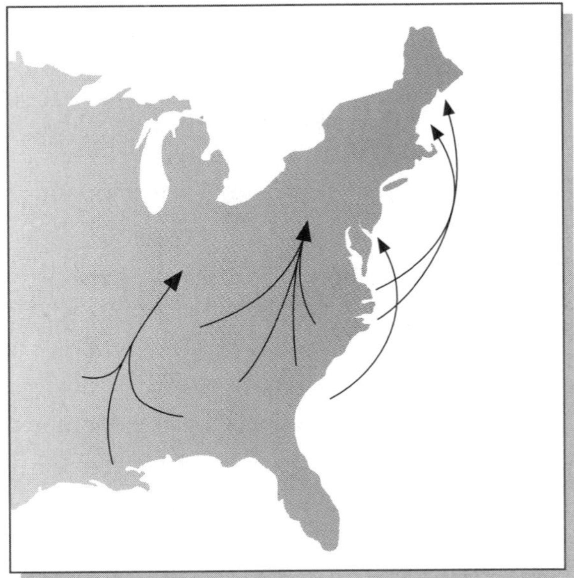

Figure 4.1 • **Routes of African-American Slaves** • Escaping slaves took several routes to reach freedom in the Northern U.S. and Canada.

and to give his answer. Larry says, "There once was a runaway slave. He escaped in 1831 and swam in the river to a city in Ohio. His owner searched for him, but he couldn't be found. His owner thought he must have escaped on an underground railroad. And that's how the Underground Railroad got its name." Mead thanks Larry and explains, "Okay. The owner was bewildered because he was so close to him. He knew he (the slave) had to be there somewhere, but he couldn't see him. So the name 'Underground Railroad' seemed to stick. *Underground* because it was secret and *Railroad* because people on it seemed to move so fast and it was difficult to catch them."

Class continues with learners giving their responses to questions such as What did it mean to be a slave? Why did slaves want to leave their masters? Where would escaping slaves go first? What dangers did escaping slaves face? What did the Fugitive Slave Law say? How did slaves hear about Canada and freedom?

COMMONPLACE CONNECTIONS

- What does Mead seem to consider important about the *subject matter* of slavery and the Underground Railroad?
- What view of *learners* does she seem to hold?
- How would you characterize her *teaching?*
- How would you describe the *classroom environment?*

When we compare Mead's and Prosy's instruction, we see some dramatic differences. Unlike Prosy's class, Mead's learners read from rich textual sources rather than from textbooks and worksheets, they work together rather than alone, and they become the "experts" on pieces of the lesson rather than look to their teacher for all the answers. Other differences show up as well. Where Prosy focuses on a narrow set of dry, decontextualized facts, Mead encourages learners to think about a series of questions related to slavery and the Underground Railroad. Some are fact-based, such as "What did the Fugitive Slave Law say?" Others, like "Why did slaves want to leave their masters?" call for relatively low levels of analysis. Still others, like "What did it mean to be a slave?" ask learners to think more deeply. Listen to Susan's response:

> To be a slave, it meant that you could not read or write. If you did, you would be punished. Being a slave meant that your owner could punish you whenever he wanted. To be a slave meant that you had to do everything he tells you to. To be a slave meant that you had to get your owner's permission to do almost everything. To be a slave meant that you could be sold away from everybody you knew.

With wonderful clarity, Susan defines the desperation of slave life: One must do "everything he (the owner) tells you" and "get your owner's permission to do almost everything." She concludes with perhaps the most wrenching dimension of slavery: "You could be sold away from everybody you knew." It is not clear that all Mead's learners are making the same substantive connections that Susan is. Still, by providing a richer instructional climate, Mead offers her students powerful opportunities to learn deeply.

Before going on to the rest of the chapter, let's consider one more teacher. Pam Derson, a European American in her forties, is a twenty-year veteran whose experience has been in suburban schools with predominantly white children. The learners in this vignette are fourth-graders.

CLASSROOM EXAMPLE

Introducing a history unit in which students will research Native Americans in the Tidewater Chesapeake region, Derson asks, "How do we know what we know?" Derson understands that historical knowledge is largely indeterminate because what we know is based only on traces of the past—residual evidence with gaps and holes. She wants her learners to wrestle with this big idea as they go about researching questions of their own design. Derson knows that the class will encounter numerous facts about native life, and she wants them to know this information, but she also wants her students to become careful, systematic researchers with a skeptical, questioning edge.

As the class considers her question, Derson continues. "Did you ever wonder how we know what we know about these Tidewater Native Americans we are studying? Have you wondered? I think about this a lot. I talk to my relatives about it, too." Students volunteer several sources of information: artifacts, bones, fossils, a wagon. On this last point, Derson asks about what would happen to a wagon over time. It would "rot," one boy replies. Sensing a teachable moment, Derson responds:

> That's right. That's exactly what happens. It makes the work historians and researchers do very difficult, because what's left of the past is so scarce many times, especially if the history you are studying happened a long time ago.

Derson then informs the class that they are going on a scavenger hunt. She tells them to look under their desks where, taped to the undersides, they find different colored pieces of paper—pink, yellow, green, and white—with drawings of native artifacts on them. Some students have one piece; others find more than one. Derson asks the children to take out a piece of notebook paper and carefully describe the nature of what they found. She draws a map of the classroom on the board and labels the rows and desks in a grid pattern with coordinates.

Students spend the next thirty minutes charting the location of each piece of colored paper and what is drawn on it. Once finished, Derson explains that the grid is an example of how archeologists map a dig site in order to understand what happened there. Having piqued their interest, Derson asks her students, "What can we

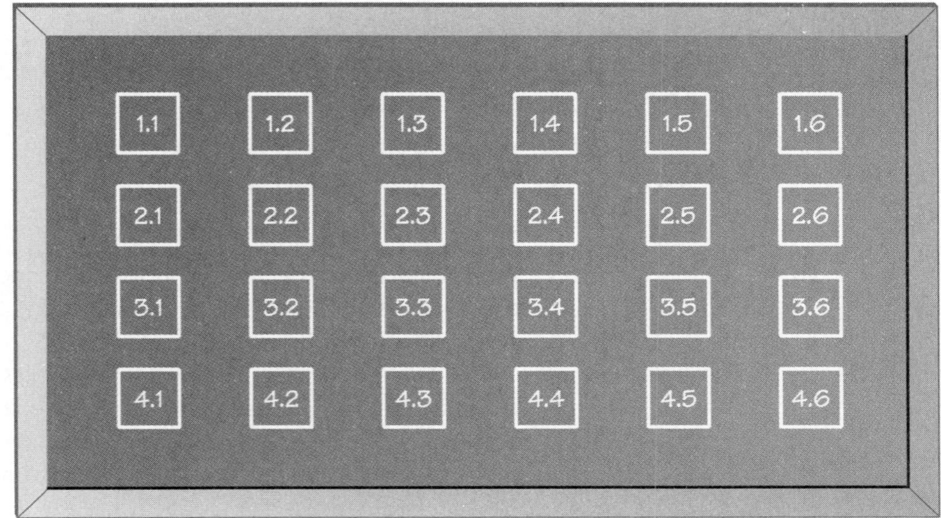

Figure 4.2 • **Derson's Blackboard Map of the Classroom**

say are the advantages and disadvantages of using artifacts to learn more about Native Americans?"

Louise: They help us know more about the Indians?
Rudy: They tell us how they lived.
Derson: Yes, but do they tell us everything? Take a look at this. (She holds up a pottery shard and walks around the room showing it to learners.) What is it?
Gina: We don't know because it's broken.
Derson: That's right. Sometimes we don't know what these things are. We have to guess, and sometimes we make mistakes. That's the problem when doing research. Often we can't be sure of the answers to our questions because what we find is not very good evidence.

Having demonstrated the difficulty of interpreting bits and pieces of evidence, Derson senses her learners are now receptive to her bigger point about the interpretative nature of history and historical understanding—how we know what we know:

Derson: What we know about history changes over time. We find new things and figure out different explanations for what went on. You would think history is dead because it happened a long time ago, but it's not. It's very much alive, and it's changing all the time. That's why I like it so much. When you are doing your research, remember to be careful; check your sources. Sometimes the facts aren't what they seem to be.

COMMONPLACE CONECTIONS

- What does Derson seem to consider important about the *subject matter* of Native history and historical evidence?
- What view of *learners* does she seem to hold?
- How would you characterize her *teaching?*
- How would you describe the *classroom environment?*

This vignette differs from the first two in several respects. First, Derson gives much less attention to facts than her peers do. Factual information emerges—for example, wagons rot over time—but the emphasis is on ideas. Second, this vignette represents a more active pedagogy than the first two. Derson makes reading and writing assignments throughout the unit. She begins, however, by grabbing learners' imaginations with an engaging map-making activity. The biggest difference between this vignette and the others, however, is that Derson aims at a big, powerful idea—how we know what we know. Her learners will do many activities and encounter a lot of subject matter over the course of the unit. But the planned subject matter and activities support and extend an idea that is substantially more meaty and complex than those attempted by Prosy and Mead.

To this point, we have looked at learners and learning and at subject matter. Here, we turn to the third commonplace: teachers and teaching.

The vignettes above suggest several ideas about teachers and teaching worth considering. One is that teachers can choose from an infinite number of teaching methods. In these three vignettes alone, we see evidence of recitation and seatwork, individual reading and note taking, class discussion, and simulation. We can supplement this list with other approaches—lecture, group projects, report and essay writing, journal-keeping, learning centers. You may remember your social studies classes largely in terms of worksheets and lectures. Clearly many other approaches are available.

This plethora of available teaching methods brings up a second point: No one "right" approach will work for all topics and students and situations. You will hear some people insist that every lesson must have a group activity, and you will hear others argue that using textbooks is always a bad idea. We disagree on both counts. Group projects *can be* a good way to teach; using only a textbook *can be* a pretty awful way. But good teaching doesn't reduce to absolutes. Teachers take many approaches to build units, structure lessons, and deliver instruction, and, as the teacher, you must decide which ones to use and when.

The third point is that good teaching demands consideration of a host of factors. In fact, one can get dizzy trying to keep track of the potential influences on one's teaching—educational goals, community needs, parents' expectations, district and state curriculum guidelines, statewide tests—well, you get the point. Many factors

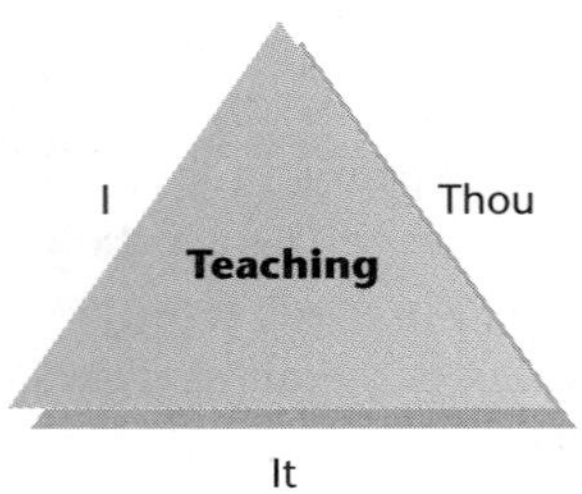

Figure 4.3 • **I, Thou, It Triangle** • Good teaching lies at the intersection of you, your students, and the subject matter.

can and should figure into your instructional decision making. We argue, however, that two factors rise above the rest: subject matter and learners. Although the other influences are important, the heart of teaching lies in the middle of a triangle consisting of you, your learners, and the subject matter. David Hawkins (1974), who calls this triangle, I, Thou, and It, notes that the "child comes alive for the teacher as well as the teacher for the child . . . [when there is] some third thing which is of interest to the child *and* to the adult in which they can join in outward projection" (pp. 57–58).

Hawkins's observation hints at one more big point. Simply put, it is that teaching is more than loving students, managing a quiet classroom, and designing "fun" activities. Instead, powerful teaching and learning develops when a teacher and her or his learners regularly engage big ideas. Good teaching is more than a repertoire of instructional strategies. Instructional methods are important, but only as they provide a vehicle for bringing students and ideas together.

In this chapter, the first of two in which we discuss the teachers and teaching commonplace, we consider how your knowledge of subject matter and learners figures into the construction of big ideas and how big ideas fit within the larger realm of pedagogical action. When you have completed this chapter, you should be able to answer the following questions:

1. ***What are the characteristics of a big idea?***
2. ***What elements frame the construction of a big idea?***
3. ***What are the phases of pedagogical action, and how does the notion of a big idea fit into that schema?***

Teachers and Teaching

Every teacher wants to think that she or he is teaching students to be smart, thoughtful, powerful knowers and thinkers. And yet observers and students alike report that little of the teaching they see and experience hits this target. Much of the social studies teaching in American schools looks like that in the first vignette: teacher-centered and textbook-driven, teachers talking and students listening (or not), discrete bits of information rather than complex, meaty ideas. As one classroom observer notes, social studies topics interest children, yet "something strange seems to have happened to them on the way to the classroom." Instead of being vivid and vibrant ideas, he continues, "the topics of study become removed from their intrinsically human character, reduced to the dates and places readers will recall memorizing for tests" (Goodlad, 1984, p. 212). The approach represented in Prosy's classroom may still be the norm, but many teachers are moving toward more and more interesting teaching.

RELEVANT RESEARCH

There are lots of reasons why teachers choose to teach in this fashion. David Cohen (1989) observes that teaching is an "impossible" profession, one characterized a great deal of uncertainty, heavy workloads, uninspiring curriculum materials, and low pay. He concludes that such factors are unlikely to "enhance teachers' inclination to take on the demanding new assignments that much innovation entails" (p. 35). As Cohen and others (for example, Cuban, 1984, Grant, 1998) suggest, however, teachers have considerable classroom autonomy, that is, the ability to make subject matter and instructional decisions. Two points, then, are clear: Teachers are choosing to teach in traditional ways, and you can choose differently. To be sure, some days you may want to give the students a stack of worksheets and be done with it, and you may even have good reasons to do so. But we can't imagine how a teacher could do so on a regular basis and assert that she or he is challenging all learners to achieve all they can.

Although good teachers use various means to develop and maintain a productive learning environment, they manage more than students' behavior: they also "manage" ideas (Shulman, 1987). In this chapter, we define good teaching in terms of managing—planning, developing, and enacting—big ideas in the classroom.

CLASSROOM MANAGEMENT

Teaching Is More Than Classroom Management and Teaching Methods

All prospective teachers worry about **classroom management.** Although they fret about knowing enough subject matter and the like, the number one concern new teachers have is managing children's behavior. It's a valid worry. We've all been in classes where the students ran wild, and the thought of them running wild on *us* is pretty intimidating. Most adults can manage a group of students through some combination of authority, persuasion, diversion, and threats. Indeed, there are some "tricks" to managing student behavior: plan more than one activity per class; provide learners with opportunities to work with their peers; give challenging assignments. Students cannot learn amidst chaos. But an enormous difference exists between keeping students quiet and in their seats and teaching them to be thoughtful, smart, and engaged learners.

Classroom management is a concern for every teacher. There are some standard practices that teachers employ, but as the fifth-graders in this photograph demonstrate, an engaging assignment often "solves" discipline problems before they start.

TEACHER REFLECTION

"Managing" Student Behavior

Although the idea of managing twenty or more active children can seem daunting, in practice it rarely is. Reflect on the ways you have observed teachers manage students' behavior. Which of those approaches seemed more effective? less effective? Which of these approaches do you think you will feel comfortable using?

If prospective teachers' first concern is discipline, typically their second worry is how to teach—what methods to use and how to use them. In fact, most people associate teaching with methodology. That is, teachers teach when they lecture, lead recitations, set up role-playing situations, organize cooperative groups.

But just as teaching is more than managing students' behavior, so, too, is teaching more than a collection of **instructional strategies.** Having a bunch of strategies or methods in your repertoire is important and useful. Teachers need to know, for example, *how* to lecture and *how* to assign group work. Such knowledge will benefit you, however, only if you also know *why* you might use one approach instead of another, and when this approach makes sense and when it doesn't.

Figure 4.4 • A Continuum of Teaching Practices

Common Teaching Practices

Explicit, teacher-centered, and prescriptive approaches	←→	Implicit, student-centered, and open-ended approaches
Lecture Worksheets Recitation		Group work Learning centers Journal writing

As Figure 4.4 illustrates, some teaching methods are more explicit (recitation); others are more implicit (group work). Some are more teacher-centered (lecture); others are more student-centered (learning centers). Some are more prescriptive (worksheets); others are more open-ended (journal writing).

While it may seem obvious that no single method is best, with so many possibilities, how do you decide? You may be tempted to choose the pet method of a favorite teacher or one that you have seen other teachers use successfully. Remember, however, that a method used to teach one idea or with one group of learners may not necessarily work, or work as well, in your classroom.

TEACHER REFLECTION

Choosing Teaching Approaches

Reflect on the following teaching approaches in light of the continuum in Figure 4.4. Where would you place each one? Is the designation always clear-cut?

group projects	report writing	class discussion
simulations	textbook reading	diary entries
pair reading	role-playing	skits/dramatizations
oral presentations	demonstrations	researching

Let's now think about the teachers profiled earlier. Prosy may want her learners to know something about the power and dynamism of American government. She may want them to feel connected to and a part of the governments that represent them. Yet what message does her instruction send? We suspect Prosy's learners now understand government as another set of names and definitions, all of which seem a great distance from their everyday lives.

We think Mead and Derson's instructional approaches mesh more closely with the ideas and learners at hand. Mead wants her class to know some of the "facts" of the Underground Railroad and, to that end, she poses questions and provides resources for learners to locate that information. But Mead also wants her learners to push below the surface, in this case, to know more about the experiences of African-American slaves. She accomplishes both of these aims within the context of the same lesson simply by asking different kinds of questions. It's a subtle difference and one that the casual observer might not catch. But the questions "How did the Underground Railroad get its name?" and "What did it mean to be a slave?" call for profoundly different levels of analysis and insight. The first calls for a factual response and, in that sense, is little different from the questions Prosy asks. The second, however, pushes much further. Here, students must put together an array of ideas to construct a sense of what the term *slave* means. We want our learners to know the "facts," but we also want them to use facts to make sense of bigger and more substantive ideas.

IN YOUR CLASSROOM: Brainstorming

Brainstorming is a teaching strategy designed to elicit the widest array of ideas students can generate around a topic, question, or issue. For example, Mead might have begun her unit by writing *Underground Railroad* on the board and asking students to call out whatever associations they had. Use brainstorming as a way to uncover and assess the ideas students bring to a topic.

It is on this last point that we see a difference between Mead and Derson. For where Mead pushes children to consider more of the slave experience than is typical, Derson goes one step further by linking the meaning learners construct to a big idea. In this case, Derson helps children understand how archeologists map and interpret evidence. This is an interesting and important idea. Derson takes it even further, however, by using this experience to illustrate the big idea of the interpretative nature of history and historical evidence. In asking, "How do we know what we know?" Derson pushes her learners toward questions and ideas that go well beyond the traditional curriculum. And the implications in doing so, as we will see in succeeding sections, are enormous.

TEACHING RESOURCES

Archaeology with Children

For some neat web sites related to doing archaeology with children see

- http://hanksville.phast.umass.edu/misc/NAarch.html

This site has a terrific index of Internet Native American resources.

- http://web.lemoyne.edu/~begieval/start.html

This site provides a virtual excavation of a medieval village.

The Teaching Act: Two Considerations

Before discussing how to develop big ideas and organize instruction around them, let's talk about some factors teachers should consider when planning instruction. These are a few:

- educational goals and objectives
- state and local curriculum
- curriculum materials available
- teaching time
- standardized tests

Although these factors are important, two pivotal elements—teachers' knowledge of the subject matter and their knowledge of the children they are teaching—figure most prominently in good teaching.

We have stressed several interrelated benefits of having deep subject matter knowledge. Teachers find that it makes the process of making connections—finding the threads—between different social science and history disciplines easier and less time consuming. Deep knowledge helps you expand your choices of curriculum possibilities by pointing you toward interesting questions and powerful ideas that can make those choices exciting and learning-worthy for your students. We also noted that deep subject matter knowledge helps you "hear" your students and decide what to do with their naive ideas.

Indeed, subject matter knowledge is important, necessary, even, but it is not sufficient. Knowing the subject well does not tell you what ideas and questions children will find interesting. Nor does it tell you the most sensible teaching approaches. Knowing the subject matter will make you a better teacher, but that knowledge alone cannot help you know what to do when you stand in front of twenty-five children.

RELEVANT RESEARCH

Suzanne Wilson, a university researcher and third-grade teacher, knows well the geography content she wants her third-graders to learn. She explains that her subject matter knowledge expands "the curricular territory I can explore with my class." She adds, however, that her content knowledge "fails to supply all the answers I need to decide what paths to take." Wilson senses that her learners need to do more than color and fill in map worksheets in order to understand the purpose and value of map-making. After several weeks of class work, however, Wilson concludes, ". . . Knowing the subject matter well and armed with good intentions, I am nevertheless unprepared to teach my learners well" (Wilson, 1990, pp. 12–13). Wilson found that knowing one's learners is as important as knowing one's subject matter.

Teachers could benefit from more research in this area, but, as discussed in Chapter 2, we do know something about what learners know. You can expect your students to have little deep knowledge about social studies concepts and ideas. Moreover, much of what your learners know comes from sources outside the classroom walls—family, television, movies, peers. An occasional child will seem to have an encyclopedic knowledge about, for example, the Civil War or Martin Luther King, Jr. Most of your students' ideas, however, will sound fragmented, over-generalized, and naive to your adult ears. These ideas make sense to students and can be hard to shake. The good news is that children can and will learn powerful ideas during the elementary years, and their thinking will become more varied and sophisticated. To do so, they need powerful learning environments and multiple opportunities to engage new ideas that are coherent and embedded in meaningful contexts and that connect with their prior knowledge and experiences.

TEACHER REFLECTION

The Power of Old Ideas

A good illustration of how hard it is to shake old ideas is to say the first thing that comes into your mind when asked the question "Who discovered America?"

If you answered immediately, we bet your response was "Columbus." If you hesitated—fumbling perhaps for a response like Native Americans, Vikings, Irish, or Africans[1]—we bet that you still saw the word *Columbus* with your mind's eye. The point is simple: Although we "know" that Columbus was hardly the first to "discover" the Americas, it is his name that we remember first.

Subject matter and learners John Dewey (1902/1969) reminds us of the necessary relationship between subject matter and learners when he observes, ". . . the child and the curriculum are simply two limits which define a single process. Just as two points define a straight line, so the present standpoint of the child and the facts and truths of studies define instruction" (p. 11). Other factors weigh into teachers' instructional decisions. Focusing on subject matter and learners, however, seems like a good place to start.

SECTION SUMMARY Teachers and Teaching

- Teaching is more than managing children's behavior and using a variety of instructional strategies.
- Although numerous factors influence teachers' practices, subject matter and learners are particularly important.

Putting It All Together with Big Ideas

Several pitfalls await teachers as they wrestle with these issues of subject matter and learners. One is to dilute social studies content under the assumption that the easier it is, the quicker learners will master it. Another mistake is to focus on classroom discipline under the assumption that learners learn more and better when they are quiet and on-task. Still another pitfall is to develop "fun" activities under the assumption that by dressing up the content, learners will find it more palatable.

We would never advocate eliminating fun (or discipline or simplicity, for that matter) from the classroom. In fact, we suspect each of these responses and the assumptions behind them has some salience. We do suggest, however, that teachers construct activities that lead toward a purpose more powerful than entertainment or quiet or ease alone. Students will remember and enjoy activities that engage them. But they will know and understand more when you construct learning opportunities that help them connect activities with a big idea.

Big Ideas: What They Are Not

While we'll have more to say about what big ideas *are* in the next section, we begin with a discussion of what big ideas *are not:*

- facts
- concepts
- topics

Facts Big ideas are not *facts*. Make no mistake: Facts such as *the colonists won the American Revolution,* or *the U.S. government has three branches,* or *a community is made up of neighborhoods,* are important and useful. By definition, **facts** express ideas that are provable and are accepted by a majority of people. In that sense, facts conveniently summarize and express ideas that most folks believe.

That said, the usefulness of facts lies in context, not in isolation. Facts express important ideas, but they are single ideas. This is a key point; knowing a bunch of facts alone does not guarantee that students will be able to think about anything in particular. Facts need to be connected in order to make sense, and those connections emerge through the construction of big ideas.

Concepts If big ideas are not facts, neither are they *concepts*. **Concepts** are ways of expressing complex sets of ideas, such as "change" or "justice." Educators often talk about children learning concepts and becoming conceptual thinkers. This seems right to us, but concepts are so big and complex that they are instructionally unwieldy. Concepts, like facts, are useful elements in thinking and knowing, but they are of limited use in constructing teaching units, and they are practically useless for developing daily lessons. Where, for example, would one even begin planning a single lesson or unit on "change?"

Topics Many teachers think of big ideas in terms of *topics* such as the American Revolution or Community. **Topics** seem like better candidates for big ideas than facts or concepts because they help group a bunch of facts together and avoid treating them in isolation. Topics are more specific and manageable than abstract concepts. Moreover, topics look a lot like the course titles and textbook chapters with which we are all familiar.

Yet, to our way of thinking, topics don't quite make it as big ideas. One reason is that they fail to help us define what content to teach. A topic tells us neither what concepts and facts are important for our particular students nor how we can figure that out. For example, one could find students studying families in both graduate school seminars and first-grade classrooms. And although both groups might find common interest in some aspects of families, we can't imagine a teacher approaching these two classrooms with the same content agenda and expectations.

The second reason that topics don't work well as big ideas is that they fail to take into account what students know and care about. Both graduate students and first-graders may be interested in how families are similar and different, but their prior knowledge and the issues they care about will greatly differ.

One last reason topics are of little use as big ideas is that they give little counsel about how to teach them. A teacher might possess an array of instructional strategies, but, given a topic as broad as families, she might still scratch her head over how to proceed. If a big idea is to help a teacher figure out what content to teach, what issues interest the students in her classroom, and how to structure both the unit and her daily lessons, topics will not do.

Looking for Big Ideas in Practice

Now let's think back to the vignettes that opened this chapter. Prosy's unit centers on a concept—government—and she seems interested in differentiating between governments at national, state, and local levels. It is difficult, however, to discern her big idea. If it is American government, that seems a daunting task. As concepts go, American government is both huge and complex. What does Prosy want her learners to know and understand about government in general and government at each of these levels? She quizzes learners over a range of facts, but where the unit is going seems unclear.

TEACHING RESOURCES

American Government

For some interesting web sites related to studying American government with children see

- http://www.uncle_sam.com

This is a "one-stop shopping" site for all things related to the U. S. government.

- http://www.execpc.com/~dboals/govt.html#STATEANDLOCALGOVERNMENT

This site has nice array of offerings related to state and local governments across the states.

By contrast, Mead's unit focuses on a topic—slavery in the United States. She too emphasizes factual knowledge; the difference is that she does not stop there. Mead pushes her learners to dig below the surface. She wants her learners to know something about the Underground Railroad, but this information serves a bigger purpose: beginning to understand the institution of slavery. In comparison, Mead's unit appears more connected and coherent than Prosy's.

TEACHING RESOURCES

Slavery in the United States

The following web sites work well for studying slavery in the United States with children:

- http://theblackmarket.com/slaveryfaq.htm

This site offers responses to many frequently asked questions about slavery.

- http://xroads.virginia.edu/~HYPER/wpa/wpahome.html

This site provides access to hundreds of first-hand accounts of slavery collected by the Works Progress Administration during the 1940s.

The problem is, if we asked Mead what she wanted learners to know about American slavery, it's hard to guess what she would say. Her unit seems more comprehensive and substantial than Prosy's, but in many ways it still lacks a big, or core, idea that gives the unit conceptual and pedagogical focus.

Big Ideas: What They Are

We have talked about what big ideas are not. Let's now talk what they are. We begin by describing big ideas, using the case of Pam Derson to illustrate and develop our descriptions. We conclude this section with an annotated sample of big ideas designed by students in our elementary methods classes.

A big idea is a *question* or *generalization* that

- *helps teachers decide what to teach* by connecting facts, concepts, and topics common to the curriculum;
- *helps teachers decide what instructional approaches* they might use by providing a framework in which to judge whether an activity or resource contributes to the understandings they hope to develop; and
- *propels and engages learners' thinking and understanding* by being meaty, complex, and open to multiple perspectives and interpretations.

That's a pretty tall order. Let's see how it plays out, by returning to the unit Derson developed. Her unit question—"How do we know what we know?"—reflects each of these big-idea qualities.

First, Derson's big idea helps her decide *what content to teach.* She follows part of the state curriculum guide in her study of Native-American tribes, but Derson chooses to situate that study within the big idea of understanding the nature of historical evidence and using it to make and support claims. She knows that her students come to class with a variety of ideas about native life and culture, some accurate and sophisticated, most not. Her big idea, *How Do We Know What We Know?,* encourages learners to think about the limits of what we know and about the evidence available as they begin their research projects. To that end, she chooses content that illustrates native life (customs and traditions, ways of living, relations among tribes) and challenges the children's preconceived ideas.

Second, Derson's big idea helps her decide *what instructional approaches she might take.* Because she wants her students to learn new information about native life and to think about how they know what they know, Derson provides a range of instructional activities. Some activities, like the archeology simulation, are opportunities to emphasize particular points. Others, like the research project, pull the entire unit together. For that project, learners use a range of trade books and expository texts to research an aspect of native culture.

Finally, Derson's big idea *promotes learners' thinking and understanding.* One of Derson's goals is to help learners understand that native cultures can be viewed from several vantages. She provides materials from the time period and from today that express the perspectives of natives and others. She urges students to see similarities and differences in the views of those who lived within native cultures

These second-graders are working on a project as part of a unit on Native American cultures. After they finish this representation, what additional assignments might help these students extend their understanding?

and those who encountered them as outsiders. Students are free to choose their own topics for the research project. To demonstrate that they understand it, however, they must show that they have considered the several ways native ideas and actions can be interpreted.

IN YOUR CLASSROOM: Shoebox Archaeology

Provide students with realistic experience as archaeologists by creating a shoebox dig.[2]

1. Lay a thin layer of soil in the bottom of three to five shoeboxes.
2. Place on top some artifacts related to your grandparents (such as, photos, coins, perfume bottles, and tools). Lay on another thin layer of soil.
3. Next, lay in some artifacts related to your parents and cover with another layer of soil.
4. Finally, place inside some artifacts specific to your time and top these off with a final layer of soil.
5. Distribute the boxes to small groups of students and ask them to complete the following tasks:

   a. Complete a Shoebox Archaeology Observation Sheet (Figure 4.5 on the next page) on which they describe, sketch, measure, and hypothesize about the importance of each artifact.

Figure 4.5 • Shoebox Archaeology Observation Sheet

Soil layer	Objects (description)	Objects (sketch)	Measurements	Importance
Layer 1				
Layer 2				
Layer 3				

Sketch artifacts found within each soil layer. Then measure, identify, and describe the importance of each artifact.

b. Write an Archaeologist's Report in which they describe the process they undertook, summarize their findings, and offer conjectures about the people who created and used these artifacts.

c. Share each group's work through short oral presentations.

Derson's unit is one example of how having a big idea can help a teacher make some tough content and instructional decisions. When we talked with her, however, Derson was a little irritated. She had set aside several fine ideas and activities because they didn't fit this big idea. Moreover, she had set aside another set of ideas and activities because she simply did not have enough time to do them. We sympathize with her frustration. Dropping a good activity either because it doesn't fit with the big idea or because of time constraints is a hard choice. Derson realized two things, however: (1) Having too many good options is better than having too few, and (2) she could always use some of the left out activities with future classes. Like all good teachers, Derson understands that one never throws away a good idea.

Derson's framing question for the Native Americans unit, *How Do We know What We Know?*, illustrates the power of teaching through big ideas. Let's look at some other examples developed by prospective teachers in our social studies methods classes:

The inspiration for a big idea can come from many sources. If you were planning a fourth-grade unit on immigration, what big ideas might this photograph of Japanese immigrants arriving in San Francisco in 1912 inspire?

- *Family History Tells a Story* is a generalization that acts as the big idea for a second- or third-grade unit on immigration. The prospective teacher who developed this unit explained, "Children begin to learn at a very early age that people are different in many ways. But they seem to lack a respect and understanding for those who are different from themselves." In her unit, she planned to use learners' interest in themselves and their own histories as a way to explore the "story" of how different people came to the United States.
- *Why Is Albany the Capital of New York?* is the question another prospective teacher used to develop a big idea for her fourth-grade unit. State studies are a common topic in fourth-grade social studies, and naming the state capital is a standard expectation. This unit, however,

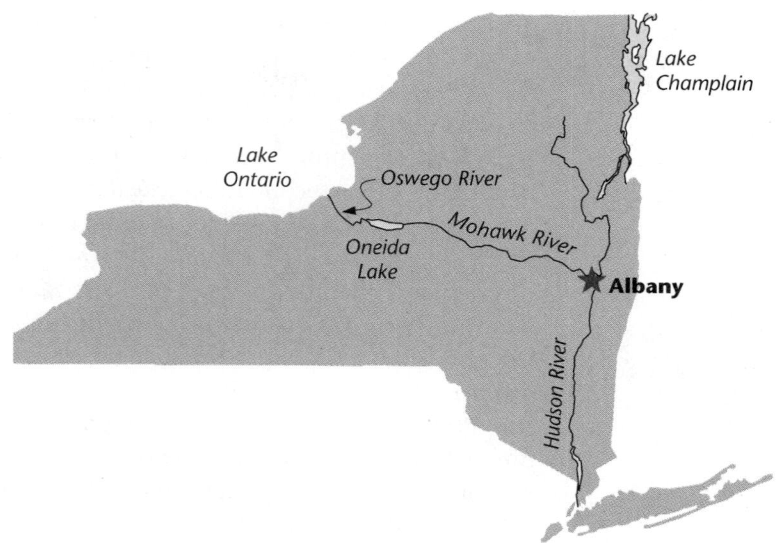

Figure 4.6 • **Map of New York** • Given only this map, what might you hypothesize as the reason Albany was named the capital of New York?

looks at a more intriguing question—*why* the state capital of New York is located in Albany. When this prospective teacher discovered no simple answer, she developed an integrated language arts and social studies unit in which learners researched the question using primary and secondary sources, interviews, and field trips.

Other big ideas that have proven fruitful:

- *Cultural Awareness: Who Are We?* (Kindergarten)
- *Family: Customs, Traditions, and Beliefs* (grade 1)
- *What Do Flags Represent?* (grade 2)
- *Unmelting the Melting Pot* (grade 3)
- *Vermont: Continuity and Change* (grade 4)
- *The Unheard Voices of the Civil War* (grade 5)
- *Savagery or Civilization: A Look at the Aztecs and the Mayas* (grade 6)

One other big-idea unit deserves some attention. Consider how Mead's unit on American slavery might have been different if she had developed it, as prospective teacher Kristen did, around a big idea like What is Freedom? Like Mead, Kristen constructed an array of activities—brainstorming, independent and shared reading of fiction and nonfiction trade books, journals, artifact centers, guest speakers, and mini-lessons—that explored the particulars of slavery. Like Derson, however, Kristen developed her unit around a big idea. The question "What is freedom?" provides a powerful context to develop and extend that topic in two ways. One is to examine multiple perspectives. This unit "teaches the histories of the United States, rather than just one story," Kristen explains. To that end, children learn about slavery from the perspective an African boy kidnapped into slavery, a white indentured servant, a runaway slave, a white slave-owner, and Abraham Lincoln. The second notable feature is that the study of slavery becomes part of a bigger issue or idea, namely, "What is freedom?" Kristen said, "To teach slavery by simply saying, 'It is bad to own other human beings does not do justice to this rich and often difficult period." She wants her learners to understand "how our country could have let the ownership of other humans continue for so long." She also wants children to think about what freedom from slavery has meant to African Americans since the Civil War. In that light, her unit includes readings and discussions that explore the on-going struggle for rights and freedom for *all* Americans (for example, people of color, women). Understanding the topic of American slavery is important, but to fully realize its importance, students need to see it in the context of bigger ideas and issues. (For more details on Kristen's unit, see Chapter 8.)

IN YOUR CLASSROOM: Dealing with Misconceptions

A common misconception many children (and adults) have is that Abraham Lincoln's Emancipation Proclamation in 1863 freed all slaves. In fact, the Proclamation dealt only with those enslaved in the southern states, which, having seceded in 1861, were no longer under Lincoln's control. After reading the Proclamation aloud to students, ask students to imagine why Lincoln might have taken this tack.

It takes more time and energy to develop units around big ideas. The payoffs seem worth it, though: Your learners will benefit from the opportunity to engage genuine ideas and the excitement that brings, and you will gain confidence and skill in your ability to create and deliver powerful instruction.

Constructing a Big Idea

If you are like our students, you are probably thinking something like this:

> Okay. I can buy the notion that creating units around big ideas is probably a good thing. It seems like a lot of work, and I wonder if I really know enough about the subject matter and what interests and engages students. I didn't like much of what my experience was in social studies classes, though, and I don't want to teach my students the way I was taught. So I'm willing to think some more about this.

Fair enough. Let's talk about how you might develop some big ideas of your own.

As we suggested earlier, teachers need to know the subject matter they are responsible for—the major facts, concepts, themes, patterns—in general as well as how those ideas were developed. They also need to know their students—what ideas interest them, what kinds of experiences they have had, what kinds of language they are familiar with, the different ways they think about ideas. These two forms of knowledge are critical; good teachers transform social studies subject matter in light of what they know about learners. It is to that process of transforming the subject matter—and constructing a big idea en route—that we now turn.

We begin with a caveat: It would be nice if we could offer a list of simple steps to big-idealand, but we know of no single path. The problem is that teaching is rarely a straightforward process. Good teachers take routes with lots of side trips, dead ends, and reversals as they develop big ideas of their own. What follows is a general framework for big-idea planning. Know, however, that each of you will find your own way.

1. Begin with a question, issue, or idea that interests you One good place to start is with a question, issue, idea, or curriculum resource that interests, intrigues, or puzzles you. Most teachers, when questioned at this stage, say something like, "Well, I've always been interested in Canada," or "I saw this really neat book on immigrants to America that I'd like to use," or "I think I want to do something where the students have to go out into the community." This might not seem like much, but these comments represent all you need at this point—an engaging idea and a place to start working. In fact, each of the units described in this chapter stemmed from the teacher's personal interest.

For example, Derson transformed her interest in Native Americans and how we've come to know what we know about them into the big idea of her unit. Similarly, the prospective teacher who developed a unit around the big idea *What Is Freedom?* said she began with vague, but strong interest in the Civil Rights movement. Wondering how African Americans could still face discrimination more than one hundred years after the end of slavery, she started thinking about the notion of "freedom" and whether black slaves were really freed after the Civil War.

In both these instances, the teachers developed units that reflect a piece of the expected curriculum for those grades. Other teachers use their curriculum guides as the starting point. In those instances, the teachers generally begin by brainstorming questions about a topic they want to learn more about. One prospective teacher, for example, noticed that recycling was listed in a district curriculum guide as a grade two topic. Always an active recycler herself, she had long wondered why many people are not. The unit she developed around the big idea *Recycling: Why It Matters* exposed students to arguments both for and against recycling and reusing products and materials.

No matter what the source, good reasons abound for starting with something that piques your interest. If you are interested in an idea, chances are your learners will pick up on that and will ratchet up their own interest. If you show a keen interest in an issue or idea, more often than not your students will follow your lead.

2. Ask yourself a series of questions With an idea in mind, you can develop your unit in myriad ways. Some teachers think through a series of questions:

- What do I want students to know and/or experience?
- Why do I think students will care about or be interested in this idea?
- What kinds of activities or experiences do I want them to have?
- What resources will I need to make those experiences happen?
- How will I know if the students understand what I want them to understand?

These are tough questions, and at this point, we wouldn't expect you to have definite answers to any of them. For now, use them as ways to jump-start your thinking if you get bogged down, and to push your thinking as it develops.

3. Express your big idea With some tentative answers to the questions above, it's time to return to the task of expressing your big idea. Let your imagination and creativity out, because the possibilities are endless. Remember, standard curriculum guide topics like Canada, Immigration, and Community Involvement are not big ideas, but they can be easily transformed. For example, if you were teaching a fourth-grade unit on Canada, you could explore past, present, and future relationships between Canada and the United States through the big idea *Canada and the United States: Friends Forever?* A unit that highlights the long tranquil border between the United States and Canada might use the big idea *Peaceful Neighbors—Canada and the United States.* Or you might use a question like *Should the United States and Canada Be One Country?* to push your students' thinking about the advantages and disadvantages of a united North America.

Similarly, a third-grade unit on immigration might support a range of big ideas. To recognize the many contributions of immigrant groups, you might develop a unit entitled *Immigrants: America's Greatest Resource.* To explore the long history of immigration to North America, you might use a big idea like *The United States: A Land of Immigrants.* Or if you wanted to explore current tensions over immigration, you might frame a unit around the question *Has America Closed Its Door on Immigration?*

Finally, big ideas can also help develop units around a standard second-grade topic such as Community. A unit that focuses on diversity might emerge from a big idea like *Many Voices, Many Faces: Life in Our Community.* Or a unit on individual and social responsibility might arise from a big idea like *Helping Each Other and Helping Ourselves: Making Our Community Work.*

4. Map out the unit We think these examples "work" because they meet the big-idea criteria we discussed above. First, they are big, meaty ideas. Like the "It" in Hawkins' triangle, they allow a teacher and learners to come alive together as they explore something of interest to the child *and* to the adult. Second, each of these big ideas helps define the important content. As topics, Community and Immigration are simply too large to teach well. Without the assistance of a big idea, teachers are forced to choose content willy-nilly or to follow a textbook outline. We would never recommend the former and, although the latter has some advantages, we believe your learners will find textbook units less engaging than those of your own design. Finally, having a big idea helps a teacher make instructional decisions. Consider the last Canada example—*Should the U.S. and Canada Be One Country?* Learners might participate in many different activities during this unit, but in framing it this way, surely some kind of debate must take place. Similarly, in a unit entitled *Many Voices, Many Faces: Life in Our Community,* we would expect the teacher to use a variety of forms—text, photographs, and audio and videotape—to illustrate the range of people who live in the area.

Our point is simple: Teaching is a complex activity, and big ideas help teachers decide which methods make the most sense. Given the wealth of instructional possibilities, any advantage in choosing one over another is worth taking.

So push on. Teaching is truly a journey, and each unit is a new and intriguing path. You are bound to take some wrong turns along the way—every teacher does—but as experienced teachers and travelers know, every trip is an occasion to learn. You will benefit, and so will your learners.

SECTION SUMMARY Big Ideas

- A big idea is not a fact, concept, or topic.
- A big idea is a question or generalization that helps a teacher (a) decide what to teach, (b) decide what instructional activities to use, and (c) propel and engage learners' thinking and understanding.
- No simple means exist to construct a viable big idea, but the process can be described as (a) beginning with an interesting question, idea, or issue; (b) asking a series of questions; (c) expressing the big idea; and (d) mapping out the unit.

The Big Idea: Key to Pedagogical Action

Turning big ideas into actual teaching units and lessons is the subject of Chapter 8. For now, we want to close our discussion of big ideas by centering it in the larger realm of pedagogical action.

We locate our notion of teaching with big ideas in the center of what John Dewey (1902/1956) calls "psychologizing" the curriculum and what Lee Shulman (1987) calls **pedagogical reasoning.** Key to these conceptions is the role teachers play in remaking or transforming the facts and concepts of history and the social sciences into instructional representations that reflect both knowledge of the subject matter and of the learners at hand. Shulman outlines his view of pedagogical reasoning this way:

Table 4.1 Phases of Pedagogical Reasoning

Phase One	***Comprehension:*** Understanding the subject matter and educational purposes
Phase Two	***Transformation,*** consisting of • *Preparation:* Preparing the text of instruction • *Representation:* Conceptualizing the range of ways to represent subject matter to learners • *Selection:* Choosing instructional representations and materials • *Adaptation:* Adjusting representations and materials to accommodate all learners
Phase Three	***Instruction:*** Teaching the subject matter
Phase Four	***Evaluation:*** Assessing what learners have learned
Phase Five	***Reflection:*** Thinking about the successes and limits of the teaching episode
Phase Six	***New Comprehension:*** Making plans for next time

Shulman's view of teaching makes a lot of sense. First, we like his emphasis on creating instructional representations that reflect the needs of the learners in the classroom. Many teachers can imagine different ways to teach an idea in the abstract. That's only half the issue, however. Powerful teaching and learning develops when teachers construct instructional representations that fit the particular learners at hand. The second point that stands out is Shulman's emphasis on reflection and change. The mental side of teachers' work is well documented (for example, Clark & Peterson, 1986; McCutcheon, 1981). Shulman reminds us that reflecting on what went well (and not so well) leads to "new comprehension," a sense of what we might do the same or differently next time. In this way, our instructional practices change and grow stronger.

Our notion of pedagogical action owes much to Dewey's and Shulman's ideas. Where we differ is in our choice of beginning point. Dewey begins with the twin foci of subject matter and learners. Shulman begins with comprehension—understanding one's subject matter and educational purposes. We begin with a big idea, a question or generalization that expresses a conceptual and instructional direction and guides the entire pedagogical process. Educational goals and the like are important, but the heart of teaching or pedagogical action lies in actively constructing a big idea that serves to frame an instructional unit.

Other factors influence how we flesh out an instructional unit: the sequence of activities, the curriculum materials and resources available, the time allotted, the connections to other subject matters, and the forms of assessment planned. These elements are part of pedagogical action and we will discuss them in succeeding chapters. For now, however, focusing on your big idea will provide the biggest payoff.

CHAPTER SUMMARY

1. ***What are the characteristics of a big idea?***

A big idea is a question or generalization that helps a teacher (a) decide what to teach, (b) decide what instructional activities to use, and (c) propel and engage learners' thinking and understanding.

2. ***What elements frame the construction of a big-idea unit?***

The actual process of constructing a big-idea unit will vary from teacher to teacher. Most, however, will work through the following elements at one point or another: beginning with an interesting question, idea, or issue; asking a series of questions; expressing the big idea; and mapping out the unit.

3. ***What are the phases of pedagogical action and how does the notion of a big idea fit into that schema?***

The phases of pedagogical action include comprehension, transformation, instruction, evaluation, reflection, and new comprehension. We argue that, although comprehension is important, pedagogical action begins with the construction of a big idea, which acts as a guide or framework for the entire process.

TEACHING RESOURCES

Print Resources

Jorgensen, K. (1993). *History Workshop.* Portsmouth, NH: Heinemann.

Levstik, L., & Barton, K. (1997). *Doing history: Investigating with children in elementary and middle schools.* Mahwah, NJ: Lawrence Erlbaum Associates.

Levine, D., Lowe, R., Peterson, B., & Tenorio, R. (Eds.). (1995). *Rethinking schools: An agenda for change.* New York: The New Press.

Each of these books offers useful ideas about teaching social studies with an eye toward subject matter and learners.

Technology Resources

Good general sites for social studies lessons and resources:

- **http://www.execpc.com/~dboals/boals.html**

This site, The History/Social Studies Website for K–12 Teachers, has an amazing variety of resources on a range of topics.

- **http://education.indiana.edu/~socialst**

Social Studies Sources has fewer links than the site above, but some are different and quite interesting.

- **http://www.ncss.org**

The home page for the National Council for the Social Studies, this site contains helpful information about the organization's activities and a link to useful teacher resources.

- **http://www.georgetown.edu/crossroads/asw**

The historical and archival resources at this site are particularly useful.

- **http://www.ecb.org/tracks**

Tracks: Impressions of America is an all-purpose site for teaching U.S. history and geography to elementary and middle school students.

- **http://www.socialstudies.com/?af@dboals**

A commercial site, this is the home page of Social Studies School Service, a leading supplier of audio, visual, computer, and print resources for teachers and students.

NOTES

1. All these groups (and more) have been proposed as the "discoverers" of the Americas. By general consensus, Native Americans were the first inhabitants in the Americas (see, for example, Morgan, 1993). After that, the arguments become intense as various authors have pitched the importance of the Vikings (Wahlgren, 1986), Irish (Fell, 1976), and Africans (Van Sertima, 1976).
2. Our thanks to Jill Korse, Reading Is Fundamental, for this activity.

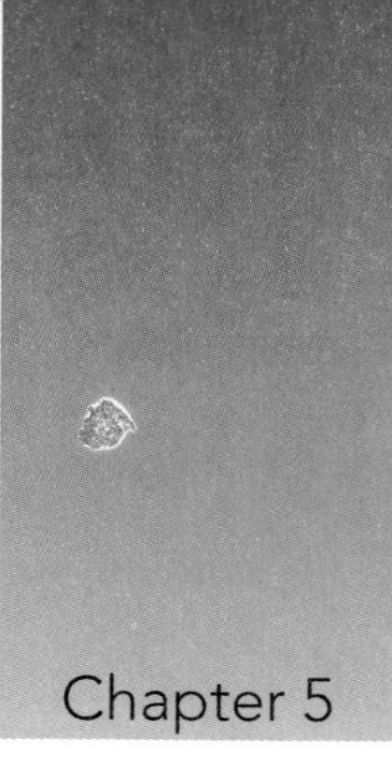

Chapter 5

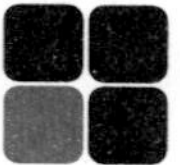

Teaching Social Studies II:
Choosing Teaching Strategies, Curriculum Materials, and Assessment Techniques

CLASSROOM EXAMPLE

Don Kite, a European-American man in his mid-thirties, teaches fifth grade in an urban magnet school with an explicitly traditional schooling mission. His twenty-four students are predominantly African American and poor. The big idea for his unit on colonial America is "America: Colonial Times and Today." His students will compare similarities and differences between the two eras along six dimensions: housing, schools, occupations, entertainment, family, and travel.

Class begins with Kite passing around an array of artifacts—a pewter candle stick, a wooden hand plane, and hand-held drill stock—all of which might have been used during colonial times. He says, "We've started talking about colonies . . . why they were founded. But what I'd really want to talk about is what life was like." As the objects circulate, Kite encourages students to handle them, ask questions, and raise conjectures. Students fill the air with ideas.

The second part of the lesson is a KWL activity.[1] Kite solicits examples of "things you know about colonial life." Students call out an array of ideas—the oldest son inherits property, no electricity, colonists made lots of stuff, freedom of religion—which Kite lists on chart paper under the label "Know." Kite labels a second chart "Want to Know" and asks students to name what they want to know about colonial life.

Students again participate eagerly, offering a range of questions—How did colonists provide food? Were all the kids in the same (school)room? How did they get heat? How did people live on so little food? Kite records these questions, praises their effort, and encourages more.

COMMONPLACE CONNECTIONS

- What does Kite seem to think is important about the *subject matter* of colonial America?
- What view of *learners* does he seem to hold?
- How would you characterize his *teaching?*
- How would you describe the *classroom environment?*

In Chapter 4 we argue that teaching is more than managing behavior or possessing a collection of teaching strategies. These things are important, but knowing how to manage kids and how to do a group activity is quite different from knowing *if* and *when* to do these to promote powerful learning. Key to knowing if and when is the construction of big ideas—questions or statements that help frame and connect the teaching and learning across a unit of study.

In this chapter, we extend that discussion by looking at how a teacher's **pedagogical plan** develops through the consideration and selection of teaching strategies, curriculum materials, and assessments. When you have completed this chapter, you should be able to answer the following questions:

1. ***What teaching strategies support individual, small-group, and whole-group instruction?***
2. ***What array of curriculum materials are available for classroom use?***
3. ***How is assessment different from evaluation, and what forms of assessment are possible?***
4. ***What factors influence teachers' content and instructional decisions?***

Pulling the Pedagogical Plan Together: Teaching Strategies, Materials, and Assessment

We believe a teacher's pedagogical plan flourishes with a big idea. A powerful big idea represents the content a teacher wants to teach. In addition to that, a big idea should help a teacher reflect on three important questions:

1. What teaching strategies will I use to represent the content?
2. What curriculum materials will I use to support my teaching strategies?
3. What forms of assessment will I use to understand what my students have learned?

The Pedagogical Plan: Teaching Strategies

Don Kite chose to begin his colonial unit with an exploration of artifacts and a KWL activity. He picked this **teaching strategy** from myriad possibilities. Before we examine Kite's case more closely, let's imagine some alternatives. For clarity's sake, we organize them in three categories: individual, small-group, and whole-group teaching strategies.

Teaching Strategies for Individual Learning

Given his purposes, Don Kite decided to use two **whole-group activities** to introduce the colonial unit. Given different purposes, he might have chosen an **individual assignment,** one in which students draw on their own resources as they work alone on various tasks.

A common individual task is for students to read and respond to a piece of text. Good teachers use a variety of resources—art, music, film—to engage their students. You will find, however, that many available resources are textual—books, magazines, diaries, and the like. Making individual reading assignments,

Learning centers can feature a wide range of materials. In this photograph, two third-grade girls are free-reading in a center devoted to books about Europe. Think about how you might respond to a parent who questioned the value of such center activities.

in-class as well as outside class, will help students understand the different kinds of text and different ways of reading them. Kite might have introduced his unit by assigning a section from the class textbook, a chapter from a trade book, or a facsimile of a colonial newspaper, and then asking questions that called for definitions, comparisons, analysis, or evaluation.

IN YOUR CLASSROOM: Trade Books

Trade books can add textual variety to your lessons. *Trade book* is a generic term for any commercially published book, either fiction or nonfiction, other than a textbook. Trade books come in a range of reading levels. Their chief advantage is their deeper story or conceptual development.

Individual and class sets of trade books are available from many book vendors, who send catalogs both to schools and to teachers. A good source of information about new trade books is the annual review published by the National Council for the Social Studies in *Social Education.*

Another common individual task is a writing assignment. Teaching social studies provides opportunities for students to learn new writing as well as reading skills. Answering questions associated with a piece of text is only one form of writing. For this unit, Don Kite might have asked each student to write two diary entries—one based on his or her experiences the previous day and one based on his or her perception of an average day during colonial times. Another approach would be to ask students to imagine how life was different for native tribes and for the colonists, and to create lists that identify those similarities and differences.

One other individual task might be developed around **learning centers.** A learning center is most often some form of classroom area where the teacher locates an array of materials and activities that children can explore. For example, instead of letting the colonial artifacts circulate around the room, Kite might have set up a series of centers. One center might have featured carpentry tools like the drill and plane, while another displayed household items such as the candlestick.

Using individual assignments to introduce a new unit has advantages and disadvantages. The obvious advantage is the opportunity to get learners on-task immediately. The principal disadvantage is that a teacher loses the opportunity to introduce the unit through an activity, such as the KWL exercise, that draws on all the learners' input. Good teachers vary their approaches depending on the unit at hand.

Teaching Strategies for Small-Group Learning

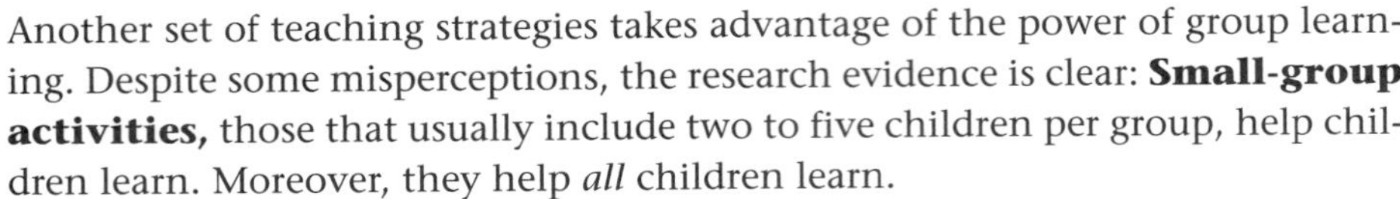

Another set of teaching strategies takes advantage of the power of group learning. Despite some misperceptions, the research evidence is clear: **Small-group activities,** those that usually include two to five children per group, help children learn. Moreover, they help *all* children learn.

RELEVANT RESEARCH

Research does not bear out the commonly held view that group learning situations enable lower-ability learners and disadvantage higher-ability learners (Johnson & Johnson, 1987). **Cooperative learning** groups benefit both students who learn more slowly and those who are faster learners. The explanation turns out to be quite simple: The more opportunity students have to read, write, think, and talk about ideas, the more they learn. Putting children in groups and giving them challenging activities succeeds because learners of all ability levels benefit from the exposure to the material and the interaction with one another.

How might Don Kite have used small groups to introduce his colonial unit? One way might have been to ask each group to develop a list of everyday needs (for example, food, shelter, protection, leisure) and create a separate **T-chart** that illustrates how colonial and present-day Americans meet each of those needs. Another small-group task could involve assigning a different reading to each group. The different readings might describe life during the colonial era from several different vantages: a black male teenage slave, a white male indentured servant, a Native-American boy, and a white woman colonist.[2] After reading and discussing each of these pieces, four new groups can be constituted in **jigsaw** fashion with one or more members from each of the original groups. The new groups' task would be to develop both ideas and questions about how life was similar and different for each individual.

IN YOUR CLASSROOM: T-Charts and Jigsaws

Use a *T-chart* activity to capture students' brainstorming on a topic or question. To make a T-chart, simply draw a large T in the middle of a page on which students can record their ideas. A T-chart based on the exercise described above would look like Figure 5.1 on the next page.

Use a *jigsaw activity* to help small groups of students teach one another. The idea of a jigsaw activity is that each group will become "experts" on a particular piece, after which they split up and share their expertise as members of newly formed groups. The piece shared can be a book review, the explanation of a concept, a draft of a newspaper article, anything that adds to everyone's understanding.

Figure 5.1 • A T-Chart • Here is a T-chart for listing the various ways colonial and present-day Americans meet their food needs.

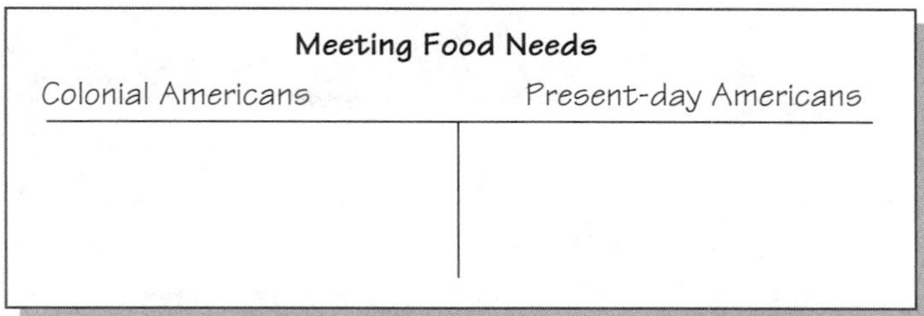

Meeting Food Needs
Colonial Americans
Present-day Americans

CLASSROOM MANAGEMENT

Small-group work can be a powerful teaching and learning experience, and many more teachers are now using such groups as a regular part of their teaching repertoire. But there is more to successful group learning than simply assigning a task to a group of students. Four considerations are crucial to successful group work:

- creating a challenging task
- teaching students how to work together
- selecting groups thoughtfully
- honoring the work of learners

1. Creating a challenging task Many factors go into developing successful group work activities, but probably the most important is the task you assign. A central assumption behind group learning is that students benefit from the ideas and interaction that develop. Consequently, assigning low-level tasks—an end-of-the-chapter worksheet, for example—is a poor use of groups. Such activities quickly turn into a game of, "I'll find the answer to the first question, you find the answer to the second, and then we'll copy from each other." This may be an efficient way to complete the assignment, but students learn little more than if they had worked alone, and maybe less. A better approach is to design activities that both challenge the majority of learners and create a situation where they need to work together in order to complete the task. As we noted earlier, learners will rise to your expectations. This is especially true in group situations where the collective effort will almost always exceed that of any individual. So aim high.

2. Teaching students to work together Creating challenging tasks is critical to effective group experiences, but so too is teaching students how to learn together. Children know how to talk to one another in social settings. That's not the same thing, however, as working together in an academic setting. Moreover, the messages learners typically hear in traditional classrooms discourage the very kind of behavior—talking with other students, sharing ideas and resources, working together to solve problems—we want to encourage in group activities.

IN YOUR CLASSROOM: Guidelines for Cooperative Learning Groups

Help your students learn how to talk and work together by constructing a set of guidelines for working in cooperative learning groups. These guidelines include the following:

- Stay with your group and help others feel welcome.
- Make sure everyone understands the nature of the assignment.
- Construct a plan for how to proceed.
- Divide responsibility for the tasks.
- Encourage others to participate in discussions.
- Discuss, rather than ignore, disagreements that arise.
- Ask for help when necessary.

Remember, though, that two key features underlie any successful rule-making activity. One is involvement. Students follow best those rules that they have some hand in constructing. The second feature is change. No set of rules is likely to cover all situations, so wise teachers sense when rules need to be revised. In the ensuing discussion, they help students articulate the problem, some possible rule revisions, and how the class might decide.

Some learners will come to you having had good group experiences and having learned how to study with others, but not all. It's important, then, to talk explicitly about how groups best function together and to give students opportunities to "practice" together before the first big assignment.

CLASSROOM MANAGEMENT

3. Selecting groups thoughtfully The third consideration in successful group work concerns the size and structure of groups. Two points are important here. One is that you should decide the composition of study groups. Students often will plead to choose their own partners. Be strong! Resist the temptation to relent, especially in the beginning when you are unsure what your learners know or don't know about group efforts. The benefits of diverse groupings—both academic and social—are well documented; mix the groups as much as you can along academic, gender, and racial lines. A second point to consider is group size. No one size works best; different tasks may require different group sizes. For example, the quick sharing of ideas is best accomplished in pairs. Pairing students is also a good first step if you suspect your learners have had little group experience. Three- and four-member groups are better suited to more complex situations where no one student could be expected to accomplish the task alone. Groups of this size also are big enough to yield a range of perspectives but

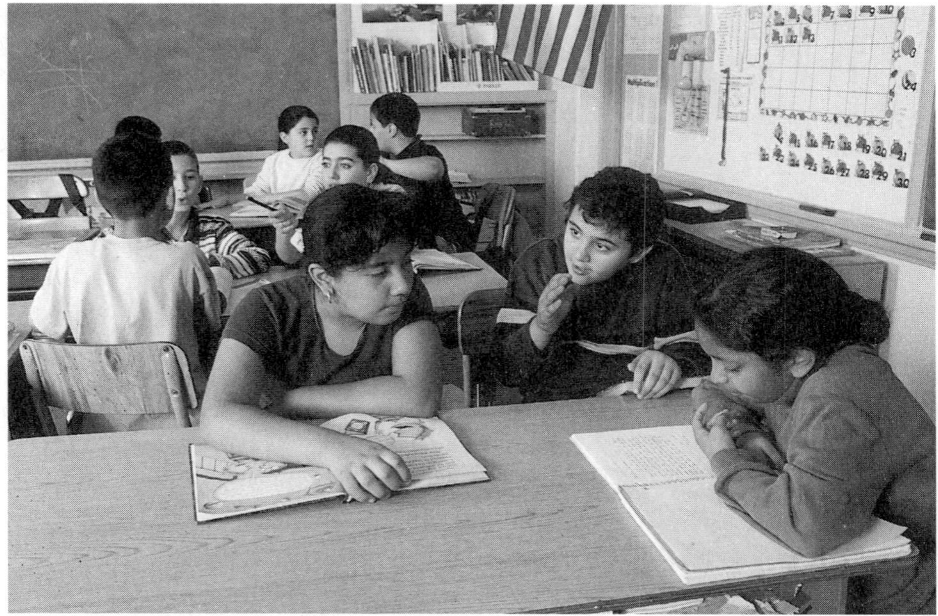

Key to successful small-group instruction is the careful selection of students for each group. What factors might the teacher who arranged these fifth-grade groups have had in mind?

small enough so that all members can participate easily. Finally, for special projects you may want even larger groups. Large groupings of five or more learners can be quite valuable, especially when assignments call for more divergent thinking. Plan to start small, though, because large groups will falter if learners have not had significant experience in smaller groupings.

4. Honoring the work of learners One last bit of advice in making group assignments is to honor learners' accomplishments. Some teachers assign group tasks, but then fail to reward learners for work well done. Reflecting traditional views, these teachers assume that jointly produced work is less important than individual work. Consequently, they may weight an individual test grade twice as heavily as the grade on a group project. Think about the message this sends: the effort students put into the group activity is worth only half as much as a test score. You may well want to assign different grade weights to different activities, but if small-group work is important, make sure you show students that you value it.

The advantages of small-group work are several. As we noted above, you should expect *all* of your students to learn more. You should also expect fewer discipline problems as students become engaged in the tasks you assign.

You may find, however, that small-group work can take a lot of time. Your learners will explore topics more deeply, but you may cover fewer topics.

Small-group work also can seem chaotic. In the beginning of the school year, as students are learning how to learn together, you may see a fair amount of misdirected and off-task behavior. You might mistake this for a sign of failure, but it isn't. Remember that, for children, learning how to talk and participate with one another is a process, and such learning is bound to look chaotic early on.

Finally, some teachers find small-group study disconcerting as their role changes from information-giver to facilitator. The better your class becomes at working and learning together, the less direct assistance they may need. That's good news for them, but you may feel awkward and left out. Remember, however, they aren't really learning without you. They could not do what they are doing if you were not helping them learn how to work in groups, setting challenging assignments, providing a range of useful resources, guiding their investigations, and the like. Small-group work, then, is not only "real" teaching, it can be particularly powerful teaching as children come to see themselves as learners and accept responsibility for their efforts.

Teaching Strategies for Whole-Group Learning

As noted, Don Kite chose to introduce his colonial America unit with two *whole-group activities*—looking at artifacts and a KWL exercise. Depending on his purposes, however, he might have employed other **whole-group activities,** those that include the entire class.

If he was primarily interested in assessing learners' prior knowledge, Kite might have given the class a short examination, known as a **pre-test.** A pre-test gives a teacher a sense of what her students already know about a topic. It can also alert learners to the information a teacher thinks is most worth knowing. If the same test is readministered as a **post-test** at the end of the unit, teacher and students can see immediately what knowledge gains have been made.

If Kite had been more interested in giving students some common information, he might have used a formal or informal lecture. Lecture gets a bad rap among educators, but if time is short and the information is relatively straightforward, we see no reason to avoid lecturing. It's a quick and efficient way to communicate explicit information.

Thus far we have been considering alternative approaches Kite might use to introduce his colonial America unit. He could, of course, also use these approaches as the unit develops. Two whole-group strategies that work nicely once a unit is underway are *role-playing* and *simulation* exercises.

Role-playing refers to teacher-created situations in which students assume roles different from those they normally play. For example, Kite might have had learners role-play the interaction between two colonists, one settled, another newly-arrived. Other examples include having children role-play different resolutions to a playground scuffle, the conversation between a police officer and a lost child, or the meeting of a slave and his owner upon the announcement of the Emancipation Proclamation.

Although **simulations** may involve some role-playing, more often they are situations in which learners confront a series of problems and decisions. Simulations usually have no right answer, but the choices learners make have appropriate consequences. A good example is *Oregon Trail*.[3] This computer simulation software presents an array of situations (for example, what supplies to take, how to negotiate with natives) and decision options. Based on their choices, groups of learners travel farther, turn back, or face imminent death.

TEACHING RESOURCES

Simulations

Simulations such as *Oregon Trail* and the *Sim* series (*SimCity, SimFarm, SimTower,* and so on) are commercially marketed instructional packages. The *Sim* series allows children to create an environment such as a city or a farm.

Free, web-based simulations are also available. For example, the National Geographic Society site, http://www.nationalgeographic.com/education/idea58/index.html, offers an Environment Explorer unit where students use their skills of observation to analyze changes that people have made to the natural environment.

Strategies such as role-playing and simulations can take a lot of class and planning time. The advantages—the chance to develop multiple concepts in one exercise, more active learner involvement, and the motivation inherent in doing something fully engaging—however, often outweigh these negatives.

A caution about "fun" Each of the approaches described above can be motivating, and that's good. A cautionary note is in order, though. All too often we hear prospective teachers talk about their teaching largely in terms of doing "fun" things with their classes. A good teacher, however, will take care that the search for fun activities does not lead to trivial teaching—lots of activity, but little real learning. A unit on colonial America, for example, is a great opportunity to develop activities students would enjoy doing—making candles, writing with a quill pen and bottled ink, and the like. Used in the right context, such activities can be terrific learning experiences—as long as each activity serves your big idea. Stringing together a bunch of fun projects may help your students enjoy the moment, but they won't be well-served in the end. Fun for fun's sake isn't very useful.

Although he might have chosen otherwise, Don Kite's instructional choices seem to work: The artifacts and KWL activity capture the learners' attention, provide learners an opportunity to share their ideas, and help Kite understand something of what his students know about colonial life before the formal unit begins. Moreover, each activity is fun (in the best sense of that term) and supports Kite's big idea. Kite's instructional choices should help you begin thinking about the range of teaching approaches from which you can draw.

What Don Kite knows about the subject matter and his students and how this all translates into his practice is pretty complex. In fact, there is even more to it; his teaching decisions illustrate a range of pedagogical issues. In the next section, we look at how Kite uses curriculum materials to support and extend his instruction.

SECTION SUMMARY Teaching Strategies

- Teaching strategies for individual work include reading and writing assignments and participation in learning centers.
- Strategies for small-group work include T-charts and jigsaw activities. Small-group activities work best when teachers create a challenging task, teach children how to work together, select groups thoughtfully, and honor learners' work.
- Whole-group strategies include pre-testing, lecturing, role-playing, and simulations.
- Prefer engaging activities that address the big idea over activities designed only for fun's sake.

The Pedagogical Plan: Curriculum Materials

Choosing teaching strategies and developing activities around them is one piece of developing a pedagogical plan. Choosing **curriculum materials**—teaching and learning resources—is another. To see how one teacher selects and uses instructional resources, let's continue to watch the development of Don Kite's colonial America unit:

CLASSROOM EXAMPLE

> Kite continues the KWL activity from the previous day. After reviewing what the students said they knew and what they would like to know, Kite breaks the class into four-member cooperative learning groups and assigns to each group one of several topics—houses, schools, occupations, entertainment, family, travel. As each group meets, they select relevant questions from the "Want to Know" list. Most groups also develop some additional questions.

Students begin researching their questions using a range of texts and videos that Kite makes available. Some students rush to the pile of U.S. history textbooks on a back shelf. Others peruse the trade books Kite keeps on a large swiveling stand. Still others ask permission to visit the school library where a large number and range of books, videotapes, and other media representations are reserved.

Before we talk about Kite's use of curriculum materials, notice that he continues to vary his instruction on the second day of the unit. Some teachers use only one or two strategies in every unit. Kite mixes whole-group instruction (reviewing the list of what students know and want to know) with a small-group assignment (investigating a set of group-selected questions around a topic related to colonial America). Blending instructional approaches is generally a good way to provide structure to the class day and keep eager minds and bodies busy. Kite knows this, but his intent is more strategic. He knows his students lack experience researching ideas on their own, so he assigns topics to small groups who then capitalize on each member's strengths as they work together. He also knows that his students sometimes have trouble knowing what kinds of questions to ask, so he gathers the whole class to generate as many questions as possible. Kite manages to challenge his students and still provide the assistance they need.

One other point: Notice that the topics Kite assigns—houses, schools, occupations, entertainment, family, and travel—represent geographic, economic, and social "threads." As the unit develops, the geographic thread is represented in discussions about where homes and schools were located, how the availability of resources influenced which occupations were viable, and how landforms made travel easy or difficult. The economic thread is represented primarily through the concept of occupations. Although they might have explored a range of other economic issues, Kite's students focus on the kinds of jobs held by colonial men, women, and children. The social thread receives the most explicit attention in this unit. Students research family arrangements, housing styles, leisure activities, and how children were educated. From his big idea—America: Colonial Times and Today—Kite astutely uses three key threads to organize his unit. This is wide territory; Kite expects his students to cover a lot of ground.[4]

Don Kite uses a variety of teaching approaches to reach his goals. He also uses a variety of curriculum materials. Because his class represents a wide range of reading levels and confidence, he makes available a wide range of materials. Some students will seek out textbooks because they are familiar sources and are easy to read. More adventurous students will seek out more challenging materials, such as trade books and Internet resources. Kite believes that his textbook presents ideas too simplistically and is bland. Eventually, he will encourage all his students to seek alternative sources. In the meantime, however, he supports those students who choose the class textbook until they are ready to move beyond it.

Using Textbooks

Like many teachers, Kite uses textbooks as part of his instructional package. Unlike many teachers, however, Kite uses textbooks as but one of several resources available to learners. Just as textbooks do not define the content he teaches, textbook reading, recitation, and end-of-chapter questions do not define his instructional approaches.

RELEVANT RESEARCH

Textbooks have in fact improved since the 1980s, when criticism of school texts in general, and social studies texts in particular, reached its zenith (Fitzgerald, 1980; Loewen, 1995). Textbooks can work effectively, especially as a quick resource for defining terms and concepts and for gaining background information. We only caution you to be wary of becoming overly dependent on them.

Using Other Texts

As educators everywhere become more and more interested in interdisciplinary connections, it makes sense to look around for both fiction and non-fiction text sources:

- Newspapers
- Reference books, such as encyclopedias, almanacs, and non-fiction trade books
- Children's literature and poetry

Newspapers One often over-looked text source is the *newspaper.* Although studies suggest that adults increasingly get their news from television, newspapers continue to be an important source of current events information and thus a vital resource for social studies classrooms.

Newspapers can be used in myriad ways. You might encourage students to bring in news clippings and to begin each day with a short discussion of these stories. Or you might ask learners to keep a current events journal where they combine their own clippings with comments on all the stories discussed in class. These two strategies help you expand your regular social studies instruction with additional opportunities to read, write, and discuss ideas.

Other strategies allow teachers to integrate newspapers more directly into their lessons. For example, a second-grade teacher introducing a unit on the local community might ask rotating groups of volunteers to monitor the newspaper for relevant articles. The content of the accumulating articles could play an important part in shaping the content of the unit. Such a strategy is a powerful student motivator, for as children participate directly in their own learning they begin to see immediate connections between their studies and the world around them. If one of our goals is to help learners see the relevance of social studies to their own lives, newspapers can be a powerful resource.

IN YOUR CLASSROOM: Surveying Newspaper Use

A natural way to incorporate mathematics into social studies is through the use of surveys. A ***survey*** is an assessment of what a group of people think about a topic at a particular point in time. You can help elementary children explore newspapers with a simple survey composed of questions such as the following.

- Where do you get most of your information about current events? a) Newspapers; b) Radio; c) Television
- Do you read a newspaper on a daily basis? Yes/No
- Do you receive a newspaper at home? Yes/No
- What section do you read first? a) Front page; b) Sports; c) Comics; d) Editorials

Students can administer the survey, tabulate the results, and graph them before discussing in class their interpretations of the findings.

Using newspapers can be a little tricky, however. Remember, newspapers are made up of many different kinds of articles—straight news, editorials, features, and the like. It is important to teach your class how to identify and read the different pieces.

- *News stories* typically describe current situations and tend to be written in a top-down manner. Reporters put the key information—who, what, when, where, why, and how—in the lead or first paragraph and develop the details of the story as the article unfolds.
- *Editorials* are expressions of opinion. An editorial writer is less concerned with reporting the facts than with interpreting those facts and persuading readers to adopt her or his point of view.
- *Features* may describe an important issue such as smoking-related illness, highlight an emerging trend such as increases in teen pregnancy, or profile an interesting person such as Bishop Desmond Tutu.

Helping your learners understand these different types of articles will help them become sophisticated newspaper readers.

Reference and nonfiction books Other text sources—reference books such as *encyclopedias* and *almanacs,* and *nonfiction trade books*—require some special reading skills, too. For example, learners need to understand that different reference books provide different kinds of information.

Encyclopedias generally offer the most global information, though not always in the most engaging fashion. Almanacs provide more detailed data on a smaller range of subjects. Almanacs provide a special challenge to beginning readers because of the concise presentation and the absence of much descriptive information.

TEACHING RESOURCES

Computer-Based Resources

The days of searching through library stacks for oversized encyclopedias are not over . . . but they are close! For example, Grolier's has produced a CD version of their encyclopedia that allows students to easily navigate the topics of their interest.

The ease of Internet surfing, however, means that students can quickly go beyond encyclopedic information. A few minutes teaching students to use a web-browser (for example, Lycos, Yahoo, MegaCrawler) combined with an opportunity to practice searching will open students' eyes to the amazing potential of the Internet.

The power of Internet access comes with some important caveats. One is the caution to avoid allowing children unsupervised access to Internet sites and services. Most school computers are equipped with programs that filter out obviously inappropriate materials. These filters are not perfect, however, so talk with your school or district computer coordinator about how to protect children from objectionable sites. Two other cautions fall under the heading of Internet literacy. With so much information available, students can easily be overwhelmed by searches that lead to thousands of hits. Helping children learn how to limit the scope of their searches, then, is an important skill. The second issue concerns how to evaluate Internet sites and the information they offer. The Internet is a boon to individuals and groups whose access to traditional means of disseminating ideas has been limited. But that democracy of access means that children need to learn how to evaluate the sources of information they see and read. Good readers always consider the source when trying to understand text; that practice is even more important in this Internet age.

Encyclopedias and almanacs are good sources for quickly finding basic information. For richer sources of information, learners can turn to nonfiction trade books. Commercial publishers continually add new titles appropriately written for and of interest to elementary-age learners. Most school and public libraries have selections of biographies, histories, and folk legends from which learners can get more detailed accounts of the topics that interest them.

Child-Friendly Resources

Internet literacy is becoming increasingly important as children (and adults) use the Internet. A useful site for teachers and children is

- http://www.yahooligans.com

Not only is this a child-friendly search engine, but the authors provide a helpful set of guidelines for teachers and children as they learn to become Internet literate.

Children's literature Many teachers believe that only nonfiction sources are appropriate for teaching social studies. Not so! *Children's literature* and *poetry* can be highly effective social studies resources.

Historical fiction refers to realistic stories set in the past. Authors combine real events (for example, the American Revolution, the Civil Rights movement) and circumstances such as slavery and immigration with fictional characters, settings, and plots. Learners benefit by vicariously reliving the times through each character's feelings, emotions, and experiences. *Roll of Thunder, Hear My Cry* (Taylor, 1976), for example, is a novel about life in the deep South during the Depression. The following passage vividly portrays the frustrations of a family of black children faced with violent racism when, while walking to school, they were almost killed by a white bus driver:

> . . . when the bus was less than fifty feet behind us, it veered dangerously close to the right edge of the road where we were running, forcing us to attempt the jump to the bank; but all of us fell short and landed in the slime of the gully.
>
> Little Man, chest-deep in water, scooped up a handful of mud and in an uncontrollable rage scrambled up to the road and ran after the retreating bus. As moronic rolls of laughter and cries of "Nigger! Nigger! Mud eater!" wafted from the open windows, Little Man threw his mudball, missing the wheels by several feet. Then, totally dismayed by what had happened, he buried his face in his hands and cried. (p. 48)

Many children have difficulty understanding life for African Americans after slavery ended. This passage and many others in this profoundly moving book dramatically illustrate the daily tensions of African Americans living in a white-dominated world. Although few of your students may have had anything like the experience described above, most will have experienced some of the range of emotion—fear, humiliation, helplessness—Little Man felt.

IN YOUR CLASSROOM: Book Talks

A good way to expose children to new books and to help emphasize the differences among texts is through **book talks.** A book talk is a brief presentation that may feature a synopsis of the whole book or a key element or concept. The idea is to give the audience enough of the book's flavor to entice others to read it. After modeling a book talk once or twice, your students should quickly pick up on the form and enjoy presenting their books.

Poetry too can be an effective means of bringing life and color to historical events. Francis Miles Finch's poem, "The Blue and the Gray," offers numerous ways to think about the tragedy of war, in this case the Civil War:

> By the flow of the inland river,
> Whence the fleets of iron have fled,
> Where the blades of the grave grass quiver,
> Asleep are the ranks of the dead;—
> Under the sod and dew,
> Waiting the judgment day;—
> Under the one, the Blue;
> Under the other the Gray.
>
> These in the robings of glory,
> Those in the gloom of defeat,
> All with the battle blood gory,
> In the dusk of eternity meet;—
> Under the sod and the dew,
> Waiting the judgment day;—
> Under the laurel, the Blue;
> Under the willow, the Gray.
>
> From the silence of sorrowful hours
> The desolate mourners go,
> Lovingly laden with flowers
> Alike for the friend and the foe;—
> Under the sod and the dew,
> Waiting the judgment day;—
> Under the roses, the Blue;
> Under the lilies, the Gray.
>
> So with an equal splendor
> The morning sun rays fall,
> With a touch, impartially tender,
> On the blossoms blooming for all;—

Under the sod and the dew,
Waiting the judgment day;—
'Broidered with gold, the Blue;
Mellowed with gold, the Gray.

So, when the summer calleth,
On forest and field of grain
With an equal murmur falleth
The cooling drip of the rain;—
Under the sod and the dew,
Waiting the judgment day;—
Wet with the rain, the Blue;
Wet with the rain, the Gray.

Sadly, but not with upbraiding,
The generous deed was done;
In the storm of the years that are fading,
No braver battle was won;—
Under the sod and the dew,
Waiting the judgment day;—
Under the blossoms, the Blue;
Under the garlands, the Gray.

No more shall the war cry sever,
Or the winding rivers be red;
They banish our anger forever
When they laurel the graves of our dead!
Under the sod and the dew,
Waiting the judgment day;—
Love and tears for the Blue,
Tears and love for the Gray. (1991, p. 159)

Your learners may have a range of ideas about the Civil War. The patterned refrains, accessible language, and vivid images of the poem, however, offer numerous ways to think about and empathize with soldiers who fought more than one hundred years ago.

Using Maps and Globes

Understanding people and events is key to a good social studies program. Also important, however, is understanding the physical space around us. Just as the different texts described above help learners understand people and events, maps and globes help them understand spatial features and relationships.

Maps and globes are amazing representations of the physical world. Consider the **Mercator projection** map in Figure 5.2.

Figure 5.2 • A Mercator Projection

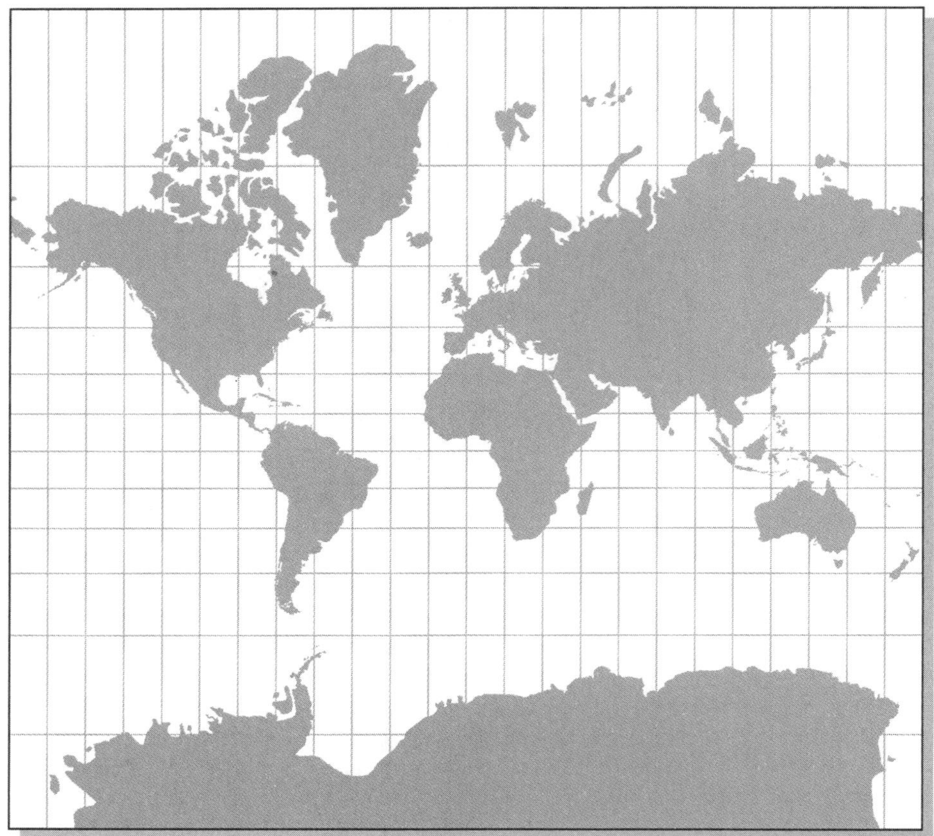

The Mercator projection provides a wealth of information in the shapes and relative sizes of continents, countries, and bodies of water; location systems that show direction (compass) and that allow us to pinpoint any spot on the earth (longitude and latitude); and a legend or key to symbols for a wide range of information—physical features, political boundaries, national capitals. In a glance, we can see stuff that would take hundreds of pages to describe in words.

Like any tool, however, maps and globes are useful only if one knows how to use them. Surveys of geographic knowledge are depressingly consistent: Many Americans simply don't know much about the world around them. The good news is that learning how to read and use maps and globes is relatively easy.

For you to effectively teach the use of maps and globes, you'll have to feel knowledgeable yourself. If your skills need upgrading, a good resource is *Geography for Life: National Geography Standards* (Geography Education Standards

Project, 1994). As you explore geography, you'll discover infinite ways to help your learners become geographically literate. Two activities we find useful are exercises where children make their own maps.

The first activity introduces young learners to map-making. The task involves making a map of the classroom and locating key features such as windows, bookshelves, and teacher and student desks. Especially good for primary-grade learners, this activity encourages students to develop their sense of space and relationship as they locate objects on their maps. Learners also can create simple legends to identify objects in the room.

A second activity introduces upper-elementary learners to mapping the world. If you have never tried it, take out a piece of paper and draw a free-hand map of the world, labeling as much of it as you can. Go ahead, we'll wait for you. . . . Okay, so what did you learn by doing this? Chances are you had some success—you drew some of the land masses fairly accurately and even correctly labeled some places. You probably also had some problems; you may have forgotten some lands (did you remember Australia?), misdrawn others (does your South America look like a big drop of water?), or created some that don't exist (did you, perchance, draw in the lost world of Atlantis?). Moreover, you may have discovered that you did not know where to locate many countries, bodies of water, and the like. That's okay; frankly, given the fact that most of you were raised on mimeographed outlines, we wouldn't expect much different. The point is that this activity has terrific potential for all kinds of lessons on locating important places, understanding longitude and latitude, and thinking about where one is in relation to the rest of the world.

TEACHER REFLECTION

Distinguishing Between Maps and Pictures

How is a map is different from a picture? What features are different? What features do both share? How might your students distinguish between them?

These map-making activities directly expose learners to key geographic concepts. Commercially produced maps (for example, the ones in your textbooks and in sets of reproducible maps) have other uses. For example, learners can get a better sense of which countries share common political borders when they look at a full-color textbook map. Reproducible maps, especially outline maps, are useful as assessments of whether or not learners can locate the features the class has been talking about. Other good sources of maps and geographic activities are computer programs. Imagine, for example, the excitement learners feel when they use their computers to locate and create maps of the hometowns of their pen pals. Using these resources reinforces the importance of geography and demonstrates another importance use for computer technology.

Teaching Geography

You can introduce your students to a terrific geography tool provided by Lycos search engine. The "Roadmaps" service invites students to enter the name of any destination in the United States and receive a map and directions to that site. An interesting feature is the ability to zoom in and out, decreasing or increasing the size of the map. The site is at http://www.lycos.com/roadmap.html.

Although many people associate using maps with dull learning, it doesn't have to be this way. Our experience tells us that kids are fascinated by maps and globes. Your students will enjoy them, too, if you look for creative ways to introduce them that spark students' imaginations.

Using Computers and Other Technologies Wisely

Although we strongly advocate the use of computer and related technology, we equally caution against misuse. New technologies can open up wonderful new worlds to learners. Video-tape, video-disks, the Internet, computer programs, and the like provide students with far greater access to ideas and information than even ten years ago. So by all means, use the technology you have available, but use it with an understanding that novelty does not always equal effectiveness.

IN YOUR CLASSROOM: Using Videotape

Videotape is a terrific classroom tool. Too often, however, teachers use more when less can be equally, or even more effective. The movie *Dances with Wolves* is a good example. This feature film has great possibilities for illustrating the complex relationships between white and native cultures. The film's length and content of some scenes undercut the usefulness of showing it in its entirety, so consider showing small clips of the film. For example, the scene where Kevin Costner's character, John Dunbar, is taught how to say the word *tatonkah* (the Comanche word for "buffalo") can effectively illustrate the problems *and* possibilities of intercultural communication.

Teachers, who have so many resources available, must use technology wisely. Remember that for thousands of years humans learned real and important knowledge without the use of computers or videotape. In your excitement to use the latest computer simulation, don't forget that powerful learning still occurs when kids use that oldest of intellectual technology—books. Our goal is not to razzle-dazzle kids, to trick them into learning, but to use the best tool for the best job.

SECTION SUMMARY Curriculum Materials

- Textual resources come in many forms: Textbooks, encyclopedias, almanacs, trade books, children's literature, and poetry.
- Maps and globes provide useful representations of the physical world.
- Computers and other technologies have an important place in classrooms, but teachers need to apply to their use the same thoughtfulness used in selecting other teaching resources.

The Pedagogical Plan: Assessment

The third issue central to developing a pedagogical plan is **assessment**—discovering what your students know. As with traditional lecture-and-recitation forms of teaching and traditional materials such as textbooks, traditional approaches to assessing learning such as multiple-choice tests are facing challenges. After all, if we are going to use different teaching approaches and materials, we need to think about assessing our learners differently. To do so, let's begin by returning to the case of Don Kite and exploring his answer to the question "How do I know what my students understand?"

CLASSROOM EXAMPLE

Don Kite's small groups research their topics for two weeks. Over that period, Kite continually returns to the "Learn" portion of the KWL activity, asking students what they are learning as a result of their investigations. As the project draws to a close, Kite reminds the class that they are responsible for two products. One is a group presentation: Each group is assigned twenty minutes to talk about the questions they asked of themselves and the information they gathered. They also should be prepared to answer questions from their classmates. The second product is an individual one. Here, each child must write an essay comparing life during colonial times to that of today. The expectation is that learners will draw information for the essay from the various group presentations.

Just as he uses multiple methods and materials, Kite also uses multiple forms of assessment. Kite knows that conventional measures such as a multiple-choice test tell him little beyond some basic facts about what learners really understand about the ideas covered. To provide learners with more opportunities to tell him what they know, Kite employs the above two less-traditional assignments. His choices feature group and individual components, public and private exhibitions, and opportunities to build writing, speaking, and group-process skills in addition to expressing the content learned.

Group and individual projects like the ones Don Kite uses represent some of the latest thinking in assessing learners' understandings. These efforts are described variously as "authentic" or "performance-based" assessments. We'll examine more closely the distinctions between these a little later. The point to consider now is that educators are rethinking the traditionally narrow use of tests and grades as they explore the issue of how to know what learners understand.

Three ideas are central to current thinking about assessment: viewing assessment as a continuous part of instruction, using multiple sources of data, and looking at a broad range of learner outcomes. Percolating throughout these issues is the distinction between *assessment* and *evaluation*. Let's look at what these issues involve.

Assessment as an On-Going Part of Instruction

For far too long, educators have thought about assessment only in terms of **evaluation,** where evaluation is a summary activity that focuses exclusively on what learners know and can do. These attributes of evaluation are a part of assessment, but only a part. We consider assessment an on-going part of instruction.

If you wait until the end of a unit to evaluate learners' efforts, you miss important opportunities. One is to understand how learners are responding to the content as they encounter it. The results of a short quiz or writing assignment given mid-way through a unit offer a snapshot of how each learner is making sense of the unit ideas. Learners who are struggling can receive extra help before they fall too far behind and become too frustrated. The second opportunity is to modify your instruction based on the outcomes of your assessments. The results of a mid-unit assessment offer an advantage in that they give you a sense of how your unit is progressing. If most of the learners seem to understand the big ideas presented, you can feel fairly confident in proceeding. If most learners seem to be missing point, however, you can take two actions. One is to do a different sort of assessment to check the results of the first. The second is to rethink how the unit has developed thus far and return to those big ideas with which learners are having trouble.

In these ways assessment helps you to understand both how learners are doing and how the unit is progressing. With this information, you can weigh your instructional plan and make adjustments as you see fit.

Using multiple sources of data A second idea that separates assessment from evaluation is using multiple sources of data. Because evaluation has traditionally meant a summary exercise, educators have generally thought in terms of one measure per study unit. If we see assessment as understanding what learners know and can do throughout a unit, it makes sense to use as many assessments as is practical.

Probably everyone has experienced the panic of having prepared for one question or type of test and been given another. Maybe you were one of the lucky ones who did well anyway; chances are, you bombed out. The point of recalling such painful memories is not to make you feel badly, but to make the point that a single measure can produce invalid results. In short, the number and kind of assessments do matter. Some students do well on **objective-type tests**—multiple-choice, fill-in-the-blanks, and matching—but other kids do better on **open-ended tasks** such as writing essays, creating political cartoons, and making journal entries. Using either as a single measure can produce invalid results. If, as teachers, we have only one end-of-the-unit evaluation, chances are some learners' knowledge and skills will not be accurately assessed.

TEACHER REFLECTION

Assessment Anxiety

Think about your past experiences with assessments, especially those that acted as evaluations . . . and the anxiety those situations produced. How did you feel in those situations? How did you respond? How did those situations compare with other assessment experiences you have had?

Just as not all assessments produce anxiety, not all anxiety is bad. The pressure to perform on an assessment can be an important motivation for learning. But good teachers know the importance of sensitivity to student anxiety and of working with those students whose anxiety levels incapacitate them during some tasks.

Because we all want all children to have opportunities to succeed, and we want to produce students who can perform well in a variety of situations, we need to build multiple forms of assessment into our teaching.

Considering a Broad Range of Learner Outcomes

One last assessment issue is the need to consider a broad range of learner outcomes. Evaluation typically implies only one kind of outcome—**cognitive** or academic. End-of-the-unit tests may have objective and open-ended questions, but they typically assess only a learner's knowledge and skill. Other learner outcomes—*affective* and *social*—are often ignored.

We want to make two points here. One is that cognitive or academic outcomes are important. Although we disagree with the conventional view that assessment should focus exclusively on evaluating learners' knowledge, we also disagree with the view that elementary school should focus exclusively on social and affective goals, and that children will get enough academics in later years. Social and affective outcomes are vital to children's development, but so too are academic or cognitive outcomes.

RELEVANT RESEARCH

In fact, some observers suggest that the kinds of intellectual experiences children have in elementary schools fundamentally shapes their cognitive growth into adulthood (Anyon, 1981; Delpit, 1988). Attending to cognitive outcomes, then—what learners know and can do—is a key component of any assessment plan.

That said, affective and social outcomes are important and should be assessed, if not graded. **Affective outcomes** refer to the attitudes, values, and dispositions learners bring with them. Of particular interest are those values and dispositions learners have toward the work they do during social studies. For example:

- Do they enjoy challenges and persist in the face of difficulties?
- Do they have an appetite for learning and a distaste for busy work?
- Do they know how to listen to someone who knows something they do not know?
- Do they understand which questions to ask to clarify an idea's meaning or value?
- Are they open and respectful enough to imagine that a new and strange idea is worth attending to?
- Are they inclined to question pat statements that hide assumptions or confusions (Wiggins, 1989, p. 48)?

Social outcomes are those behaviors that concern how learners work, both individually and in groups. For example, when working on an individual assignment, can learners stay on task and avoid unnecessarily disrupting their neighbors? When working with others, do learners fulfill their responsibilities and take an active interest in ensuring a quality product?

Few people would argue against the significance of learners' affective and social development or the importance of understanding them. Instead the concern has been how to assess these behaviors. As noted assessment expert, Grant Wiggins, argues, "*If* you value the outcome that students collaborate effectively on complex tasks, *then* you ought to assess it" (Nickell, 1992, p. 91).

CLASSROOM MANAGEMENT

Let us consider one more point here: Assessment is not the same thing as *grading*. Assessment is about understanding what a learner knows and can do. *Grading,* like any evaluation, is about judging that learner's performance (and often about managing student behavior)—his performance on a test might be judged as 88 percent; her performance on a small-group project might be judged an "A." The more you come to know about assessing learning, the more likely you will squirm at having to render a final judgment. If you are like us, you'll always wonder if the grades you give truly represent the learning that has occurred. Compelling arguments exist for doing away with grades, and some schools have eliminated them. Equally compelling, however, is the tradition of giving grades, and most likely you will teach in a school where virtually everyone expects you to comply. We wish we had some good advice on how to deal with this, but we don't. We do know some social studies teachers who take the time to write short narratives about each child. These narratives go some distance in explaining the letter grade. We think this is a good practice, but can take a lot of time.

These three ideas—thinking about assessment as a regular part of instruction, using multiple sources of data, and the need to look at a broad range of learner outcomes—are central to new thinking about assessment. Older notions that focused on end-of-unit evaluations have given way as educators make assessment a bigger and more natural part of teaching and learning and as they assess (and therefore emphasize) a broader sweep of outcomes.

Matching Assessments with Purposes

Bearing in mind these issues of assessment and evaluation, we can now discuss specific assessment measures. As with teaching methods, you will be able to choose from a range of assessments. And, just as it makes sense to choose teaching strategies wisely, so too does it make sense to consider carefully which form of assessment you use to meet your pedagogical needs.

Assessment is a hot topic these days. As teachers rethink traditional methods of teaching, they are also rethinking how they understand learners' work. With the increased attention to assessment, however, has come a somewhat confusing array of ideas and terminology. Depending on the source, you can read about "alternative," "authentic," "constructivist," "performance," and "realistic" assessments. We won't try to sort through all this here. Instead, we propose some assessment basics—definitions, examples, and the like—to prompt your on-going thinking.

This photograph illustrates the power of authentic assessment. This fourth-grader, working from his detailed drawing of barter systems, holds his peers' attention as he presents his ideas.

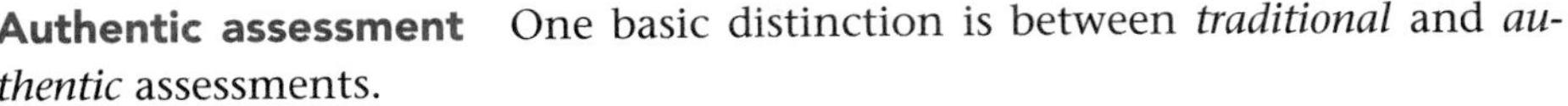

Authentic assessment One basic distinction is between *traditional* and *authentic* assessments.

RELEVANT RESEARCH

According to Wiggins, **traditional assessments** such as multiple-choice tests "are not authentic representations of subject matter challenges. They are more like checkup tests and quizzes and drills." Wiggins is not saying that students need not know content or that all testing is bad. Instead, he is saying that most traditional measures tell us only "whether kids mastered some facts." This is not the same as helping us understand whether learners can perform "the authentic act of mastering historical analysis and information" (Nickell, 1992, p. 92).

Authentic assessments are those that push learners to demonstrate their understanding in real and genuine ways. As Wiggins notes, an authentic as-

Figure 5.3 • Authentic Assessment

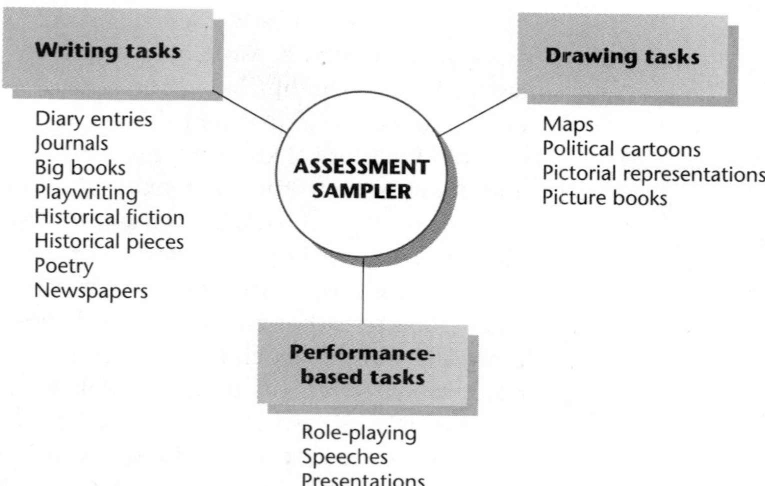

sessment "would be much more a simulation or representation or replication of the kinds of challenges that face professionals or citizens when they need to do something with their knowledge" (Nickell, 1992, p. 92).

What do authentic assessments look like? A rainbow of options are available depending on your pedagogical purpose. For the colonial America unit, Don Kite's learners might write diary entries for various colonial residents, construct maps of important features of colonial towns, or draw pictures of meetings between natives and colonists. Small groups of learners might create a colonial newspaper, assemble a big book[5] on colonial life, or write and perform a play dramatizing an interesting colonial experience. Writing tasks can include keeping a daily journal, writing poetry and other creative works (including historical fiction), and writing small pieces of "real" history. Drawing tasks can include making picture books and creating political cartoons. **Performance-based** tasks can include role-playing, making presentations, and giving speeches. Figure 5.3 illustrates the many ways one might approach assessment.

You have considerable discretion in choosing classroom assessments. As you do, however, keep two considerations in mind. One is variety. Think about ways to give learners a range of opportunities to demonstrate what they know and can do. You need not include every form of assessment in every unit, but keep track of the assignments you make and rework them over time—a varied diet is always more appetizing. The second consideration is thoughtfulness. Think about what your learners might actually be able to do that demonstrates a thoughtful understanding of the material at hand. Not every learner will be able to meet your highest standard, but if you have thought about what constitutes a substantive effort, you will better understand your learners' products.

Test-based assessments School tests get knocked pretty hard in the current assessment literature. Most observers agree with Wiggins that "school-given tests, whether bought from vendors or designed by teachers, are typically *inauthentic,* designed as they are to shake out a grade rather than allowing student to exhibit mastery of knowledge in a manner that suits their styles and interests and does justice to the complexity of knowledge" (Wiggins, 1989, p. 58). Although we think this makes sense, we recognize that traditional testing has a place in every teacher's classroom.

Test-based assessments are important for two reasons. First, we can construct good tests that measure more than low-level knowledge. Test questions, especially those that call for students to do more than circle the right answer, can be an effective way to get at what students know and can do. The caution is not to rely on tests as the sole measure of learning. The second reason tests are important is that standardized testing, state and local, is a fact of classroom life. Such tests are heavily criticized, and for good reason. Nevertheless, because they are unlikely to go away, smart teachers must help their learners deal with them. Those teachers study the tests their classes take to understand

- how the questions are formatted (for example, multiple-choice, essay);
- what kinds of content they cover (for example, content that is part of the school curriculum or general knowledge);
- what levels of knowledge are tested (for example, knowledge and comprehension versus analysis and synthesis).

Smart teachers also provide learners with opportunities to practice answering those kinds of questions. The caution here is not to go overboard. Turning your classroom into one continuous practice test not only will bore the class, it won't guarantee better test scores (Wiggins, 1993). Learners need practice with different test question formats. More important, however, are opportunities to engage interesting and challenging ideas. Go ahead and give your classes some practice questions, but focus on developing powerful units and assessments.

Informal assessment In addition to authentic and test-based assessments, one other way to understand what learners know and can do is through *informal assessment.* The difference between the former and the latter is that authentic and test-based assessments can also be used to evaluate learners' performance. **Informal assessment,** however, is strictly informative, to understand what sense learners are making of the material to date and to make adjustments in your instruction as necessary.

Learners cannot always articulate what they do not understand. Some times they think they understand something only to discover later that their understanding was thin or flawed. Good teachers help avoid such confusions by using a variety of informal assessments throughout their instruction. The simplest is observation, and most good teachers are good observers. They "read" the faces and actions of their learners and make educated guesses about whether to slow down, provide another example, or reiterate an idea. But expect to be fooled occasionally: Sometimes learners understand when it appears they don't. Other times they don't understand when it appears they do. Observation isn't foolproof, but the more you observe, the better you will be at gauging learners' understanding.

CLASSROOM MANAGEMENT

Another informal assessment method is asking questions. Good teachers ask a lot of questions, and they ask them in a variety of situations—individual, small group, and whole class. Sometimes teachers ask questions to spot-check understanding (and to see who is paying attention). In those cases, the questions tend to be fact-based, and the emphasis is on right answers. You know the type: "Why did English colonists come to America?" "What hardships did they face?" "Where did they settle?" Another purpose for asking questions (and a more important one, we would argue) is to understand children's thinking. Fact-based questions tell a teacher little more than if a learner knows a specific piece of information. To better understand learners' thinking, teachers must ask open-ended questions that push below the surface. Questions like "How do you know that?" "What makes you think that?" and "Are there other ways to think about that?" push learners' thinking and provide valuable insights into how they come to know what they do. Even a question as simple as "Can you give me another example?" can yield helpful information about how kids think. Figure 5.4 below illustrates the components of informal assessment.

Portfolios

Although not a form of assessment per se, using portfolios as part of a comprehensive assessment strategy has gained much attention of late. In simplest terms, a **portfolio** is a collection of student work used to demonstrate learning over time.

Figure 5.4 • Informal Assessment

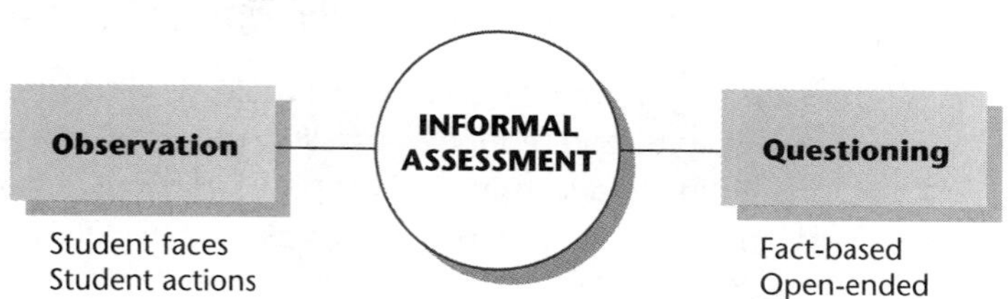

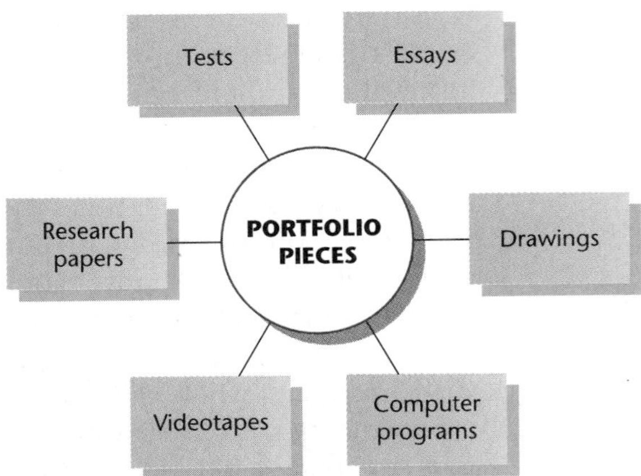

Figure 5.5 • Portfolio-Based Assessment

Any number of student pieces can make up a portfolio (see Figure 5.5). Whether teacher or learner-selected, these works generally represent the range of assessments assigned throughout the school year. Some items may be individual assignments such as test-based assessments, essays, and drawings. Other items—copies of projects, research papers, videotapes, even computer programs—may reflect work done in group settings.

Portfolios serve a variety of purposes. Learners may see portfolios as a means of charting their own progress and a source of pride and motivation. For teachers, portfolios can clarify a learner's strengths and weaknesses, information that can be passed along to the next teacher. And for parents, portfolios can make clearer the work the class does in general and the work their child does in particular. On first encounter, some parents may seem impatient with portfolios, preferring to look at test scores and grades. Our experience tells us, however, that a teacher's patient explanation pays off. If helped, most parents come to see the value of collecting a range of their child's work and take an active interest in seeing growth over time.

TEACHER REFLECTION

Developing a Professional Portfolio

Think about developing a professional portfolio as a way of capturing your best work and representing yourself to others. Consider including a statement of your teaching and learning philosophy, sample unit plans, examples of classroom assessments, and copies of evaluations of your teaching.

SECTION SUMMARY Assessment

- *Assessment,* which is about understanding what learners know and can do, differs from *evaluation,* which is about evaluating and ranking students.
- Assessment is best considered as an on-going part of instruction.
- Assessment plans should include multiple sources of data.
- Well-rounded assessments aim at cognitive, social, and affective measures.
- Assessments can take many forms—authentic, test-based, informal, or portfolios—but should always be matched to instructional purposes.

Influences on Teachers' Content and Instructional Decisions

As noted earlier, Colonial Life is a topic traditionally covered in fifth-grade social studies. We have seen, however, that Don Kite's unit owes little to traditional approaches. He crafts his unit around a big idea that picks up geographic, economic, and social threads. He employs a variety of instructional strategies instead of a single method. He uses the textbook to support the instructional plan he develops, but it does not define either the content or his instruction. He assigns group and individual projects, but not only to evaluate students' products. Kite bases his decisions on a mix of personal, organizational, and policy factors.[6]

Personal Influences

Observers often try to explain the influences on teachers' content and pedagogical decisions in terms of **structural factors.** Those structural factors often include state and district curriculum guides, the organization of the school day, the availability of resources, and the norms and expectations of teachers. Although structural factors tend to get more attention (especially from policymakers), the importance of **personal influences** such as teachers' knowledge, beliefs, and experiences is widely acknowledged in the general literature on teaching (Eisenhart, Shrum, Harding, & Cuthbert, 1988). In this section, we explore the influence of personal factors on teachers' classroom actions.

RELEVANT RESEARCH

Personal factors represent the lived character of individual teachers. We can talk about these factors generally as

- personal knowledge and beliefs
- personal and professional experiences
- personal history or narratives

No two people live the same lives nor are they influenced by their experiences in the same ways. Much like their pupils, what teachers know and do is shaped generally by their unique pasts, and these in turn influence teachers' content and pedagogical decisions.

Don Kite is no different. We see the influence of personal factors on Kite's instruction in two ways. One is that Kite's decisions reflect his *knowledge of history as a school subject*. Kite believes fifth-graders are more familiar with social considerations (for example, family, entertainment, schooling) than with any of the other thread categories. To that end, he puts primary emphasis on social constructs and gives less attention to geographic and economic ideas. Because this is his students' first formal encounter with U.S. history, he focuses on colonial life instead of the structure of colonial government or the nature of colonial economic outputs.

A second personal factor reflects Kite's *belief in interdisciplinary instruction*. One reason he likes social studies is that it provides a site to "work it together with some of our other subject matter." Kite often combines his language arts and social studies instruction. This unit is no different. For example, during the time allotted for language arts instruction, Kite's students read the nonfiction trade book *Colonial Life* (Kalman, 1992) and write sample diary entries that reflect various colonial perspectives—blacksmith, farmer, teacher, child. Kite has a basal reading series that most of his peers use and he uses, too, but sparingly. Instead, he teaches the same skills the basal covers, but with trade books that support his social studies curriculum.

Choosing to emphasize social history over political and economic, and linking language arts and social studies, are two examples of personal beliefs influencing Kite's instructional decisions. Personal factors encompass diverse experiences, formal and informal, in and out of school, and current and past. Some of the more influential include a teacher's experiences as a learner, interactions with family members, personal and professional beliefs, and the sense of social studies as a school subject.

You may be surprised to find that teachers make important classroom decisions based on personal beliefs rather than curriculum guides, textbooks, and the like. As a prospective teacher, you can expect some guidance from these sources, but you will balance that with your own important knowledge, beliefs, and experiences.

Organizational Influences

We are beginning to build a more dimensional picture of teachers' content and instructional decision making. Teachers do not work in a vacuum. Instead, they work in a complex system of roles and relationships, norms and expectations, resources and constraints, all mixed in with the personal factors of their lives. A second category of influences on teachers' instructional decisions can be described as *organizational,* as in the way schools and classrooms are organized for teaching and learning. **Organizational influences** include

- roles and relationships
- norms and expectations
- resources

The colonial America unit Don Kite constructed is influenced by several organizational factors. One set of factors involves *roles and relationships.* Though it might seem odd, the role of "student" is an important organizational influence on teachers. As students, the children who sit in Kite's classroom help shape his instructional plans.

Don Kite knows several things about his students. First, he knows that students find their social studies textbook dull and plodding. Second, Kite knows that, while his students can become engrossed in some activities, their attention span is often short and unpredictable. Finally, Kite knows that different students know different things and that what they know is more or less historically accurate.

Each of these ideas, in turn, helped shape the unit Kite constructed. To take advantage of students' changing attentions, he used a variety of instructional approaches. To obviate the monotony of the textbook, he offered a range of instructional materials. To address the differences in students' knowledge, he organized students into groups so that they could benefit from one another's abilities.

These are good strategies in and of themselves. The point here, however, is that Kite takes these actions *because* of the particular learners he has in front of him. Many factors compete for his attention, but a key factor is the nature of the children he teaches.

A second organizational influence on Don Kite's colonial unit involves *norms and expectations* in his school. We might focus on several examples here, but let's focus on Kite's use of the social studies textbook. Many of Kite's colleagues use their textbooks to teach most of their lessons. Kite chooses not to, and an important part of his decision comes from the organizational norm that supports his instructional autonomy. It is not the case everywhere, but in most schools, teachers have considerable say over how they plan and teach lessons and units. And so although Kite's peers use their textbooks, he would be shocked if anyone criticized his decision not to.

Kite's colonial America unit is also influenced by a third organizational factor: *resources.* This influence is straightforward; Kite could not put the textbook aside if he lacked other resources to take its place. This is a critical point. Many teachers would like to move away from their textbooks, but, for them, alternative resources are either unknown or unavailable. Kite has no surfeit of available books and videos; like most urban schools, money is tight. Still, he knows well what is available and, with the help of a resourceful school librarian, he shapes his instruction around what he has.

In each of these examples, we see how Don Kite's instructional decisions are shaped by organizational factors. Other teachers work with organizational influences unique to their situations. Their decisions are in part influenced by colleagues, school administrators, central office administrators, and parents. They balance choices with reference to school-based norms and expectations such as the amount of homework assigned, how student grades are calculated, and how much classroom "noise" is tolerated. Few, if any teachers can completely escape the need to consider resource limits such as computer and software availability, equipment for projects, and, in some severely underfunded schools, even a supply of lined paper. Needless to say, lack of resources—especially those basic to instruction—can severely constrain teachers' instructional decisions. Most teachers, like Don Kite, are resourceful: They make good things happen whether or not the latest technology is at hand.

Policy Influences

Policies—national, state, and local—are a third source of influence on teachers' instructional decisions. Schools and school districts are like any large, complex, bureaucratic organization in that certain tacit norms and expectations become formalized and codified as policies. **Policies** include

- curriculum frameworks
- tests
- policy statements

Policies can take many forms. **Curriculum frameworks** or guides might come from a national organization such as the National Council for the Social Studies, a state education department such as the *History-Social Science Framework for California Public Schools* (California Board of Education, 1988), the central office of a school district, or even a group of grade-level teachers in a single school building. *Tests* are also a common policy item as many teachers must administer standardized state and district-level tests. Issues like the inclusion of special education students into mainstream classrooms may also be covered by state and local *policy statements*.

Just as personal and organizational factors influence Don Kite's decisions, so too do policy factors. Kite teaches the unit on colonial life as he does partly because of a district assessment policy: Kite, like his fifth-grade teaching peers, is required to administer a district-developed social studies test. The test includes one question that asks students to compare colonial and present-day life. The question begins, "Life is different today from the way it was in colonial America. Some things that have changed are houses, schools, occupations, entertainment, family, travel." The question is then divided into two parts. Part A states: "From your list, choose three of the above six, list your choices, and for each of those choices, describe it as it existed in colonial America and describe it as it exists in America today." Part B states: "Using your notes from Part A, write an essay of about one hundred words describing the changes in America from its colonial days until today."[7]

Kite's unit shows impressive planning and instruction. The unit sprang from a decent big idea with some intellectual meat to it. Instructional activities and materials seemed engaging and appropriately diverse. The assessments gave learners multiple opportunities to show what they had learned. One criticism might be that Kite focused exclusively on European settlement. The unit ignored native cultures and their views on housing, family, schooling, and the like. Including native perspectives would have enriched the unit by providing a third point of comparison.

Upon reflection, designing the unit in part based on the district assessment question made sense. Kite really could not ignore the district assessment; one way or another he was going to have to administer it. Clearly, he brought intelligence and insight to a constrained situation. Policies like this district assessment test do matter, but as Kite's response suggests, they matter in no particular way. Don Kite "taught" to this test. He did so, however, in a way that remained faithful to the instructional goals he holds dear. In that sense, Don Kite's colonial America unit demonstrates the power of teachers to seize the instructional value from even the most pedantic source. Like good teachers everywhere, Kite turned a sow's ear into a silk purse.

Cross-Current Influences

One way to test the notion that Kite's pedagogical decisions relied not only on the district test requirements, but on personal and organization factors as well is to imagine how some of Kite's colleagues might have approached the same task. A teacher who believes that children simply need to know the "facts" might have developed lessons and units that focused on imparting basic information through textbook readings, worksheets, and end-of-the-chapter questions. A teacher whose chief concern is getting through the information as quickly as possible, might have rejected the notion of constructing a unit in

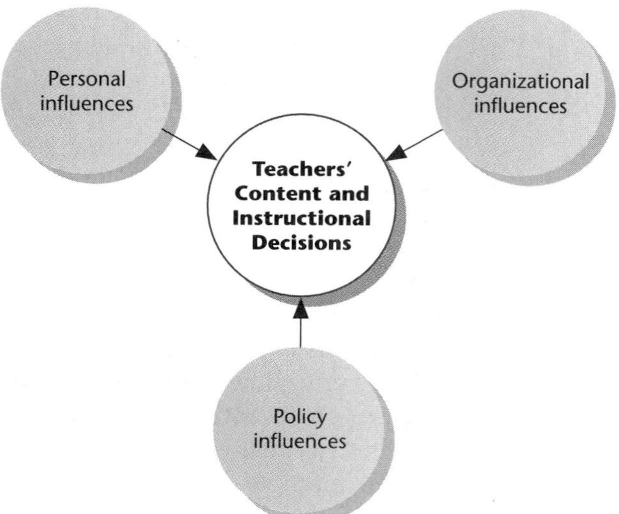

Figure 5.6 • Cross-Current Influences

favor of delivering a series of short lectures. A third teacher might not have even addressed the test question explicitly. This teacher might have dealt with the issues relevant to the test question—housing, occupations, family, and the like—as part of a larger and perhaps quite different instructional unit.

If asked, each of these teachers would likely cite the district exam as influential, but each could also cite other factors, personal and organizational, that influenced their decisions, as illustrated in Figure 5.6. As an example of a policy influence, then, testing pushes in no particular instructional direction and ultimately may hold no more authority over teachers' practices than personal or organizational considerations. Instead, each teacher's content and instructional decisions probably reflect a mixture of personal, organizational, and policy influences.

Let's discuss a few other important points pertaining to the interaction of personal, organizational, and policy influences. One is that influences are potential rather than real. A survey of the influences on teachers' classroom decisions would produce a staggering list. But "influence" is a socially constructed phenomena; what one teacher counts as influential another might downplay, dismiss, or ignore. Moreover, what counts as an influence may change over time and circumstance. That is, what a teacher counts as influential at one point and in one context, may be supplanted by other influences as time and situations change.

If these two points ring true, we begin to see both the promise and problem of teaching: The promise of considerable opportunity to construct engaging and powerful learning situations balanced by the problem that teachers are likely to feel pushed in multiple directions.

So what does one do? First, recognize that, although you will discover many potential outside influences on your practice, how *real* these influences become (that is, how much influence they have over your practice) depends on how you perceive them. Second, understand that the bottom line is that ultimately you must make classroom decisions, and those decisions will reflect as much your own personal preferences as any outside influences. Third, realize that having all this autonomy may feel like a heavy responsibility. The good news, however, is that you really can transform the classroom lives of your learners. It will take a lot of work. Don Kite, like all good teachers we know, puts in long days. Fortunately, the payoff—learners engaged in powerful learning because of your pedagogical decisions—is well worth it.

CHAPTER SUMMARY

1. ***What teaching strategies support individual, small-group, and whole-group instruction?***

   A wide range of teaching strategies can be drawn on to support either individual, small-group, or whole-group instruction. Strategies for individual instruction include reading and writing assignments and learning centers. T-charts and jigsaw activities work well in small-group settings. Whole-group strategies include pre-testing, lecturing, role-playing, and simulations.

2. ***What array of curriculum materials are available for classroom use?***

   Curriculum materials are limited only by a teacher's imagination. For simplicity's sake, the most common can be grouped into textual materials (nonfiction and fiction), maps and globes, and computers and other technologies.

3. ***How is assessment different from evaluation and what forms of assessment are possible?***

   Teachers use assessments to understand what learners know and can do. They use evaluations as a means of judging and ranking students' work. Teachers may use authentic, test-based, informal, and portfolio assessments.

4. ***What factors influence teachers' content and instructional decisions?***

   Although they can be separated for analytic purposes, personal, organizational, and policy factors interact as they influence teachers' classroom decisions.

TEACHING RESOURCES

Print Resources

Alvermann, D., & Phelps, S. (1994). *Content reading and literacy: Succeeding in today's diverse classrooms.* Boston: Allyn & Bacon.

Conley, M. (1995). *Content reading instruction: A communication approach* (2nd ed.). New York: McGraw-Hill.

Two good resources on the range of issues that surround teaching reading in the content areas in general, and in social studies in particular.

Cohen, E. (1994). *Designing groupwork* (2nd ed.). New York: Teachers College Press.

Johnson, D., Johnson, R., & Holubec, E. (1993). *Circles of learning: Cooperation in the classroom* (4th ed.). Edina, MN: Interaction Books.

Two excellent resources outlining the advantages of small-group instruction.

Finn, P. (1993). *Helping children learn language arts.* New York: Longman.

This is a useful guide to the issues and approaches around teaching language arts within the social studies.

Jorgensen, K. (1993). *History Workshop.* Portsmouth, NH: Heineman.

Levstik, L., & Barton, K. (1997). *Doing history: Investigating with children in elementary and middle schools.* Mahway, NJ: Lawrence Erlbaum Associates.

Each of these texts offers helpful advice about how to encourage and support students writing about history.

Irvin, J., Lunstrum, J., Lynch-Brown, C., & Shepard, M. (1995). *Enhancing social studies through literacy strategies.* Washington, DC: National Council for the Social Studies.

Tunnell, M., & Ammon, R. (Eds.). (1993). *The story of ourselves: Teaching history through children's literature.* Portsmouth, NH: Heinemann.

Two useful books on teaching social studies through children's literature.

Sanders, N. (1966). *Classroom questions: What kinds?* New York: Harper & Row.
An older but still valuable discussion of and guide to asking good classroom questions.

NOTES

1. Recall that the KWL teaching strategy (Ogle, 1986) calls for students to (1) list what they *K*now about a topic, (2) list *W*hat they would like to learn, and (3) after the instructional unit is complete, describe what they have *L*earned.
2. Sources of these readings include: *A Colonial Town, Williamsburg* (Kalman, 1992), a story told from the viewpoint of a black male teenage slave; *From Forge to Fast Food* (Greene, 1995), a history of child labor in New York State for the view of an indentured servant; *Sign of the Beaver* (Speare, 1983), the story of a native boy; and *Colonial Life in America* (Farquhar, 1962), a story about a white woman's life.
3. This software program is produced by MECC, 6160 Summit Drive North, Minneapolis, Minnesota 55430-2100.
4. We will have more to say on this later, but notice that two threads—political and global—are not mentioned at all.
5. A "big book" is a large-format book written and illustrated for beginning readers.
6. For a full discussion of this idea, see Grant (1996).
7. This essay is one component of the district assessment. The two other parts are a multiple-choice examination of social studies concepts and a project that each teacher designs individually. Kite's students did individual projects on the states of the United States.

Chapter 6

The Classroom Environment:
Creating a Genuine Community

We've covered a lot of territory thus far—notions of learners and learning, subject matter, and now two chapters on teachers and teaching. What else is there to talk about? Well, hold onto your seats, for in one sense we're only halfway there. Although creating big-idea teaching units sensitive to your learners and your subject matter *will* make a difference in your learners' lives, encouraging the growth of democratic values and attitudes demands more (Angell, 1991; Ehman & Hahn, 1981). It goes by many names—classroom climate, atmosphere, milieu—the point is, that the classroom

RELEVANT RESEARCH

environment itself can have a dramatic effect on how learners experience your class, on what they learn, and on the values and attitudes they develop.

In other words, if you want smart, thoughtful kids who also believe in justice, equality, opportunity, and the like, you need to think hard about the full range of experiences they'll have in your classroom and school.

Classroom environment, the fourth commonplace, is a general term that describes the range of activity that occurs in a classroom. Part of that activity is instructional—issues of teaching, learning, and subject matter. Also important is the environment in which instruction takes place. That's a lot of territory, so, for simplicity's sake, we'll talk about three elements of environment: discourse, classroom organization, and dispositions.

Discourse refers to the nature of the talk that goes on in a classroom. For example, what patterns of interaction arise between teacher and learners? What kinds of questions are asked, who asks them, and what do the answers look like? Who decides what the classroom conversations will be?

Classroom organization refers to the ways in which we structure learning activities. For example, how are learners organized for teaching and learning, and who decides? What classroom rules are evident, and who chooses them?

Dispositions refer to those values and attitudes a teacher and her learners create and practice during classroom activity. For example, does the classroom climate reveal an honest respect for and commitment to inquiry? Open respect for and commitment to ideas and people? Patient respect for and commitment to argument and evidence?

Attending to these elements is no easier than attending to the pedagogical plan, and it's every bit as important. Your learners will remember some part of the content you teach; they will remember much more about how your class *felt*—whether or not they genuinely felt welcome, involved, respected.

CHOOSING GOALS

We want students to develop as thinkers and knowers; we also want them to develop as concerned and caring human beings. And we can help them on both scores if we work to create genuine spaces where growth can happen.

In this chapter, we unpack the notion of classroom environment and construct an image of these genuine places through extended discussions of discourse, classroom organization, and dispositions. When you have completed this chapter, you should be able to answer the following questions:

1. ***What are the discourse, classroom organization, and dispositional patterns found in traditional classroom environments?***

2. ***What are the discourse, classroom organization, and dispositional patterns found in* genuine *classroom communities?***
3. ***What stakeholders are involved in the negotiation of a genuine classroom community?***

The Complex Nature of Social Studies Classrooms

Let's be honest: Few classrooms reflect the kind of genuine classroom environment we envision. Too many are places where teachers try hard and kids try hard (sometimes), but where the classroom environment is a jumble of conflicting messages.

Consider this example from Carol Sheldon's fourth-grade class. Sheldon, an African-American teacher in a suburban school, is teaching a unit on the geography of the United States[1]:

CLASSROOM EXAMPLE

> The class has been working on a textbook lesson on different uses of land and water resources. Before the students close their books, Sheldon directs their attention to the picture on the last page of the chapter. The picture depicts a harbor scene at dusk. Fishing and tourist boats are tied up to a dock; a large mountain looms in the background. No people appear in the picture.
>
> While students look at the picture with various degrees of interest, Sheldon explains that they are to write a story or poem based on what they see. The assignment clearly excites a few learners; they immediately begin taking out pencil and paper and talking quietly, but enthusiastically, with their neighbors. Most, however, appear uninspired. They roll their eyes, shake their heads, groan. These protests escalate when Sheldon, perhaps feeling the need to raise the stakes, announces, "Maybe we'll have show and tell at the end. Maybe I'll have you go to the front of the room and read your story." She pauses, "That's what I'll do."
>
> A chorus of complaints fill the room. Even some of the children who initially favored the assignment protest. When one student calls for a vote, several classmates come to his side. Calling for order, Sheldon declares, "No, there is no choice this time. There won't be any votes. We already voted once today (on a question involving playground equipment). We'll vote on something later today." As the class quiets, she explains, "You vote on the things you like, not on the things you don't." She pauses, "Besides, I know I'll get out-voted."

COMMONPLACE CONNECTIONS

- What does Sheldon seem to think is important about the *subject matter* of geography?

- What view of *learners* does she seem to hold?
- How would you characterize her *teaching?*
- How would you describe the *classroom environment?*

In terms of classroom environment, this is a complex case. Sheldon promotes creativity and freedom of expression when she gives students an open-ended writing assignment. She indicates that she values cooperation as well as individuality when she allows students to work with one another. Other messages are more complex, however.

CLASSROOM MANAGEMENT

The most obvious is the mix of messages Sheldon sends around voting. In the playground equipment vote, she sends one message about learners' roles in decision-making and majority rule. She sends quite another message in the issue of voting on the classroom assignment.

In the case of the playground equipment, Sheldon implies that because class members have a stake in the outcome, their voices and votes should be heard and counted. Taking a vote is not the only way of resolving such issues. The class might have devised a compromise that better satisfied all learners' desires. *How* the issue was resolved, however, seems less important than that the students themselves decided. That's a strong message about the environment of this classroom—the kind of talk, classroom rules, and values that are respected and encouraged.

TEACHER REFLECTION

Allowing Students to Make Choices

When students have the opportunity to make choices as a class, teachers often allow them to vote on a majority-wins basis. What are the benefits of this practice? What are the drawbacks? How else might children make decisions?

CLASSROOM MANAGEMENT

Sheldon's message becomes muddied later in the day during the story-writing activity. This time the disagreement is over a classroom assignment rather than a playground activity, and the disagreement is between learners and their teacher rather than among classmates. Given the earlier episode, the call for a vote is hardly surprising. Sheldon's abrupt response, however, is. In dismissing the call to vote, she not only entertains no alternatives to the assignment, she even seems to suggest that the only votes she is willing to endorse are those that have no real classroom consequence. Individual voice, free discussion, majority rule—all these fall by the wayside as Sheldon asserts the traditional teacher prerogative of just saying no.

Here's the tricky part: Sheldon had good reasons for her actions in both instances. Although dismissing the call to vote seems harsh, not every instructional decision can be decided by a vote. We don't fault Sheldon for asserting her authority.

CLASSROOM MANAGEMENT

We do question, however, the way she handled it, especially given the earlier vote. Two actions she might have taken would have moved the class along (presumably, her main intention) and preserved some of the good from the first incident. She might have explained that the class had to move on. Children understand that discussion and decisions can take a lot of time, and few would have begrudged their teacher's concern about time *if* she had explained it. She might also have put the voting idea aside in favor of exploring some alternative assignments. It's not clear why the learners were unenthusiastic about the original assignment, but Sheldon could have defused the situation by taking a few minutes to discuss alternatives and either have the class choose one, or allow each student to choose for him or herself.

Classroom life is often crazy: Teaching is not called the "impossible profession" (Cohen, 1989) for nothing. Our purpose here is neither to make Carol Sheldon look silly nor to suggest that a teacher can always do the right thing if she thinks about it. Teaching is just not that simple.

Traditional Classroom Environments

The case of Carol Sheldon helps illustrate some of the perplexing issues that arise when one considers the classroom environment. Let's look deeper into those issues by exploring the kinds of discourse, classroom organization, and dispositions that exist in traditional American classrooms.

RELEVANT RESEARCH

Discourse in the Traditional Classroom

In many classrooms, teachers talk and kids listen (or not). No big surprise there. Studies of who talks and how much yield consistent results: Teachers talk—by some estimates more than 80 percent of the time (Goodlad, 1984; Wilen & White, 1991). When learners talk, they usually speak to a teacher, usually in response to a teacher's question, and usually briefly—a word or phrase at most.

CLASSROOM MANAGEMENT

Aside from procedural discourse (that is, taking roll, giving directions), the prevailing pattern of "school talk" is **recitation,** which looks like this:

teacher **I**nitiation—student **R**esponse—teacher **E**valuation **(IRE).**

In short, the teacher asks a question, a student answers, and the teacher judges whether the answer is right or wrong. We already have seen several examples of this kind of interaction. Recall this exchange from the first lesson on U.S. government in Sandra Prosy's fifth-grade classroom from Chapter 4:

CLASSROOM EXAMPLE

Prosy: What kind of government do you think we will talk about?
Angela: Public schools?
Rashona: City?
Prosy: Who runs the city?
Michael: The mayor?

Prosy writes *city* on the board and asks, "Who is the mayor?" A girl calls out, "Luciano." Prosy nods and writes *Luciano* on the board. "What other kinds of government are there? What other areas need to be run?" she asks.

Deion: Community.
Tina: State.
Prosy: Yes, what state?
Michelle: New York.
Prosy: Who runs our state?
Tom: The governor.

Prosy nods and writes *state, governor,* and *Pataki* (the current New York governor) on the board. As she does, a boy calls out, "What about county?" Prosy says, "Well, yes, but I'm looking for something that starts with an *F*." A girl guesses, "Federal?" Prosy responds, "Right. And who runs the federal government?" A boy offers, "Rush Limbaugh!" while the rest of the class shouts out, "Bill Clinton!"

RELEVANT RESEARCH

In Chapter 4, we looked at this vignette in terms of the ideas represented. Here, we return to it as a means of exploring traditional classroom discourse. It is a classic case of the IRE (initiation-response-evaluation) pattern so long a part of U.S. schools (Wilen & White, 1991). Prosy asks the questions: What kind of government do you think we will talk about? Who runs the city? Who is the mayor? Learners answer them: public schools/city; mayor; Luciano. And Prosy evaluates the responses; she nods, says "right," records the answer on the board, or goes on to the next question. So dominant is this form of talk that even primary-grade children can mimic it with ease (Edwards & Westgage, 1987).

But *who talks and how much* is just one component of classroom discourse. A second component emphasizes *classroom questions:* the kinds of questions asked, who asks them, and what the responses look like.

RELEVANT RESEARCH

Again, we see no surprises here. Most of the questions asked (upwards of 80 percent in some studies) look like those above—knowledge or fact-level questions to which learners spit back a remembered piece of information (Gall, 1984;

Goodlad, 1984). Make no mistake: Memory and facts are useful. Humans could not think if they had no memories, and facts bundled together, represent the stuff of thinking—ideas. Still, if we only ask low-level questions, we're likely to get only low-level thinking.

CLASSROOM MANAGEMENT

Teachers ask the vast majority of questions. In such classrooms, students learn quickly that factual knowledge counts, and so when they do ask questions, their questions tend to look like their teachers'. Questions that probe deeper sometimes become the basis for interesting conversations. More often than not, however, they are perceived as either "off the subject" or, as in the case above of the boy's question about county government, they are not what the teacher was looking for.

One last element of classroom discourse concerns the nature of *classroom conversations*. Most classrooms are teacher-centered, which means the teacher, like Sandra Prosy above, controls the substance, form, and duration of classroom talk. In other words, the teacher determines what the class talks about, how they talk about it, and how long they talk about it. Learners participate, but their participation is passive—listening, for the most part, and talking only when spoken to.

TEACHER REFLECTION

Classroom Discourse

Think about the kinds of discourse you have experienced. How did you feel in classrooms where the discourse was strongly teacher-centered? How did you feel in classrooms where students were more actively involved in the discourse?

CLASSROOM MANAGEMENT

Pretty bleak, eh? Such traditional classrooms remind us of old factory scenes where workers do their jobs in drone-like fashion overseen by supervisors whose primary concern is getting the work done efficiently. Few classrooms are quite this bad, but the notion of school as a factory, a place where teachers and learners march through their work, has a long tenure. In fact, Marshall (1990) argues that the "workplace metaphor" is so strongly held that "we hardly notice this root metaphor when teachers talk about 'homework' or 'seatwork' or tell students to 'get back to work' or grade them on 'work habits' " (p. 94). As workers, then, it is the learner's job to accumulate as much knowledge as possible in the shortest period of time. Teachers are the supervisors who push learners to work harder and test them to see if they had succeeded. And the work itself? In reading, it is breaking words into syllables and building oral fluency; in mathematics, it is practicing algorithms; and in social studies, it is gathering facts. (The factory model of schooling also gives us school buildings that look like industrial plants, bells that divide up the workday and keep teachers and students moving efficiently through the halls, and the like. But more on that later.)

It may not be fair to lay the prevalence of recitation solely at the feet of the factory model. After all, the notion of education as teachers asking questions and students answering them is at least as old as the ancient Greeks. Nor is there anything particularly wrong with recitation per se. But when the factory model of schooling becomes linked with views such as the behaviorist model of learning (Chapter 2), teaching becomes staid and formulaic. When it never pushes beyond mere facts, problems surface.

Organization in the Traditional Classroom

When we think about traditional classrooms, our first image is of teachers talking and students listening. The second is of students sitting in long rows, in individual seats, working quietly on individual assignments. Let us explore another element of classroom environment by looking at

- how classroom activities are organized
- how classroom rules support traditional instruction.

The influence of behavioral theory and the factory model of schooling is not limited to classroom discourse. The assembly line—where workers work silently

This photograph of an early 1900s classroom presents something of a stereotypical traditional environment. What elements of such settings do you remember from your own school experiences?

on individual, repetitive tasks—is an American idea. (Quick—who invented this manufacturing approach? Henry Ford? Yup. See knowing facts *can* come in handy!) Only recently have American industrialists learned what the Japanese have known for some time—that people working together produce more and better products than they do as individuals.

Transferring this model to the classroom, traditional teachers *organized their instruction* such that learners spent a good part of the day working quietly at their desks on individual assignments. Doing so provided a means of determining the quantity and quality of each child's output and a way of managing rambunctious children's behavior. Quiet classrooms where learners studiously did their lessons became the model of good teaching and learning.

CLASSROOM MANAGEMENT

Quiet classrooms are still the norm. Many teachers report getting nervous when they schedule group work for fear that their principal or their peers will perceive their class as too loud, off-task, or out of control. These teachers typically avoid potential problems by arranging the instructional day around individual assignments that learners do quietly at their desks.

CLASSROOM MANAGEMENT

Classroom rules often reinforce the instructional message of quiet, efficient, and individual work. If you walk into most traditional classrooms, you'll inevitably see a list of rules posted. Many look like the one in Figure 6.1.

Such rules are almost always developed by teachers, and they send strong messages about proper classroom behavior. The sentiments behind admonitions about not putting classmates down and encouragement to do one's best work seem sound, but think about the messages some of the other rules imply. Although classroom rules about being prepared and including proper headings urge students to be responsible and ready to work, such exhortations recall factory rules that tied workers to their tools and closely prescribed and governed their behavior. Rules about no talking and no cheating send even more subtle

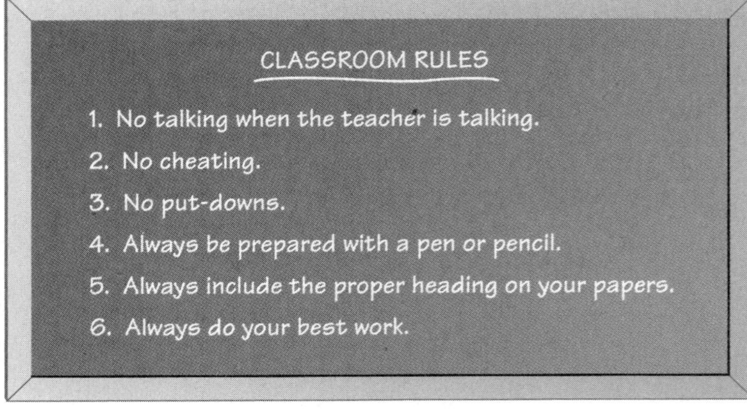

CLASSROOM RULES
1. No talking when the teacher is talking.
2. No cheating.
3. No put-downs.
4. Always be prepared with a pen or pencil.
5. Always include the proper heading on your papers.
6. Always do your best work.

Figure 6.1 • Rules in the Traditional Classroom

messages. Both rules have long histories in U.S. classrooms that blessed quiet, individual work. The messages are clear: Learners can talk only when their teacher allows them to, and talking to one another is discouraged.

Of course, sometimes teachers need to talk and children need to listen, and sometimes teachers must assess each learner's individual work. These are normal parts of classroom life. We believe that's all they should be: *parts* of classroom life, actions that come up and are important as necessary. That's much different from *rules* that imply an expectation of every day and every situation. A few classroom rules are probably helpful (especially if they come from the class), but you must think carefully about the messages your rules send.

Dispositions in the Traditional Classroom

The third element of classroom environment looks at dispositions, those *values and attitudes* a teacher and her learners create and practice throughout the school day.

CLASSROOM MANAGEMENT

The factory model of schooling promotes an array of dispositions. One is the value of hard work, the notion that learners benefit from diligence and persistence in completing their assignments. A second disposition is efficiency, which emphasizes working quickly and quietly and without distraction. A third disposition is deference to authority. The traditional classroom has only one power or authority, the teacher. Learners are expected to do as they are told and to ask questions only about those things that interfere with their individual learning. One last disposition is a focus on external rather than internal rewards. Motivating learners, in this view, is a matter of creating the right incentives—praise, grades, promotion. Internal rewards—joy from learning something new, satisfaction from overcoming a problem—are nice, but only explicit rewards produce consistent effort.

Given the world of possibilities, it is hard to argue with any of these values. In fact, none are problematic in and of themselves. Even the goal they support—the efficient acquisition of knowledge—has its purpose, but we think it's a pretty thin view of teaching and learning. We can, and must, do more.

CHOOSING GOALS

Few classrooms combine the worst of these features. Moreover, some of these ideas, like the disposition to work hard, are well worth cultivating. The challenge is for you as a teacher to think carefully about the messages you send through the discourse, classroom organization, and dispositions you create and support.

We've spent time defining the traditional classroom environment because we can't know where we're going until we understand where we've been. We see elements of these classrooms that are worth keeping, but we also can do better. One way to do better is by working toward the notion of a genuine classroom community.

SECTION SUMMARY Traditional Classroom Environments

- The standard pattern of *discourse* in traditional classrooms is recitation (initiation, response, evaluation), where teachers typically control the nature of the classroom conversation.
- Traditional classroom *organization* favors quiet, individual work.
- The chief *dispositions* found in traditional classrooms include hard work, efficiency, deference to authority, and external rewards.

The Promise of Genuine Classroom Communities

Those who advocate changes in the classroom lives of teachers and learners often focus on curriculum, teaching methods, assessment, and the like. Yet, attention to classroom environment is growing.

RELEVANT RESEARCH

That attention goes by many names—"learning communities" (Johnson, Johnson, & Holubec, 1993), "democratic classrooms" (Dreikurs, Grunwald, & Pepper, 1971; Wood, 1990), and "just communities" (Kubelick, 1982; Lickona, 1977). Our notion of a genuine classroom community shares many characteristics with these models—commitment to inquiry, cooperative learning, democratic values, and respectfulness. Where we differ is that we believe the teaching and learning of social studies is intricately linked to the classroom environment. These other models tend to make the mistake of focusing on the environment and either ignoring the teaching and learning of subject matters or treating teaching and learning as a generic activity. That's a mistake. Remember, the commonplaces—learning, teaching, subject matter, and environment—must work together, each supporting and extending the others. That's the goal in creating a *genuine classroom community*—ambitious teaching that is sensitive to the needs of learners and the subject matter and occurs in classrooms where discourse, classroom organization, and dispositions encourage the development of thoughtful, caring, active human beings.

CHOOSING GOALS

How do you get there? A genuine classroom community is not something one gets to by checking off items on a list, and it's not something one achieves once and then never has to worry about again. We can offer some insights into what a genuine community looks like and how to build one. The hard work of constantly working toward that goal, however, is yours.

CLASSROOM MANAGEMENT

Teachers who try to understand what their learners know and can do, who develop and teach from big ideas, and who use an array of teaching approaches, materials, and assessments will inevitably, we believe, establish classroom climates that are significantly different from the traditional norm. In the following sections we use discourse, classroom organization, and dispositions to illustrate what we mean by a genuine classroom community.

Discourse in Genuine Classrooms

The talk between teachers and learners and among learners sounds different in a genuine classroom. Consider this example from Suzanne Wilson's third-grade class as they explore the purpose, meaning, and construction of maps.[2]

CLASSROOM EXAMPLE

While working on a class book about the school, Wilson plans three weeks of work with maps. Rather than distribute completed maps, however, she prepares learners to construct maps of the classroom by asking them how they might use graph paper to aid their work. Several children note that the linoleum floor is made of square tiles and, after counting them, that the classroom is forty squares wide and fifty squares long. Some conclude that they could mark off the requisite number of squares on their graph paper to mark the boundaries of the room. Wilson next asks what features of the classroom might be included in the maps. The list—student and teacher desks, flagpole, bookcases, rugs, and chalkboards—goes on the board. With that, students begin work on their individual maps while Wilson circulates around the classroom asking questions and probing each learner's understanding of what they are doing.

Figure 6.2 • **Map or Picture?** • Some of the representations drawn in Wilson's classroom probably looked like this. Which is a picture and which is a map?

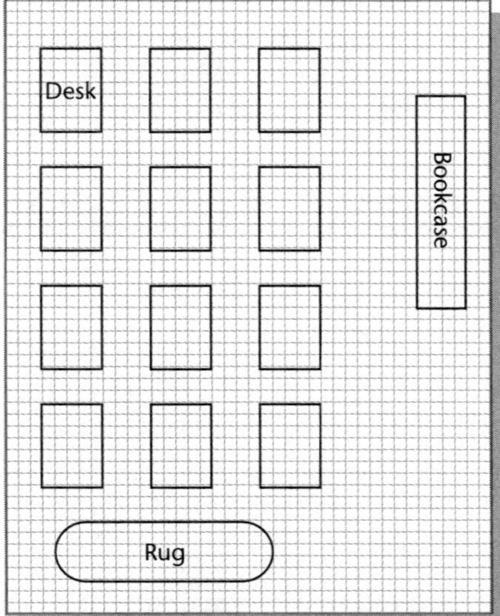

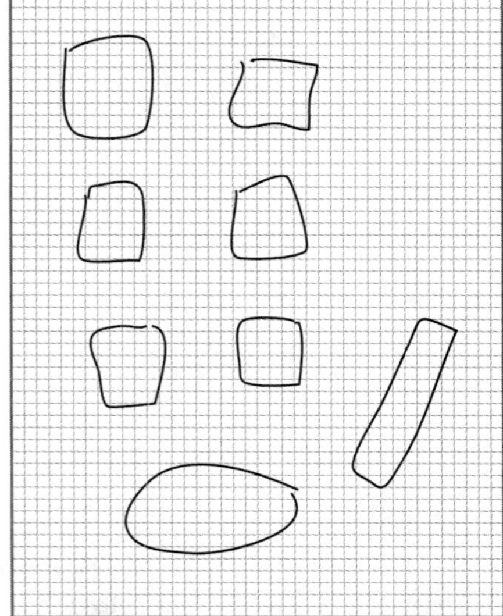

After a couple of days and uneven results, Wilson starts a class discussion with a question: "What makes drawing a map hard?" The question falls flat as most of the students sit silently. Wilson surmises that those learners who had drawn pictures of the classroom rather than maps simply do not see anything hard about that and therefore see no substance behind the question. She has more luck the next day with the question, "What is the difference between a map and picture?" The lively discussion that follows produces a range of hypotheses. Some, like the idea that maps have keys, are agreed on, and others, like the idea that pictures are colored and maps are not, are dropped. To test students' developing ideas, Wilson picks up Mary's carefully delineated drawing and asks, "Is this a map or a picture?" When disagreement ensues, Wilson asks, "How can we decide?"

Several students call out, "Let's try to find something!" Sean suggests trying to locate the rug. Agreeing, Wilson asks the class to count the number of squares (fifteen) on Mary's map from the front of the room to the edge of the rug. Eileen then counts the number of floor tiles and announces a match—Mary's drawing, the class agrees, is a map. Melissa's freewheeling drawing is evaluated next. The test—to locate the bookcase—is unsuccessful and the class decides Melissa has drawn a picture instead of a map. The third trial features Ned's drawing. Wilson describes what happened as follows:

CLASSROOM EXAMPLE

> Ned's depiction of the classroom was smaller than Mary's, but my class was sure that it too was a map because they could find things. However, instead of being fifty by forty squares, Ned's map was only twenty-five by twenty squares. "How can this be a map," I asked the class, "when he has twenty-five squares between the front and the back of the room, and there are fifty tiles on the floor?" [After a long discussion] Katharine stood and stated, "If you divide fifty by two, you get twenty-five. I think he made every square two tiles instead of one." Ned nodded smugly. My heart smiled, for I had witnessed the birth of the idea of scale. (p. 9)

COMMONPLACE CONNECTIONS

- What does Wilson seem to think is important about the *subject matter* of mapmaking?
- What view of *learners* does she seem to hold?
- How would you characterize her *teaching?*
- How would you describe the *classroom environment?*

CLASSROOM MANAGEMENT

Some observers would object: Surely, Wilson could have saved a great deal of time and frustration by simply describing the concept of scale and giving students worksheets to practice on. Perhaps, but Wilson's class is directly encountering a profound geographic construct. Rather than receiving information, these kids are co-constructing the meaning of scale in a way that can't help but be more powerful than a worksheet approach. And this happens, in large part, because of the way Wilson helps shape the classroom discourse. There is no IRE interaction here where the teacher merely checks to see if the kids have the same knowledge in their heads that she does. Instead, Wilson uses big questions to frame the discussion and the students carry the conversation. Moreover, it is a student, Katharine, who observes and describes the key point—Ned's use of scale. Wilson is clearly the teacher in the classroom, but her willingness to share the floor with her learners sends strong messages about the importance of everyone's voice.

Discourse looks different in a genuine classroom. This is not to say that traditional forms of lecture and recitation are never appropriate. At times, you will need to transmit basic information to the class or check students' understanding of basic facts. In those instances, lectures and recitations are in order. The point is that in a genuine classroom, the discourse frequently moves beyond fact and teacher-centered talk. Wilson is trying to teach her learners about a vital concept—scale. In doing so, however, she keeps two key points in mind. One is that it's better to work with the complexity of the idea than to avoid it. The other is that learners need to make their understanding their own. In using big questions and in sharing the talk with her students, Wilson promotes an environment that supports these two points well.

Organization in Genuine Classrooms

If discourse is different in genuine classrooms, so too is *classroom organization.* Teaching with big ideas demands new kinds of talk and new ways of organizing learning activities and of using classroom rules to support those activities. In traditional classrooms, the demands of keeping learners quiet and on-task drive the manner in which activities are structured and classroom rules are structured. In genuine classrooms, ideas drive activities and rules.

Organizing classroom activities around ideas In Suzanne Wilson's classroom, we see the power of interweaving individual and whole-class activities. She initiates the unit on mapmaking with a whole class discussion of how to draw a map of the classroom.

Two key aspects of maps surface in the ensuing conversation. One is the notion of size and shape. Students quickly realize that their classroom is rectangular and can be measured by counting the number of floor tiles from front to back and from side to side. Representing the size and shape of objects is a key feature of mapmaking, although it is one that teachers often take for granted.

These third graders have created a 3-D representation of their town. How does such a project fit with the research (described in Chapter 2) on students' understandings of geography?

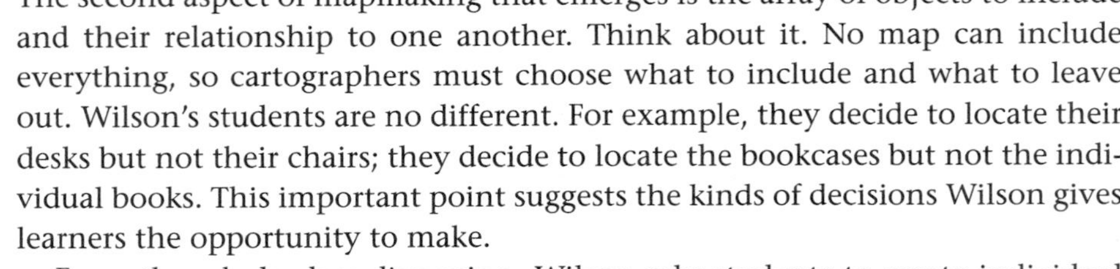

The second aspect of mapmaking that emerges is the array of objects to include and their relationship to one another. Think about it. No map can include everything, so cartographers must choose what to include and what to leave out. Wilson's students are no different. For example, they decide to locate their desks but not their chairs; they decide to locate the bookcases but not the individual books. This important point suggests the kinds of decisions Wilson gives learners the opportunity to make.

CLASSROOM MANAGEMENT

From the whole-class discussion, Wilson asks students to create individual maps. She often has them work as partners or in small groups, but in this case we suspect she wants to see how each learner understands the task of mapmaking, especially in light of the preceding discussion. This assignment functions both as a piece of instruction and as an assessment of what each child can do at that point in time.

As so often happens when one assesses, Wilson learns that her students know and can do different things. Some, like Mary and Ned, produce relatively accurate representations of the classroom. Others, like Melissa, do not. Wilson might pull aside Melissa and the others whose drawings look more like pictures than maps for a mini-lesson on mapmaking. Sensing, however, that the whole class would benefit, she asks two questions. The first, "What makes drawing a map hard?" falls flat; the second, "What is the difference between a map and picture?"

makes more sense to students and sparks a lively discussion whereby they can test their ideas using classmates' drawings. Out of that comes yet another key geographic concept, the idea of scale.

IN YOUR CLASSROOM: Encouraging Inquiry

Early elementary teachers rarely worry about encouraging their children to talk about their ideas; thoughts of all kinds tend to fill the air of most K–2 classrooms. Older students can be more reserved, though, especially as concerns about getting the "right answer" begin to surface. Although no teacher wants students to come away with inaccurate information, too much stress on right answers can stifle children's thinking.

Good teachers distinguish between situations that require factual information and those where hunches, conjectures, or guesses are appropriate. In the latter, teachers help students open up their thinking by encouraging divergent ideas and perspectives. Help your students develop and make public their emerging insights by giving them frequent opportunities to brainstorm ideas.

By weaving whole-class and individual activities together, Wilson provides opportunities to introduce new ideas and for learners to try out those ideas individually and with their peers. She might have used other work arrangements such as small groups and partners, but, given her purposes and her sense of her learners, her decisions make considerable sense.

Using classroom rules to support instruction Wilson's example helps us understand one more point about the organization of a genuine classroom community, and that involves the kinds of rules or norms that govern this classroom. We don't know what expectations Wilson and her class talked about at the beginning of the year, but we can infer some of the norms that govern this class, and they seem decidedly different from those common to traditional classrooms.

CLASSROOM MANAGEMENT

First, we sense that talk is important—it appears to be a fundamental way of exploring, developing, and negotiating meaning in this classroom. We wouldn't expect Wilson to spend much time scolding her students to be quiet. We expect that she agrees with the traditional norm of no put-downs or meanness between students. It's also clear, however, that she values ideas and she knows that talk may not always be comfortable. Take the case of Melissa and her drawing. Some might worry about showing the girl's sketch, which was clearly not a map. Wilson acknowledges that she chose Melissa's paper deliberately:

CLASSROOM EXAMPLE

> I selected Melissa's on purpose—she had drawn hers freehand, and for a key she had drawn a picture of a house key. Melissa is a smart but lazy student who has been testing my limits. I chose her picture because I thought that she, rather than being devastated by a decision that she had not drawn a map, would pick up the gauntlet and prove that she too could draw one. (p. 9)

Wilson has two ideas in mind here. On the one hand, she wants the class to see and discuss an example of a picture, as opposed to a map. On the other hand, she wants to challenge Melissa to raise the level of her work. Rather than trying to be mean or expose the girl to ridicule, Wilson believes that the frank examination and discussion of Melissa's work will benefit both Melissa and the class. Talk is an important feature of teaching and learning, and Wilson encourages norms about talk that promote multiple goals.

CLASSROOM MANAGEMENT

Second, we suspect Wilson and her learners think more in terms of sharing than of cheating. We don't know for sure, but we suspect considerable sharing of ideas and approaches occur while the students work on their individual maps. If so, the possibility exists that one or more children simply copied the work of another without any learning. We think two factors undercut that possibility. One is that Wilson does not sit at her desk while the class works. Instead, she circulates throughout the room, continually stopping to examine and to ask questions about each learner's work. The second mitigating factor is that learning in this classroom is less about getting work done and more about exploring and refining what one knows and can do. To that end, Wilson knows that some of the most important learning that transpires in classrooms is between learners. As a result, she promotes the norm of working together as a means of helping all students learn.

CLASSROOM MANAGEMENT

Finally, we sense that Wilson is little concerned about the nit-picky details that sometimes consume traditional teachers, such as putting proper headings on papers. Maintaining a certain level of structure is important in every class, and we expect Wilson's is no different, but as we see in the vignettes, most important are the multiple, varied, and sustained opportunities children get to work with big ideas.

TEACHER REFLECTION

Setting Rules

Think about the discussion of rules in Wilson's classroom. How might these tacit rules have been made more explicit? Why might Wilson not post such a list of rules?

In genuine classrooms, learners and activities take myriad shapes across the school day, and those few rules that do exist encourage rather than discourage a lively atmosphere. These are important qualities, ones that transform a classroom where children simply put in their time into one where ideas live and breathe because of the opportunities learners have to engage them.

IN YOUR CLASSROOM: Using Classroom Rules to Support Instruction

Should you decide to develop a list of classroom rules governing students' classroom behavior, we would encourage you to make this a class discussion and decision. A rule like "No put-downs" carries much more meaning when it comes from students themselves.

Just as important as behavior rules, we think, are rules that support the kind of teaching and learning envisioned in genuine classrooms. You might create this list of rules yourself, but we have another suggestion:

- Soon after the start of the school year, engage your class in a discussion in which you think all or most students will participate. The topic matters less than the opportunity created for everyone to participate.
- Assuming that the discussion goes well, encourage the children to identify features that helped make the conversation work. Examples might include instances where a student tried to understand another's perspective, where all or most students were actively listening, where a student constructively challenged another's point of view.
- Make a list of these actions and decide what to call them. Some possibilities include "Our learning rules," "Rules for how we learn," or "How to help everyone be smarter."
- Add to and modify this list each time an activity goes well.

Dispositions in Genuine Classrooms

Like discourse and organization, *dispositions* are different in genuine classrooms. Dispositions are those values and attitudes teachers and learners work toward that contribute to learners' development as thoughtful adults. A list of those dispositions would be long indeed. Justice, inquiry, freedom, fairness . . . the list could go on and on. Instead, we collapse that list into three groupings:

- respect and commitment to inquiry
- respect and commitment to ideas and people
- respect and commitment to argument and evidence

Figure 6.3 • **Where is Lansing?** • Who's right, Susie or Matthew?

These three sets of ideas reflect the values and attitudes we believe are both important and possible.

As the context for a discussion of these dispositions, let's return to Suzanne Wilson's third-grade classroom. In another set of lessons, Wilson's students try to figure out how the state capital came to be located in Lansing. Students fill the air with possibilities, but when Susie volunteers that it made sense to locate the capital in Lansing, " 'cause it's kind of in the middle," Matthew scoffs. "It's not in the middle of the state," he laughs. "Haven't you ever looked at a map?"

CLASSROOM MANAGEMENT

Wilson points out that Matthew is correct, if one looks at a map of Michigan that includes the Upper Peninsula, for then Lansing is nowhere near the middle of the state. (If one considers only the lower peninsula, however, Susie's observation makes more sense.) Wilson, however, wants to support Susie's contribution and keep open the classroom conversation. Sensing that Matthew's derisive tone might discourage the offering of other ideas, Wilson subtly reproves him: "We're just making guesses right now, Matthew. Anything goes. Later we'll find out which of our guesses were right." She adds, "Any other reasons why Lansing might be the capital?"

Respect for and commitment to inquiry One disposition found in genuine classrooms is an open *respect for and commitment to inquiry.* If education is about people and ideas, it's also about asking questions and exploring alternative answers. **Inquiry**—the passion for pulling ideas apart and putting them back together—drives learning.

CLASSROOM MANAGEMENT

Ideas have power, but that power goes unrealized unless teachers and learners read and think, discuss and argue, compromise and disagree, ask questions, answer them, and then ask and answer them anew. We hear a lot of yak about active learning today. Some people mistakenly believe this means that learners are active only when they are doing something with their hands, feet, and bodies. Active learning, however, is as much about cognition and inquiry as it is about physical activity.

In the vignette above, we see the importance Wilson attaches to inquiry. Although it is convoluted, the "answer" to the question of why Lansing is the capital of Michigan has something to do with land speculation, bogus maps, and some political wheeling and dealing. Wilson and her learners will have the complete picture in due time. What is important at this point, Wilson explains, is generating possibilities. She knows that, although her students live in Lansing, few have given much thought to what a capital is and what it represents. She uses the children's developing interest in why Lansing is the capital as a means of generating interest in the larger and more complex issues of government, decision-making, politics, and power. By reminding Matthew that their purpose was to make guesses, Wilson keeps the question open and the ideas flowing.

Respect for and commitment to ideas and people A second important disposition is an honest *respect for and commitment to ideas and people*. We believe as Hawkins (1974) does that education is about bringing together people (the I and Thou) and ideas (the It). Teachers and learners should hold values and attitudes that promote the power of ideas and the right of individuals to hold various perspectives. We are all individuals and, as such, we have a right to hold our own particular views. But we are also social beings.

CLASSROOM MANAGEMENT

Classroom groups—whether the whole class, a small work group, or a pair of classmates—have a responsibility to hear and try to understand one another's views. Each member, however, also must understand that holding a perspective confers no special privilege to be mean or inconsiderate to others.

IN YOUR CLASSROOM: Drawing Out Children's Ideas

Drawing out children's ideas, especially if they are not fully formed, is not easy. Self-conscious and timid students often remain silent for fear of embarrassment, but even confident children may be quiet if an easy answer is not apparent. Good teachers have a repertoire of questions at hand with which to prompt students' participation. Some of those questions are

- Can you say more about that?
- Can you give me an example?
- Who can add to what has been said?

CLASSROOM MANAGEMENT

In Suzanne Wilson's third-grade classroom we see a teacher who deftly demonstrates the balance between respect for ideas and for people. Wilson knows that, in some sense, both Susie and Matthew are right in their ideas about Lansing. She accepts both, sensing that each, in turn, will be useful as the class continues to wrestle with this issue. At the same time, however, she clearly disapproves of Matthew's mocking approach in making his point. She knows that students need to feel safe in offering their ideas and that Matthew's behavior may undercut less confident students' willingness to share their thoughts. Think about how she admonishes Matthew, however. Wilson knows that Matthew's actions are unhelpful, but she also knows that he's a third-grader and still learning how to respect and talk about the ideas of others. Rather than come down hard on the boy, Wilson firmly, but gently, explains to Matthew that all ideas are acceptable at this point. And though directed at Matthew, Wilson expects her point will resonate throughout the class: We're here to wrestle with hard ideas, but we'll do so thoughtfully and respectfully.

Respect for and commitment to argument and evidence Among many other possible dispositions, we believe teachers and learners in genuine classrooms hold one in particular: patient *respect for and commitment to argument and evidence.*

CLASSROOM MANAGEMENT

Sometimes you'll want your learners to begin exploring an idea simply by talking to one another. Other times, you'll want them to brainstorm, a form of inquiry that emphasizes generating as many ideas as possible. Still other times, though, you'll want learners to be more systematic in their thinking. One key to systematic thinking is the notion of **argument.** Argument, in this sense, is the ability to make a series of points that build to a reasonable conclusion. **Evidence** is the support one calls on for those points.

After the brainstorming activity described above, Wilson and her students compare their initial ideas with the resources available as they attempt to construct a satisfactory answer to the question of why Lansing is the capital of Michigan. In the course of their deliberations, students consider whether Detroit would be a better capital site (rejected ultimately because, at the time, it was too close to French settlements in Canada), where other important institutions (for example, the state prison and the University of Michigan) are located, and why it might be advantageous to locate a state capital near the geographic center of a state. After considering all the arguments and the evidence behind them, Wilson asks the class to compose letters to then–Governor Greeley making a case for Lansing as the best site for the new capital. Figure 6.4 represents Katharine's letter, with her original spelling (Wilson, 1990).

Wilson notes that Katharine's account is "more sophisticated" than those the class read during their investigation. Her account also demonstrates that Katharine and her peers are "capable of complicated thinking and critical analysis." No one would expect these third-graders to handle the full complexity of this issue. Clearly, however, they are on their way to the adult process on making arguments and supporting them.

Actively pursued, the dispositions described above—respect for and commitment to inquiry, ideas and people, and argument and evidence—will help your learners become smarter, more thoughtful, and more reflective people. They will also help your learners become more mindful and responsible members of society.

Figure 6.4 • **Letter of Argument and Evidence**

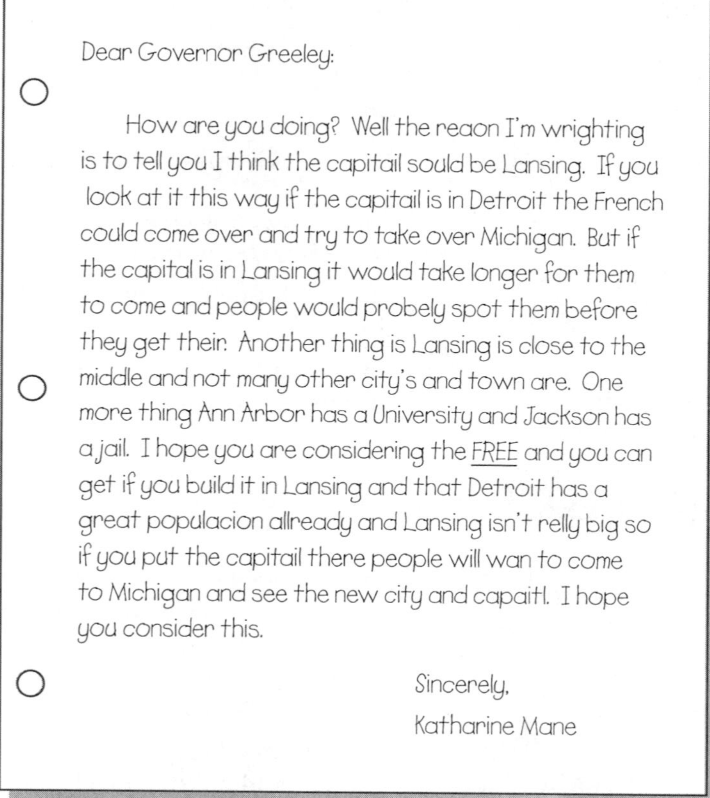

Dear Governor Greeley:

How are you doing? Well the reaon I'm wrighting is to tell you I think the capitail sould be Lansing. If you look at it this way if the capitail is in Detroit the French could come over and try to take over Michigan. But if the capital is in Lansing it would take longer for them to come and people would probely spot them before they get their. Another thing is Lansing is close to the middle and not many other city's and town are. One more thing Ann Arbor has a University and Jackson has a jail. I hope you are considering the FREE and you can get if you build it in Lansing and that Detroit has a great populacion allready and Lansing isn't relly big so if you put the capitail there people will wan to come to Michigan and see the new city and capaitl. I hope you consider this.

Sincerely,
Katharine Mane

CHOOSING GOALS

These dispositions promote a view of the "good citizen" different from the one that emerges from the traditional classroom. There, the emphasis is on passive, respectful obedience. Certainly, there is nothing wrong with obeying laws, respecting authorities, and trying to get along. If we lived in a perfectly just society, that view would probably suffice. But we don't, and while being passive is one way to deal with problems, there are others. In our view, the good citizen is one who embodies the dispositions we describe above.

Before this chapter, we focused on the academic side of schooling—the teaching, learning, and subject matter of social studies. Although these elements are important, so too are the less apparent but equally consequential elements of classroom life—discourse, classroom organization, and dispositions. We talked about those elements by sketching two noticeably different classroom environments, traditional and genuine. As a prospective teacher, you will choose what kind of classroom environment you and your learners will work toward. The traditional classroom may not inspire many learners, but it will be familiar to them and to you. The genuine classroom has the potential to inspire learners, but it demands a lot more work from everyone. Clearly, we believe the extra work is worth it. We hope you do too.

SECTION SUMMARY: Genuine Classroom Communities

- *Discourse* in genuine classrooms is framed by big questions, and students play an active role in the conversation.
- In genuine classrooms, ideas drive the *classroom organization* of activities and rules.
- The *dispositions* in a genuine classroom include respect for and commitment to inquiry, ideas and people, and argument and evidence.

The Genuine Classroom Community: Moving Forward

The image described above is just that—a picture of what a genuine classroom might look like. Images or pictures are important, for they illustrate possibilities, but they can't tell you how to get there. Moreover, once you think you're there, an image can't tell you how to stay there. We'd love to whip out a list of surefire do's and don'ts, a prescription for, or a road map to Genuineville, USA. Instead, we offer some ideas based on our collective experience and that of the several hundred student and practicing teachers we have known. We can't promise a smooth ride, but maybe, together, we can move forward.

The Genuine Classroom: How to Know If You're Getting There

Sometimes it's easy to know if your classroom is a genuine one:

- A girl approaches you after class one day and says, "You know, I used to hate social studies, but that thing we did in class today wasn't too bad."
- During parent–teacher conferences, a parent "complains" that his child wants him to start buying the newspaper because of the current events you've been discussing in class.
- You see kids who seemed to hate each other earlier in the year now hanging out together after working on a group project.
- A boy who hasn't said anything all year offers a comment or asks a question or does a piece of a group presentation, and he smiles.

When trying to figure out why a lesson is not going as you planned, don't neglect an important source of information: your students!

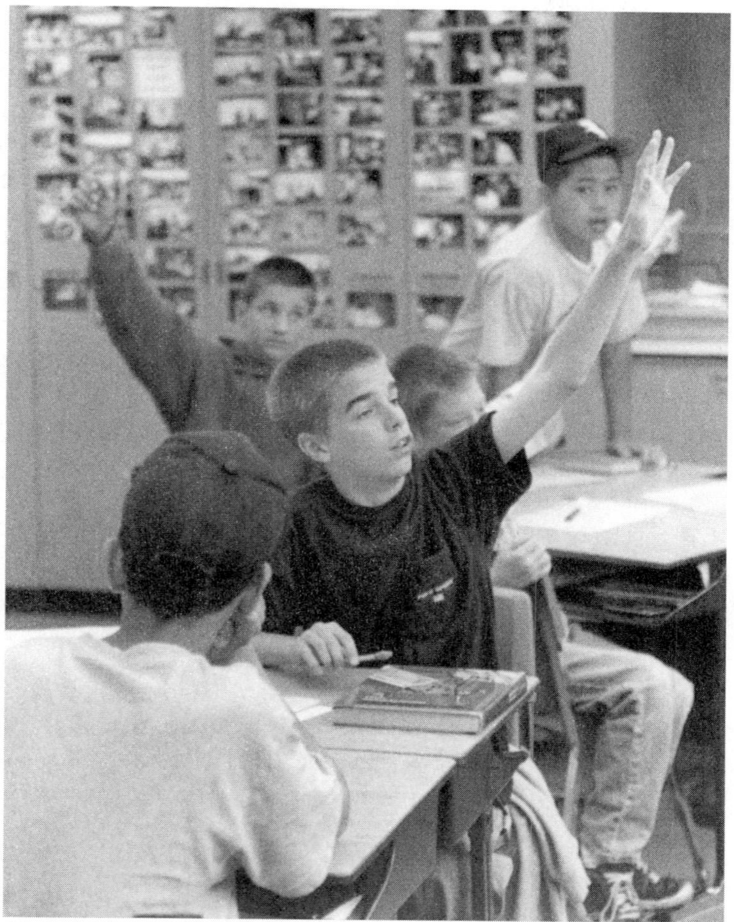

These snapshots may reflect little more than moments in time, yet they speak volumes about what is happening in your classroom. In the first, the girl is telling you that you've made this subject, social studies, something worth paying attention to. In kid-talk, if something isn't "too bad," then it's pretty good! In the second, the parent is saying that his child's interest in the world has so expanded that he wants to read for himself about the events of the day. The child's emerging questions have been validated and given importance, yielding a burst of curiosity. The third situation reveals the big impact you've had on how children view themselves and others and the importance of giving them opportunities to interact with a range of peers. And the last image is one teachers tend to carry around with them for weeks, months, and even years—that time when your patient efforts paid off, and the child you always worried about stepped into his own.

RELEVANT RESEARCH

You will have many of these moments in your career. They are **psychic rewards,** the gratification teachers experience when they believe that they have positively influenced a learner, which many teachers say mean far more to them than, for example, their principal's yearly evaluation (Lortie, 1975). These moments will confirm your sense that you are doing something right, that learners are benefiting from your teaching and from the classroom environment you are building.

TEACHING RESOURCES

Talking with Other Teachers

Check out this site for teacher-developed ideas on classroom management:

- http://www.pacificnet.net/~mandel/ClassroomManagement.html

The site below is linked to the site above. In this site teachers talk on-line with other teachers about a range of issues related to teaching and learning.

- http://www.pacificnet.net/~mandel/ircinfo.html

You will also have many moments of doubt, anxiety, and concern, moments where you *think* that what you are doing makes sense and has value, but the class reactions make you wonder. What do you do? Proceed as if nothing is wrong and hope the kids "get it" later? Switch to a new topic, activity, or instructional approach? Let the kids go to gym early? Give them a test? At any particular time, you might do any of these.

We have an additional suggestion: Sometimes, it makes sense just to stop and ask the class what's going on. Doing so sends several important messages.

CLASSROOM MANAGEMENT

First, it shows that you care enough about the students' learning to halt the lesson and make sure that they are with you. Good teachers may not mind their learners' being confused and uncertain at particular points in a lesson because they know that greater clarity is around the bend. If that is not the case, however, stopping the lesson tells kids that your purpose is not simply to cover material, but to help them learn and understand. Second, stopping a lesson shows you trust and value what learners think. Although children are not always able to articulate what they are confused or uncertain about, when they do their insights can prove invaluable. We're reminded of a teacher who, frustrated that her learners did not seem to know or care much about the material at hand, said, "Let's stop here and try to figure what's going on." Five minutes later she understood: The children lacked the necessary background knowledge she assumed they had acquired during the previous year. She learned differently when a student said, "Mrs. Thomas, you're acting like we know what you're talking about, but we don't." She reconsidered what the class needed to learn, made adjustments in her unit and lesson plans, and found the students much more cooperative and engaged.

Not all such incidents have happy endings, but many do. The constant and complex challenges teachers face drive some away after a year or so. Most, however, find those challenges endlessly interesting, and the headaches and heartaches well worth the costs, especially when *that* boy smiles with understanding.

Parents want their children to be well educated, so do not hesitate to enlist their support and cooperation. Key to garnering that support and cooperation, however, is good communication.

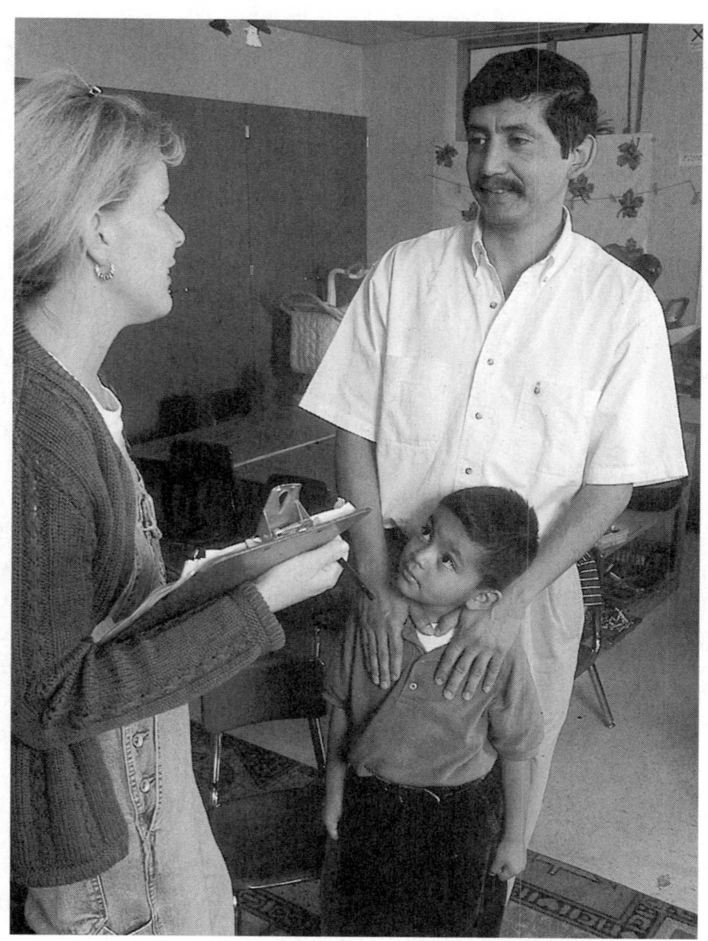

Negotiating the Genuine Classroom Community

RELEVANT RESEARCH

Before we leave the subject of classroom environment, we must remind you that you're not alone in there. As the discussion above suggests, classroom atmospheres are negotiated (Grant, 1996). Your stake in that negotiation is important, and much that you do will shape the classroom environment. Other stakeholders' needs and interests also will influence, to one degree or another, the kind of classroom environment that develops. Those stakeholders include

- students
- parents
- principals and teacher colleagues
- district-level actors
- state departments of education

CLASSROOM MANAGEMENT

One large group of stakeholders is your *students*. Like you, students have a big stake in the kind of classroom that emerges. Nothing will happen without at least their tacit consent and cooperation. This point is tricky for two reasons. First, although you might expect otherwise, learners may balk in their first encounters with your overtures at building a genuine classroom. Instead of enthusiastically engaging in real discussions, classroom rule-making, and the like, students may act out, refuse to participate, or remain silent. These behaviors will likely catch you off-guard because, after all, wouldn't any learner want to be part of a genuine classroom environment? The answer is probably yes, but this may be entirely new to the children in front of you, and when you confront them with a new and uncertain situation, you may see a range of disruptive, unhelpful, and silly behaviors. Take heart. It's not that they don't want to work with you, they just don't know how.

That brings up a second point: Until you help them learn how to act in a genuine classroom, both you and the children will be frustrated. Talk with them about what classroom rules make the most sense, model ways they should talk to one another, give them opportunities to practice making and supporting arguments. There is no magic formula here, just the idea that if you want learners to think and act differently, you'll have to teach them.

You and your students are the primary actors in shaping the classroom environment. As we described in Chapter 5, however, the factors that influence your teaching may also influence the classroom environment you and the learners attempt to develop.

Parents are likely to exert some influence on your classroom. Like their children, many parents have only experienced traditional classroom settings. New discourse patterns, classroom organizations, and dispositions may confuse them at first. A call from a skeptical parent is every novice teacher's nightmare. Again, patience and understanding will serve you well. You will need to listen calmly to the parent's concerns with the knowledge that she or he simply may not grasp your purposes and practices. The vast majority of parents want good education for their children, and so they will often give you the benefit of the doubt as long as they sense that you are dealing with them honestly. Help them understand what you are trying to do.

Others who may attempt to influence your class include your *principal and teacher colleagues*. Like any social organization, schools have norms and expectations of the people who work there. We would like to think that all principals and teachers will support the development of genuine classrooms, but we're not that naive. Some of your co-workers will continue to support traditional aims, and if they set the school norms you can expect to take some flack. Two realities mitigate that tension. One is that, although genuine classrooms are far from standard, they are increasingly evident and accepted. The other reality is that, despite the presence of school norms, teachers generally hold a wide degree of professional autonomy. A colleague or two may grouse about the "noise" coming from your classroom as your learners actively engage ideas and each other. You may even find the principal stopping by more often than she or he does in other classrooms. The simple fact, however, is that results, in the form of smart, thoughtful, excited learners, count. You may still encounter some grumbling, but you and almost everyone else will see it for what it is: professional jealousy.

Less direct influence can come from other quarters. Most teachers work for a school district rather than a school itself, so several actors—*the district superintendent, central office staff, and the school board*—will make decisions that may influence the classroom environment you strive to create. One of those decisions concerns district-level testing. Like Don Kite in Chapter 5, most elementary school teachers administer some sort of local test. Intelligence tests may have little influence; they are presumably unrelated to instruction. Achievement tests are a different story. Some are broad-brush tests of general knowledge and skills (usually in literacy and mathematics) and so, like IQ tests, will have little immediate implication for your practice. Others, however, will be more directly relevant. Recall that Don Kite administered a district-developed test based on the district social studies curriculum for fifth grade. Recall also, however, that Kite still retained considerable autonomy in the way he interpreted the influence of that test. In truth, you will hear many teachers talk about the influence of testing as if it completely and single-mindedly drives their instruction.

RELEVANT RESEARCH

No evidence supports that claim (Cohen & Barnes, 1993; Grant, in press). Testing influences teachers' practices, but like everything else, how it influences teachers depends in large part on how an individual teacher interprets it. We believe its influence should relate to how you construct your classroom community: If testing practices support your goals and approach, they should be quite influential. If not, they would be less so.

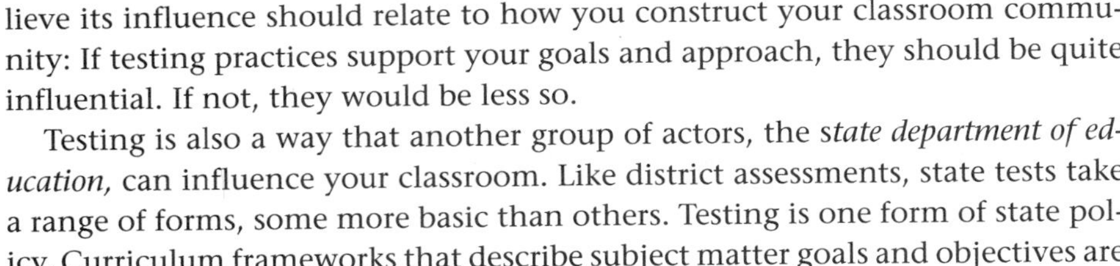

Testing is also a way that another group of actors, the *state department of education,* can influence your classroom. Like district assessments, state tests take a range of forms, some more basic than others. Testing is one form of state policy. Curriculum frameworks that describe subject matter goals and objectives are another form of state policy, but so too are more specific actions which may set maximum class sizes, the length of the school year, and the like.

With all these interested parties, it should be clear that the classroom environment is a negotiated affair and that teachers and students are not the only negotiators. Those influences outside the classroom are many and may, at times, seem overpowering. But the nature of teaching remains such that teachers, even untenured ones, retain considerable control over the basics of teaching, learning, subject matter, and environment.

Teaching, learning, and subject matter are all important. In his wisdom, however, Joseph Schwab saw fit to include milieu or environment as the fourth commonplace of schooling. It's a fuzzy concept, though, more tacit than explicit. But if we are to believe the research on classroom environments, creating a vibrant atmosphere for learning will energize you and your teaching, your learners and their learning, and the big ideas of the subject matter at hand.

CHOOSING GOALS

Every classroom has some sort of environment. Most reflect traditional approaches to discourse, classroom organization, and dispositions. Still, we see increasing evidence of teachers promoting what we call a genuine classroom community. In those classrooms, the talk is more open and more balanced between teacher and learners, the learning opportunities are organized in a variety of ways, classroom rules support rather than hinder social learning, and the dispositions evident encourage respect for and commitment to inquiry, people and ideas, and argument and evidence.

Creating genuine classroom communities is no mean feat, in large part because doing so challenges much of what we have all experienced as schooling. Teachers who take the leap, who strive to create such classrooms will find no blueprint or master plan for getting there. Moreover, they may be discouraged as others struggle to understand their efforts. That said, teachers who do take the initiative to push beyond the norms of traditional schooling will, in the end, sense that they have done something real and important for their learners. And that's a great feeling.

CHAPTER SUMMARY

1. ***What discourse, classroom organization, and dispositional patterns are found in traditional classroom environments?***

   Traditional classrooms are characterized by recitation, by quiet individual seatwork, and by values of efficiency, hard work, deference to authority, and external rewards.

2. ***What discourse, classroom organization, and dispositional patterns are found in genuine classroom communities?***

   Genuine classroom communities are characterized by active student involvement in classroom conversations, classroom activities and rules driven by ideas, and a respect for and commitment to inquiry, ideas and people, and argument and evidence.

3. ***What stakeholders are involved in the negotiation of a genuine classroom community?***

   Students, parents, principals and teaching colleagues, district-level actors, and state departments of education represent a range of interests in and influences on the classroom environment teachers foster.

TEACHING RESOURCES

Print Resources

Burke-Hengen, M., & Gillespie, T. (Eds.). (1995). *Building community: Social Studies in the middle school years*. Portsmouth, NH: Heinemann. Although intended for middle-school students, this edited book has much to offer elementary school teachers interested in thinking about how their approach to teaching interacts with the classroom environment.

Cohen, E. (1994). *Designing groupwork* (2nd ed.). New York: Teachers College Press. In addition to being useful as a guide to constructing small-group instructional opportunities, this classic offers many insights into how to develop and sustain a genuine classroom community.

Fraenkel, J. (1973). *Helping students think and value: Strategies for teaching the social studies*. Englewood Cliffs, NJ: Prentice-Hall. An older, but still useful book that nicely integrates attention to the commonplaces.

Jorgensen, K. (1993). Children's historical understanding, *History Workshop* (pp. 3–25). Portsmouth, NH: Heinemann. This is an excellent resource for exploring how teacher-student discourse can look in classrooms.

Technology Resources

Most of the web sites that offer lesson and unit plans for social studies teachers also offer suggestions for various approaches to classroom organization. Some particularly useful sites include the following:

- **http://ericir.syr.edu/Virtual/Lessons/crossroads/sec6/preface.html**

This site is the introduction to the CROSSROADS K-16 American History curriculum developed by the Sage Colleges (Troy, NY) and the Niskayuna School District (Niskayuna, NY).

- **http://www.pacificnet.net/~mandel/**

This site, Teachers Helping Teachers, has many unit plans on a variety of subjects and a chat line for teachers who want feedback on their ideas.

NOTES

1. For a fuller account of this vignette, see VanSledright and Grant (1994).
2. See Wilson (1990) for the full version of this and the following episodes.

Part TWO

Putting the Commonplaces into Action

Chapter 7

Purposes, Goals, and Objectives for Teaching and Learning

In this chapter we talk about selecting a social studies *goal framework* and how one goes about working from it to construct powerful learning opportunities for students. Our discussions in the previous chapters have explored social studies in a teaching-learning context that we hope will help you reflect on the education process and make the sometimes difficult choices required. We've presented many rich stories from classrooms that we trust have given you a distinct feel for this teaching-learning context. Now we offer you some ideas and guidance about choosing and working from goal frameworks so that, in the end, you will feel prepared to make your own choices.

You can build from a variety of different goal frameworks, several of which we will describe later in this chapter. These goal frameworks are clusters of goals that help teachers decide how to design and organize learning opportunities and evaluate their importance. They not only reflect different purposes of education, but also different views of what it means to be a good citizen in society. Each framework tends to make good sense in and of itself, and the arguments often seem persuasive, which can make the decision process difficult. Trying to build your own educational goal framework in teaching social studies by picking and choosing from the best and most attractive features of all the arguments, often leads to trying to put incompatible elements together.

Instead, we'll begin with examples from teachers' classrooms; we'll describe four of the most common frameworks that influence social studies education, illustrate how they play out in those classrooms, compare them, note some of their incompatibilities, and offer some guidance about being a reflective and independent decision maker.

This chapter builds on the commonplaces discussed in Chapters 2 through 6: learners and learning, subject matter, teachers and teaching, and classroom environment. We draw on learners and learning because social studies goal frameworks inevitably center on students and their learning processes. We draw on subject matter because it deals with what students are learning. We fuse these two commonplaces together with teachers and teaching and environment because the classroom is the context in which your goal frameworks will take root and grow.

When you have completed this chapter, you should be able to answer these questions:

1. ***What are several common educational goal frameworks that influence social studies teaching and learning?***
2. ***What enduring arguments support different goal frameworks?***
3. ***Where can teachers go for guidance in choosing a goal framework?***
4. ***What goes into building a goal framework?***
5. ***What is the case for working from the liberal education goal framework?***

Goal Frameworks and Good Citizens

CHOOSING GOALS

How do seasoned social studies teachers work from goal frameworks in their teaching? This is a tough question. While teachers rarely talk much about their goal frameworks and sometimes even disparage talk about **goals,** nonetheless teachers do teach toward goals. What do we mean by goal frameworks? A **goal framework** expresses those aims teachers hold for their students that help them decide *how* to design learning opportunities, *what* those opportunities should consist of, *when* to put them in place and in what order, and how to explain to parents, administrators, and other teachers *why* engaging these opportunities is important. In many ways, a teacher's goal framework is the very heart of her or his teaching. These crucial learning aims form the basis for making sound decisions about learning opportunities. A teacher simply cannot teach effectively without a goal framework.

RELEVANT RESEARCH

In social studies, goal frameworks have been expressed in differing and often competing visions of what it means to develop "good citizens" (see, for example, Engle & Ochoa, 1988; Parker & Jarolimek, 1984; VanSledright & Grant, 1994). The debate, as you can probably anticipate, centers on how you define the idea of **good citizenship.** In other words, what does it mean to be a good citizen in this country and in the world? What should good citizens do? What are their characteristics? How you answer these questions makes all the difference in understanding how you will design learning opportunities for your students. In the next section, we look at four elementary school social studies teachers who work from different goal frameworks that express competing visions of what it means to develop good citizens. We use these examples to illustrate types of goal frameworks from which you might choose to anchor your own social studies teaching practice.

Let's begin with a series of short stories about four teachers. All four teach units on the American Revolution to predominantly white fifth-grade students. Each teaches in the same school district, so the social studies curriculum guidelines and objectives are identical. We will talk more about curriculum guides and other sources of information about goal frameworks in a moment, but let's first look at the teachers in action.

Tom Simpson: Good Citizens Are Good Workers

CLASSROOM EXAMPLE

The first teacher, Tom Simpson, employs a common approach to teaching and learning social studies. He relies almost exclusively on the fifth-grade history textbook used by the school district, follows its order of contents, has students answer the follow-up questions at the end of each chapter section, and finishes the unit with a slightly modified version of the end-of-chapter test supplied by the publisher. Classroom instruction generally is a predictable daily dose of reading the chapter and reciting answers to the section questions that have individual students recalling specific facts from the book. This approach is spiced with an occasional videotape or filmstrip. Students do reasonably well on the unit test, in part, because the questions are as predictable as the daily order of instruction.

Students seem more than occasionally bored and lifeless, and sometimes they find diversions that cause minor disruptions. Simpson, nonetheless, retains tight control of classroom activity and ends the disruptions almost as quickly as they begin. His management style is designed to create an orderly, some would say strict, atmosphere in which the work he assigns gets done efficiently and his students all accomplish the tasks at the same pace. Tom Simpson's classroom is structured in ways quite similar to the factory model we describe in Chapter 6. Students study the history textbook by consuming facts and work to produce good scores on the test in something akin to an assembly line. Good citizens, by Simpson's lights, are good workers, following his rules by diligently consuming and reproducing historical knowledge (that is, the key terms and ideas of American culture as defined by the textbook) in his classroom as preparation for later adult roles that require similar consumption-production roles.

Ramona Palmer: Good Citizens Are Knowledgeable and Informed

CLASSROOM EXAMPLE

Across town but still within the same school district, Ramona Palmer, whom you met in Chapter 3, is doing something quite different with her unit on the American Revolution. She also uses the textbook, some videotapes, and an occasional filmstrip, yet all sparingly. Her students read historical fiction accounts for different perspectives on the past and richer more varied accounts than the textbook provides. They also play the roles of angry colonists writing letters to relatives back home in England on the eve of the passage of the Stamp Act. Palmer engages them in a simulation exercise where she plays King George and collects "taxes" from her charges to help her students feel what the colonists might have felt. Later, she invites her fifth-graders to pursue a deep discussion of the Bill of Rights.

Palmer operates from a much different goal framework than does Simpson. She asks her students to become deeply engrossed with this historical period, to make the period come alive. She pushes them to analyze and assess events as a portion of their historical heritage as American citizens. She encourages them to imbibe the period, wrestle with its events, study it from different angles, judge causal connections, and learn by constructing their understanding of the period and its consequences for Americans.

In short, she urges children to engage history with panache and commitment. Why? Because she defines the good citizen as one who is deeply knowledgeable and well informed about many things, including his or her own history. Through history, she believes, children learn deeply about their collective past, a process necessary to helping them become well-educated citizens who know enough about their country to effectively and passionately discharge their roles and responsibilities as citizens.

Tina Roberts: Good Citizens Are Well-Rounded Human Beings

CLASSROOM EXAMPLE

Tina Roberts spends much of her non-classroom time at the local teacher store. There, she hunts down activities to use with her students that they will find interesting and fun. Roberts wants her students to enjoy school and learn to feel good about themselves. Rather than make schoolwork drudgery, Roberts's goal framework promotes as pleasant and as rewarding a school experience as possible for her students.

The unit Tina Roberts constructs on the American Revolution is less about the history of events that occurred and more about arranging activities that enable children to interact in multiple ways, to learn how to get along with each other, and to assist them in developing positive self-esteem. Roberts worries less about the content itself. She is far more concerned with the nature of activities and if her students are enjoying themselves.

Roberts begins the Revolution unit with a series of tradebook stories about key figures who contributed to the Americans winning independence from Britain. Roberts is careful to avoid the uglier aspects of the war with England, such as the early struggles of Washington's ragged army, the details of the Boston Massacre, attitudes and actions against the loyalists, and the conflict between slavery and the idea of inalienable natural rights in the Declaration of Independence. Much of the unit features students creating period costumes, art projects, dioramas, and stories designed to ensure that each student succeeds in accomplishing something that he or she can be proud of. Students receive grades, not on the basis of test scores as in Simpson's class, but on the relative quality of their projects. Roberts assists students as much as she can to enable them to get the best grades possible.

The way Tina Roberts organizes learning opportunities for her students differs greatly from both Simpson and Palmer. Tom Simpson focuses on the importance of helping students understand and be prepared for work and their future as citizen consumers and producers in a complex, competitive adult work world. Ramona Palmer trains her eye on getting students to deeply engage in the social studies subject matter because she believes it is important for helping them become articulate, thoughtful, and knowledgeable citizens. Tina Roberts, on the other hand, focuses on her students as human beings with unique talents, personalities, thoughts, and emotions. She is primarily interested in her children as children. Educating good citizens, for her, is about creating well-rounded human beings.

Sara Atkinson: Good Citizens Are Social Activists

CLASSROOM EXAMPLE

In a fourth school in the same district, Sara Atkinson is treating the American Revolution unit differently from any of her three colleagues. Like Simpson and Palmer, Atkinson uses the textbook, filmstrips, and videotapes, but all sparingly. The textbook acts as a guide, a method for organizing the order of the content. Students read it and occasionally address the section questions by writing responses in their social studies notebooks. Sometimes, as a form of review, they make a game out of answering the questions, a sort of American Revolution *Jeopardy!* Students also read from alternative texts such as historical fiction. Atkinson connects these readings to language arts as a method of integrating content.

But what really gets Atkinson excited about teaching history is the opportunity to discuss with students what she often refers to as the "mistakes of the past." She wants her students to see how such events as the Boston Massacre can be understood from different perspectives, that the colonists who were killed in this so-called massacre had been agitating the British sentries, who fired their guns. Atkinson wants her students to consider whether this agitation was justified, whether or not it might have been a mistake, and whether the British could have handled the situation differently. Were these all errors in judgment? Could disaster have been averted? What do we learn by these lessons from the American Revolution? In short, Atkinson uses historical knowledge as a tool for getting her students to think about what they might gain from understanding historical mistakes in judgment and how they might avoid repeating similar mistakes. She frequently approaches this task by using analogies to students' lives that reflect bad judgment and unfortunate consequences. She links the past with the present and attempts to extend the lessons learned to the future. She wants her students to recognize and avoid those mistakes, to work to correct those that create injustices.

In short, Atkinson wants to develop students who can detect social problems and do something about them. The content she teaches serves as a vehicle to this end. Students become historical detectives, but detectives with an activist mission to undo the damage that has been done by incorrect or unjust decisions made in the past. What animates Atkinson about history, and social studies generally, is that it serves her purpose of educating young social activists who sense wrong and injustice and who are willing to extend their energies toward change. By her definition, this is what it means to educate the good citizen.

TEACHER REFLECTION

Reflecting on Goal Frameworks

Having read the goal frameworks of the teachers profiled, think about these questions:

- Which of these frameworks have you experienced as a student? How do they seem similar and different?
- Which of these frameworks seems closest to your sense of yourself as a teacher? If you are having trouble deciding, think about why that might be so.
- If you could ask any or all of these teachers a question or two about the goals they hold, what would those questions be?

SECTION SUMMARY Goal Frameworks and Good Citizens

- A goal framework should help teachers decide *how* to design learning opportunities, *what* the opportunities should consist of, *when* to put them in place and in what order, and how to explain *why* engaging these opportunities is important.
- In social studies, most goal frameworks center on the education of "good citizens."
- Four common goal frameworks define good citizenship alternatively as a) good workers, b) knowledgeable and informed thinkers, c) well-rounded human beings, and d) social activists.

Educational Goal Frameworks and the Supporting Arguments

Above we have four teachers who all work from the same curriculum guidelines, yet take four quite different approaches. How do we account for these differences? Why do they have such disparate views of the curriculum? of citizenship? As we discuss in Chapter 5, one part of the answer is the many personal, organizational, and policy influences that affect teachers' decisions about subject matter, teaching approaches, and most importantly, the goals they pursue. In many ways, these four teachers represent four ways these various influences play out in the social studies classroom.

You may be wondering if it is good practice for these teachers—all from the same school district and ostensibly following the same curriculum guidelines—to be working from such different goal frameworks, with different definitions of what it means to educate the good citizen. It's a good question, for it illuminates the fact that each of the goal frameworks and definitions of good citizenship is rooted in a long history of arguments about how schools should educate children and create citizens. As a larger culture, we cannot agree on what a good citizen is; it is no surprise that these teachers do not agree either.

Arguments are efforts designed to persuade. It is essential to recognize the ongoing debate over what makes a good citizen, and that this debate is among groups of people who value certain ideas and wish to persuade others to share their values. For our purposes here, we will discuss only those arguments that address and support the goal frameworks embedded in the stories of the four teachers you just read. However, these are only four of perhaps twice that many arguments about how schools educate good citizens.

Educating Workers

Because much of adult life relates to being a productive worker in whatever capacity, one could say that the social studies role in educating good citizens ought to be to teach in ways that help train children for life's adult work roles. Those who support this view argue that children should learn to get their work done efficiently and effectively, to follow rules, to listen to authority figures, and to become disciplined competent members of the work world. Doing so helps to create citizens who participate in the economy via the process of being wise producers and informed consumers.

Teachers like Tom Simpson emphasize the importance of individual achievement and good work habits.

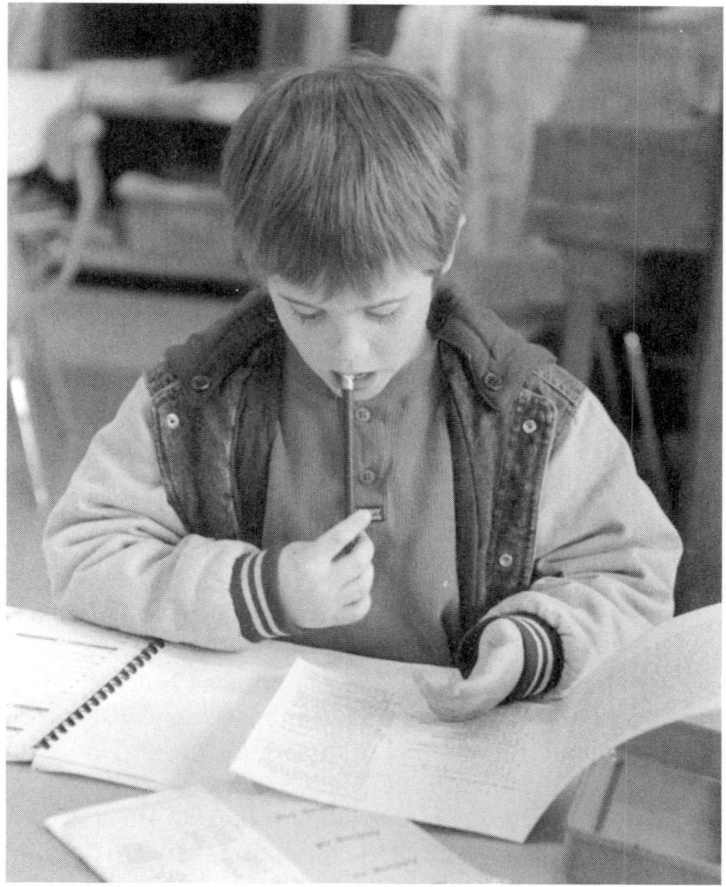

You have probably heard much talk recently concerning America's place in the burgeoning world economy. This talk spawns increased calls for training students more diligently in school subjects, so that they will be better able to help America compete in an increasingly competitive and information-driven world. You may have heard teachers talk about the importance of helping students become good workers in the classroom as a prelude to becoming valued contributors to the life of work after school.

Embedded in Tom Simpson's approach is just such a view: Learners become good citizens when they become good workers. Students learn to consume the culturally 0authoritative textbook content and reproduce it on tests and worksheets. Simpson's classroom tends to mirror the world of workers going to work and doing their jobs (studying the textbook), producing things (test results), earning their paychecks (grades) and reaping the rewards by exchanging their earnings for what they want (praise from parents, academic degrees, good jobs). Simpson structures his classroom to serve his goal of getting students ready for the world by creating an environment that tries to mirror that world. In short, it is education as work and as preparation for the world of intelligent consumption and competitive production in our democratic, capitalist system.

Providing a Liberal Democratic Education

CHOOSING GOALS

A second, rather different way to understand messages about school goals comes from what some call the liberal democratic educational ideal. *Liberal democratic education* as a goal framework means, generally speaking, that students are taught about the society's culture and ways of doing things, such as its political methods and its social and economic interactions. This knowledge, so the argument goes, enables them to become intelligent, creative, adaptive members of their communities and of our democratic society as a whole. It encourages them to be wise consumers, who are actively involved participants in the democratic process. This goal stance can be traced to Thomas Jefferson and to European Enlightenment Age social philosophers such as John Locke. But it has deeper roots. The early Greeks talked about *phronesis,* the well-educated wise person making informed decisions on the basis of the greatest good for the community. This liberal education ideal is deeply melded to American culture, its history, and its cultural institutions. As a goal framework, it drives much of what public schools choose to do, how they organize their curricula, and how they make value choices.

Knowledge in this framework is usually thought of as a product of universities, through scientific research, careful study, and published scholarship. This is why schools typically have built their curricula around subject matters that sound like university departments and colleges. Students amass a liberal educa-

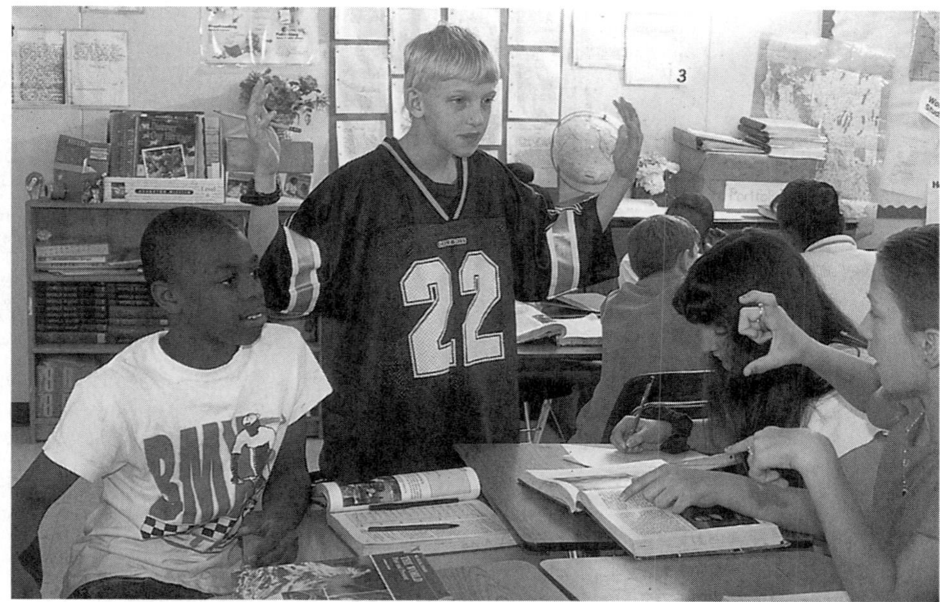

Ramona Palmer and other teachers who espouse a liberal democratic philosophy of education believe in the importance of ideas. What elements of this photograph support the liberal democratic stance?

tion in chemistry, sociology, art, history, literature, and so on, and therefore become capable of accepting their democratic rights and exercising their responsibilities soundly, reflectively, actively, and with respect and concern for their community. Although the stress here is on becoming knowledgeable about ideas already created within the culture, this goal framework also leaves room for students to invent new ways of seeing and understanding the world through a focus on the importance of curiosity about and systematic inquiry into how things work.

You have probably heard some teachers talk about their goal frameworks using these ideas. They might say "I want my children to be well-educated, so that when they leave school, they can think for themselves and evaluate ideas, political propaganda, sales pitches, and the like. I want them to make wise choices when they vote and become involved in their communities, to do good for others, and participate in making society a better place to live. This requires them to earn a good education and be knowledgeable and also to be curious and inquisitive, to question and assess. And it all starts right here in my classroom."

Ramona Palmer believes that history is one of those academic disciplines that provides a rich store of the knowledge Americans need to be liberally educated, to develop rich habits of mind that allow them to think and reason intelligently about issues they confront in their daily lives and in the world around them. From history they learn about the struggles inherent in building of their country, about its political, economic, and social systems, about its successes and its failures. Without this understanding and deep knowledge, Palmer believes that her students simply will not be educated enough to become good citizens in American democratic cultural life.

Although she is working from the same curriculum guidelines and using the same textbook, Ramona Palmer differs from Tom Simpson in that she operates from a goal framework that goes beyond preparation for adult work roles and the consumer-producer environment he creates in his classroom. One could argue that Palmer's approach tacitly encompasses some features of Simpson's work world, but she explicitly goes beyond it by asking students to engage the subject matter more deeply, to think, argue about, and assess what they are learning. Students in Palmer's class are more independent and self-engaged than are Simpson's students because Palmer organizes their learning that way. She interprets the curriculum guidelines differently from Simpson, largely because she is working from different arguments about what good citizenship is, arguments designed to support her quite different goal framework.

Nurturing a Humanist Perspective

CHOOSING GOALS

Did you ever meet a teacher who talked about the importance of students learning to feel good about themselves, to search for the meaning of their experience and the experiences of others, to develop strong interpersonal skills? This sounds like Tina Roberts, whose talk is usually coupled with commentary on how these personal growth factors are essential to the development of healthy, competent, well-rounded people who serve society in admirable ways and are therefore exemplary citizens. This view centers on introspection, learning to appreciate one's self and developing a fun-loving sense of self and others, resulting in a deep commitment to care and concern about human beings. This view of good citizenship as well-rounded humans is expressed in schools and classrooms that nurture and support the social growth of children.

Such is the humanist educational goal framework. It has its roots in much the same period as the liberal democratic educational goal, but with social thinkers such as Jean-Jacques Rousseau. In fact, the two approaches share much common language. The principal difference between them is in the nature of how knowledge is directed and understood. In the humanist stance, knowledge is directed inward, toward knowing one's self, and it is understood, in part, through self-reflection. In the liberal educational approach, by contrast, knowledge is directed outward, toward self-in-the-world, and it is understood largely, but not entirely, through academic scholarship.

Tina Roberts appears committed to the humanist approach in her teaching. She wants her children to develop into citizens who care about others because

Activities such as this one, in which students paint African ceremonial masks, are typical of classrooms where humanist perspectives are enacted. The academic benefits of this activity may be clear, but what individual and social benefits might the students be realizing through this activity?

they have learned to care first about themselves. Because they participate in the pleasant activities Roberts organizes in her classroom to enhance their own self-esteem, they develop into citizens who wish to do well by their fellow citizens, or so Roberts hopes. She develops fun and enjoyable in-class activities that reduce conflict and dispute, and allow budding citizens to work together toward ends that actualize their full potential and, by extension, the potential of the culture as a whole.

Encouraging Social Change

CHOOSING GOALS

The fourth argument sounds something like a call to arms. Here, the goal framework involves the desire to create citizens who are competent, intelligently informed, and socially engaged precisely because they are activists intent on changing the system locally, nationally, and internationally. Educational goals, so this argument suggests, ought to be about showing students the injustices and mistakes we make as a society and as individuals, and what to do to change them. Schools and education are used to level the playing field by, for example, providing the poor with opportunities to avoid poverty and obtain the same wealth the rich hold, thus making for a more just and humane society.

The students in this photograph are helping serve a Thanksgiving dinner in their community. Their involvement, facilitated by their teacher, demonstrates that student learning can take place just as easily outside as inside classroom walls.

Some observers suggest that, in fact, American public schools are the embodiment of equal educational opportunity. Others claim that our schools are stratified into rich and poor just as is society itself, that they perpetuate the status quo, and that fundamental changes need to occur.

RELEVANT RESEARCH

You might wish to read Jonathan Kozol's (1991) book, *Savage Inequalities,* as a case in point.

In this goal framework, effective citizenship education is about creating knowledgeable people who can inquire into, recognize, and challenge the problems of and injustices in local, national, and international communities. Such people become involved in that they actively seek to organize themselves in ways that allow them to fight for better living, working, and general sociocultural conditions. The civil rights workers of the 1960s, by this definition, are a pointed illustration of social change activists.

According to this argument, teachers should help students understand and create knowledge about the world and use it to act upon the injustices inherent in that world. Teachers also have a responsibility to challenge assumptions learners typically have about the world, especially those assumptions held by students who come from privileged backgrounds.

This sounds like Sara Atkinson. Compared to Tom Simpson's ideas, for example, Atkinson's definition of developing a good citizen is notably different from educating future workers. In fact, she rejects the students-as-future-workers goal framework because she finds injustices in it, such as exploited workers and unsafe working conditions. She differs from Tina Roberts in that she teaches the very content Roberts studiously avoids as a lesson in detecting injustices and moving toward social activism. In some ways, Atkinson is more like Ramona Palmer. However, she worries less about engaging students in the content as deeply as Palmer does. She's more interested in those elements of the American Revolution that allow her to pursue her goal framework and more willing to bypass content that provides no lessons for the future. Atkinson, too, wants knowledgeable citizens, but for a different purpose. Good citizens, to her, are social and political activists; they use their knowledge of history, for example, to seek out and attack social and cultural injustices.

TEACHER REFLECTION

Changing Ideas, Changing Goals

Reflect back on the set of questions we posed at the beginning of this section. After reading the arguments supporting the various goal frameworks, have any of your responses to those questions changed? In what ways? What questions are you now thinking about?

SECTION SUMMARY Arguments Supporting Goals Frameworks

- The goal frameworks most teachers employ have their roots in enduring arguments about the nature of schooling in general and in the education of good citizens in particular.
- The good-worker goal reflects the educating-workers argument; the knowledgeable-informed-citizen goal reflects the liberal education ideal position; the well-rounded human-being goal reflects the humanist perspective; and the social-change stance reflects the social-activist goal.

Sources for Guidance About Goals

CHOOSING GOALS

A visit to classrooms in any school is likely to turn up examples of all four goal frameworks; they tend to be fairly ubiquitous. But which one is right for you? Remember, each goal framework is comprised of arguments about what it means to be a good citizen. You must decide which argument (or perhaps none of them) is most persuasive to you, and use it to construct your own goal framework. At the moment, you probably are leaning toward one or more that resonate with your own values, education, history, and community background. However, before choosing, let's look at several places where you might get further guidance about developing a goal framework. After all, if your framework influences your decisions about the when, what, where, and why of creating learning opportunities for your students, you will need to think hard about formulating it. One way to do this would be to consult a variety of sources about potential social studies teaching and learning goals.

The Standards Movement

The 1990s have seen a move toward establishing national curriculum standards. Many different organizations have weighed in on this effort, including state boards and departments of education from Maine to California and federally-funded organizations such as the National Center for History in the Schools. Let's see what several of these groups say about establishing a goal framework.

National Council for the Social Studies standards The National Council for the Social Studies (NCSS) created a set of standards called *Curriculum Standards for Social Studies: Expectations of Excellence* (National Council for the Social Studies, 1994). These thematic standards, listed in the accompanying box, represent ten curriculum target areas in which to situate goals.

TEN THEMATIC CURRICULUM STANDARDS FOR SOCIAL STUDIES: FROM THE NATIONAL COUNCIL FOR THE SOCIAL STUDIES

1. Culture
2. Time, Continuity, and Change
3. People, Places, and Environments
4. Individual Development and Identity
5. Individuals, Groups, and Institutions
6. Power, Authority, and Governance
7. Production, Distribution, and Consumption
8. Science, Technology, and Society
9. Global Connections
10. Civic Ideals and Practices

PERFORMANCE EXPECTATIONS FOR NCSS SOCIAL STUDIES CURRICULUM STANDARD #2

A. To demonstrate an understanding of how different people describe the same events over time

B. To correctly use language connected with history (change, continuity, timeline, etc.)

C. To compare and contrast different historical stories and accounts

D. To use source material in reconstructing an understanding of the past

E. To understand how time has shaped our differing views of history

F. To use knowledge of history and methods of inquiry to help with decision-making and taking action on public issues.

Because we cannot study all ten standards here, we'll take a detailed look at just one, Standard 2, Time, Continuity, and Change, to see if we can ferret out the goals NCSS is recommending. We focus on this standard because the four teachers above teach history and this standard deals with that subject area.

One way to understand the goals behind this standard is to explore the student "performance expectations." From these expectations, one can detect specific goals behind each standard. Consider the elementary-level expectations for Standard 2 as listed in the accompanying box.

Here, and throughout NCSS standards, the authors appear to assume that the primary goal of schooling is for students to engage and learn subject matter. Thus, akin to their definition of social studies, NCSS seems to embed its goal framework primarily in the liberal educational ideal. But also notice the trace of social activism connected to this target area, as when the authors suggest "taking action on public issues."

TEACHER REFLECTION

Interpreting Performance Expectations

Think about how each of the teachers presented earlier might interpret these performance expectations. What similarities might emerge? What differences?

NCSS Standards

For more on the ten NCSS Thematic Social Studies Standards and each of the performance targets, visit the NCSS web site at http://www.ncss.org. Follow the links on "Thematic Curriculum Standards."

National history standards If, like the four teachers we have discussed, you find yourself teaching a heavy dose of history, you might take a close look at the *National Standards for History, Basic Edition* (National Center for History in the Schools, 1996). In the first chapter of these standards, the authors discuss the importance of understanding history for the "educated citizen." Reading this preface quickly takes one back to Thomas Jefferson, and sounds like a full embrace of the liberal educational ideal. Again, this should be no big surprise; this ideal has deep roots in our culture.

At one point, the authors state:

> *Knowledge of history is the precondition of political intelligence.* Without history, society shares no common memory of where it has been, what its core values are, or what decisions of the past account for present circumstances. Without history, we cannot undertake any sensible inquiry into the political, social, or moral issues in society. And without historical knowledge and inquiry, we cannot achieve the informed, discriminating citizenship essential to effective participation in the democratic process. . . . (National Center for History in the Schools, 1996, p. 1, emphasis in the original.)

This statement clearly attempts to define good citizenship. It expresses the liberal educational ideal through its view of citizens as knowledgeable, able to inquire about issues, and able to make informed judgments and act on them. In many respects, it relates the importance of history to preparation for life in our democracy, for life as an active participating citizen. It does not spell out a form of social activism per se, but it hints at it nonetheless.

For elementary teachers who teach American history, the *National Standards for History* are well worth reading. These standards go farther than many documents in spelling out important and engaging content and examples of student learning expectations.

Ideas for Teaching History

We recommend that you read *Bring History Alive! A Sourcebook for Teaching United States History* (Ankeney, Del Rio, Nash, & Vigilante, 1996). This books gives insight into how the authors of the *National Standards for History* think history should be taught in schools. It also reveals more about the goal frameworks behind the history standards.

Other content-standards documents Among the host of other national standards documents, many, like the *National Standards for History,* were commissioned and funded by the federal government. They deal with such subject areas as world history, geography, economics, and civics. We lack the space here to look at all these standards, but they are out there and might be worthwhile reading as you construct your own goal framework. In the accompanying box see some of these other standards organizations, their documents, and the social studies subject areas they address.

TEACHING RESOURCES

Curriculum Standards by Social Studies Subject Area

Standards Document (Organization)	**Subject**	**Grade Levels**
Geography for Life: National Geography Standards (National Geographic Society, 1994)	Geography	2, 3, 4, 5 Middle School
National Standards for Civics and Government (Center for Civic Education, 1994)	Civics/Government	2, 3, 4, 5 Middle School
Voluntary National Content Standards in Economics (National Council on Economic Education, 1997)	Economics	3, 4, 5 Middle School
National Standards for World History: Exploring Paths to the Present (National Center for History in the Schools, 1994)	World History	Middle School

National Board for Professional Teaching Standards The National Board for Professional Teaching Standards (NBPTS) (1994) also has produced a set of social studies-history teaching guidelines. The NBPTS consists of eleven target

NATIONAL BOARD FOR PROFESSIONAL TEACHING STANDARDS TARGET AREAS

1. Knowledge of Students
2. Knowledge of Subject Matter
3. Advancing Disciplinary Knowledge and Understanding
4. Promoting Social Understanding
5. Developing Civic Competence
6. Instructional Resources
7. Learning Environments
8. Assessment
9. Reflection
10. Family Partnerships
11. Collaboration

areas or standards teachers should attain if they wish to be certified by the NBPTS. These target areas are a rich source of ideas related to creating a goal framework. The accompanying box lists the eleven areas.

In each area, the NBPTS makes a series of recommendations social studies teachers should work toward in order to become master teachers. The areas make no explicit statements about what students need to learn, but they do suggest a goal framework through the standards they recommend. For example, drawing from several of the areas, the NBPTS believes that master social studies teachers know their subject matter (for example, history, geography) deeply; know their students just as well; teach social studies for intellectual and social understanding and for civic competence; seek out and use high-quality instructional resources; and create classroom environments and assessment practices that support the attainment of the foregoing. In several ways, the NBPTS appears to promote specific teaching practices and approaches that support the liberal-educational goal framework.

Definitions of Social Studies

It should be clear by now that many resources exist to help teachers clarify what they want to accomplish with students in schools. But is this always the case?

To take a closer look at this question, return with us for a moment to the definition of social studies offered by the National Council for the Social Studies, which contains some important statements that suggest guidance on goals.

The NCSS definition of social studies In the following NCSS definition of social studies, pay particular attention to the first and last sentences. These essentially are goal statements that we will analyze more carefully as we look for guidance about choosing teaching and learning goals.

> Social studies is the integrated study of the social sciences and humanities to promote civic competence. Within the school program, social studies provides coordinated, systematic study drawing upon such disciplines as anthropology, archeology, economics, geography, history, law, philosophy, political science, psychology, religion, and sociology. The primary purpose of social studies is to help young people develop the ability to make informed and reasoned decisions for the public good as citizens of a culturally diverse, democratic society in an interdependent world. (National Council for the Social Studies, 1993, p. 7)

What do the first and last sentences mean? What does it mean to "promote civic competence," and to "help young people develop the ability to make informed and reasoned decisions for the public good?" Does the latter phrase define the former? It seems as though the root message here is about educating good citizens, but what is a "good" citizen? As we have seen, it can be defined according to one of several different arguments designed to persuade that certain values are better than others in developing citizens. Also, upon closer scrutiny, we see that the goals implied in this definition are difficult to see clearly, largely because the definition is broad and all encompassing. This is often the case with such goals and standards documents because, to satisfy many different educational groups, they try to include many elements of different goal frameworks at once, and therefore produce goal frameworks that are quite vague. Based on this NCSS definition, it's tough to say for sure what the argument is here, so let's explore this further.

Similarities in language between the liberal and humanistic goals make it easy to read the NCSS definition and its goal sentences as *either* an example of a liberal education *or* the humanist goal position. In other words, the NCSS statement is roomy enough to allow a Palmer or a Roberts to find herself in it and to claim she is teaching social studies in the name of creating good citizens. At the same time, the NCSS definition language is open enough to suggest other possibilities. A social activist like Atkinson could appropriate the NCSS statement, claiming that competence be defined as the basis for social action. Yet, Simpson might also feel comfortable with this definition because competence could easily be interpreted to mean learning basic facts. The point here is that statements that reflect goal frameworks require careful study. Often what seems good in print means little in practice because terms and statements need further interpreting and defining. Our point is simple: In the pursuit of a thoughtful goal framework, understand that not all resources are equally useful.

Variations on the Definition of Good Citizenship

The debates and discussions around the definition of social studies in general, and around the definition of good citizenship in particular, have fed a small industry of groups who have tried to define with greater clarity what they think good citizenship should be and the social studies role in helping to shape it. As you develop as a social studies teacher, we invite you to consult the expanse of social studies literature that has grown up around various ways to define and to specify a curriculum for social studies and good citizenship. But for now, let's briefly examine some examples of this literature.

Issues-centered social studies One example is **issues-centered social studies,** or ICSS (Engle & Ochoa, 1988; Evans & Saxe, 1996; Goodman, 1992). Advocates of ICSS seek to use the social studies as a vehicle for developing knowledge in students that can enable them to address public issues that need attention in the nation and world. ICSS is rooted in the social-activist goal approach (although this assumption too can be questioned; see Grant & Tzetzo, 1997) that we see most clearly in Atkinson's treatment of the American Revolution. To a large degree, proponents of ICSS believe that the goal of social studies teaching and learning is the education of democratic citizens who are deeply knowledgeable about their world, can use their knowledge to understand social justice issues, and employ this understanding to address and redress those issues.

Multicultural education Another approach to good citizenship can be seen in **multicultural education,** or MCE (Banks, 1994; Ladson-Billings, 1994; Sleeter & Grant, 1994). Proponents of MCE look to social studies as one area of the curriculum that can help students to develop greater awareness of the ethnic and racial diversity of our culture. This awareness promotes a view of good citizenship that turns on a greater appreciation of the strengths of cultural diversity, a tolerance for different world views, and a culture that is free from bigotry, intolerance, and racism.

Caveat Emptor (Buyer Beware)

Each of the above definitions is broad. None defines good citizenship in specific, concrete terms; each leaves that to the reader. We can understand why these authors might have avoided this task; there is nothing straight-forward about defining these terms. Their potential to provide guidance, however, suffers from such a wide array of possible interpretations. As odd as it may seem, goals documents and definition statements may lack both clear goals and specific definitions, and so they must be studied carefully.

Beginning teachers, and many more experienced ones look at all these standards and definitions and wonder, do they cohere? Does one voice unite them all? Unfortunately the answer is no. As we have said, goal frameworks are about arguments, arguments about what's best for students. Within our culture, we are not in complete agreement about how to educate students for the society at large. We differ politically, racially, ethnically, and socially, and therefore we argue about and differ with regard to educational goals. This is the case also among those who recommend goal frameworks for teaching social studies. In some respects, disagreement over goal frameworks gives you some autonomy in choosing them because we have no *final* authoritative source to which we can appeal to settle the debate. This may seem like a mixed blessing, particularly when you first are learning to teach. But you will cherish this autonomy after you become more masterful at your chosen profession.

SECTION SUMMARY **Guidance Toward Goals**

- Teachers have additional sources for finding guidance in developing a goal framework. These sources include, for example, documents emerging from the curriculum standards movement, a definition of social studies developed by NCSS, and several other ways of defining social studies and its relationship to citizenship (for example, ICSS, MCE).
- None of these sources, however, has a corner on the goal framework market, leaving to you the task of constructing a goal framework for yourself from the resources available.

Building a Goal Framework

CHOOSING GOALS

By now you can see that making goal choices involves embracing some ideas and letting others go. This is important, for most teachers we know have difficulty attending to a whole mixed bag of goals. You might blend together some of the goals evinced by the four teachers profiled, but quite frankly, we suspect that you would end up sending your young students confusing and mixed messages about what is important. A few features of each goal framework may be compatible, but for the most part, the four arguments for good citizenship are different enough that blending *all* of them together would be difficult and futile.

A better approach is to locate your teaching practice primarily within one goal framework and add compatible pieces such that you tailor-make a framework that reflects your values, beliefs, and strengths. The metaphor of a restaurant meal may help you conceptualize this: Think of your primary goal framework as the entree and the compatible pieces from other goal frameworks as side dishes. *How* you mix your goal framework and compatible pieces—entree and side dishes—is less important than the product—a complete and satisfying meal, er . . . goal framework.

Consider how Tom Simpson and Ramona Palmer have seasoned their goal conceptions. Simpson thinks good citizenship is all about competitive, hard work; adept consumption and production; and other such efforts that prepare his charges for their adult roles as workers in a market economy. This stance reflects the goal of educating workers as the means to producing good citizens. At the same time, however, Simpson adds something of the flavor of the liberal education agenda in that he expects his students to know the facts of American history. We might disagree that factual knowledge is sufficient, but many observers would argue that Simpson's focus on facts defines a good education (see, for example, Hirsch, 1987, 1999). Ramona Palmer's goal framework also reflects some diversity. Palmer teaches her students the importance of being informed about the past in order to enhance their own decision-making capabilities—a standard expression of the liberal education ideal. Palmer augments that focus, however, with elements of the good-worker stance, in that, like Simpson she values some types of competitive work settings.

Both teachers give attention to the educating-workers and liberal-education positions, yet each focuses on one position: Simpson's goal framework features an entree of educating workers with a side order of liberal education; Palmer's goal framework is just the reverse, educating workers is the side order to her main meal, which is creating knowledgeable and informed citizens in the liberal education tradition.

TEACHER REFLECTION

Compatible or Incompatible Goals?

Now think about Tina Roberts and Sara Atkinson. What compatible elements, side orders if you will, can you detect encompassed within their goal frameworks? Do any elements seem incompatible?

Thinking about your goal framework as an entree with complimentary side orders should help you begin building your own goal framework. To push yourself to greater clarity on this issue of social studies goals, ask yourself the accompanying reflective questions, and make a list of your responses as you go.

Clarifying Social Studies Goals

1. What should be the purposes of social studies teaching?
2. What should students learn from social studies and be able to do once they learn it?
3. What is my definition of a "good citizen"?
4. In what ways do my responses to the first three questions reflect my values?
5. How are my responses to the first three questions complementary?
6. In what ways are my responses contradictory? How so?

You also might talk over and perhaps debate these questions with fellow practicing and prospective teachers in order to get a sense about how others think about these goal issues. Making your ideas public is a good way of deepening your understanding.

SECTION SUMMARY **Building a Goal Framework**

- Building a goal framework is no easy task.
- When you build your framework, avoid blindly choosing a mix of elements from various other frameworks.
- A better approach is to build your framework around a primary goal stance to which you add complementary elements.

Some Parting Thoughts

CHOOSING GOALS

So far, our effort here has been to (1) familiarize you with a nonexhaustive range of possible stances you could take, (2) ask how your stance reflects your values, and (3) argue that your goal framework influences the way you make teaching and learning decisions in your social studies classroom. We are hoping this quick trip through the goal menu will help you become more reflective about your goal positions and help you avoid the trap of thinking that teaching is nothing more than teaching technique. Thinking more clearly about your goals will help you to think more clearly about what learning opportunities to provide your students, when and how to provide them, and why.

Our Choice: The Liberal Education Goal

CHOOSING GOALS

As both school and university teachers, we hold to the liberal-educational ideal argument for the following reasons:

- It appears to drive much of what we ideally know schools, teaching, and curriculum to be.
- It likely will have the most profound influence on you as you move into teaching elementary school social studies because of its deep roots in American cultural institutions.
- It holds the greatest promise for allowing aspects of other goals to be embedded within it.

The liberal educational ideal is a broad framework, which may account for much of its appeal in a culture that prides itself on the importance of democratic participation in the affairs of community, state, and nation, from political to sociocultural, economic to familial, and so on. We think that appeal is well-deserved.

The liberal educational ideal requires thoughtful, well-educated, well-rounded citizens who are willing to engage deeply in the lives of their communities, both large and small, close and distant. They value historical and social science knowledge, for example, and use such knowledge to benefit their communities. They also value constructive debate about courses of action, are concerned that all voices are heard in such debates, and are sensitive to the consequences of possible choices. In several ways, Ramona Palmer, comes the closest of the four teachers we've profiled in this chapter to working toward this ideal. We consider something like this ideal a worthy place to set up *your* social studies goal framework. It gives you considerable flexibility to adjust and modify it as you go. However, that's *our* argument. We still recognize that it's up to you to decide, and decide you must. We simply hope that you choose wisely.

CHAPTER SUMMARY

1. What are several common educational goal frameworks that influence social studies?

A goal framework is a means by which you decide *how* to design learning opportunities, *what* the opportunities should consist of, *when* to put them in place and in what order, and how to explain *why* engaging these opportunities is important. In social studies, goal frameworks commonly revolve around definitions of good citizenship. There is no one definition that all teachers work from, instead numerous definitions are in circulation. These definitions characterize good citizens as good workers, knowledgeable and informed citizens, well-rounded human beings, and social activists. Teachers build goals to match the definition that they most support.

2. What enduring arguments support different goal frameworks?

The competing goal frameworks reflect enduring debates about the nature of schooling and of citizenship. The good-workers goal comes out of the educating-workers argument; the knowledgeable-citizens goal comes out of the liberal-educational ideal; the well-rounded human-being goal comes out of the humanist perspective; and the social-activist goal comes out of the social-change position.

3. Where can teachers go for guidance in choosing a goal framework?

Several sources are available for teachers seeking guidance in developing a goal framework. None of these sources—curriculum standards and definitions of citizenship—is all-encompassing, but they serve a useful purpose as ways to provoke teachers' thinking.

4. What goes into building a goal framework?

Although teachers may feel comfortable, firmly ensconced in a single perspective, many will want to broaden their frameworks. One way to do that is to develop a goals stance that has a primary focus (for example, one of the goal positions outlined), to which the teacher adds complementary elements.

5. What is the case for working from the liberal-education goal framework?

Although we can see pros and cons within all goal frameworks, we find ourselves drawn most consistently to the definition of good citizens as knowledgeable and informed, which is reflected in the liberal educational ideal. The ideal is deeply wedded to our culture, it's had a profound impact on educational practice, and it offers enough room to accommodate other goal framework elements within it.

TEACHING RESOURCES

Print Resources

Butts, R. F. (1980). *The revival of civic learning.* Washington, DC: Phi Delta Kappa Educational Foundation. This classic text on citizenship education offers some valuable insights into the various definitions of the good citizen.

Technology Resources

- **http://www.civiced.org**

One of the functions of the Center for Civic Education is to act as a clearinghouse for programs, materials, and professional growth opportunities related to citizenship education. You will find much of value by searching the Center's web site.

- **http://www.ncss.org**
- **http://www.sscnet.ucla.edu/nchs**

These two sites, the National Council for the Social Studies and the National Center for History in the Schools, offer useful places to examine standards documents in light of the goal frameworks they offer. For state-level standards documents, visit the respective state education department web sites, such as http://www.nysed.gov for New York State.

Chapter 8

Unit Planning and the Commonplaces

Now it's time to start thinking about how we fit together the many ideas and practices described in this book. This is no small task. Let's get to it.

Unit planning is central to successful teaching and learning. In your unit plan you will outline your instructional intentions. But you don't simply pull a unit plan off the shelf or off the Internet! A successful unit plan will exemplify your best thinking about the interaction of learning, teaching, and subject matter in the content of the classroom environment in which you teach.

We divide this chapter into two sections. In the first, we revisit the commonplaces of education as you think about some of the teachers you have read about in earlier chapters and about how you might use the commonplaces to think through some typical classroom problems. With this background, we turn to the practical issues of writing a unit plan. To do so, we offer unit plans developed by two of our students to illustrate the unit planning process.

When you have completed this chapter, you should be able to answer the following questions:

1. ***How do the commonplaces help teachers understand and analyze classroom situations and problems?***
2. ***What are the components of a unit plan?***
3. ***What purposes does unit planning serve?***

Pulling It All Together: The Commonplaces

The commonplaces of education—learners and learning, subject matter, teachers and teaching, and classroom environment—offer a useful framework for understanding social studies classrooms.

- Thinking about *learners and learning* pushes us to remember that teaching is not a solitary act. One does not prepare, deliver, and assess lessons in a vacuum. Instead, teaching is about interacting with real, live children who come to class with a variety of experiences, and who will make various sense of the ideas you teach.

- Thinking about *subject matter* encourages us to remember that teaching is always about teaching something—the It in David Hawkins' (1974) triangle of I (teacher), Thou (learner), and It (subject)—and that subject matter is about ideas. In the case of social studies, those ideas relate to the human condition and to how and why people live (and have lived) as they do.

- Thinking about *teachers and teaching* spurs us to remember that teaching is more than delivering instruction, and that what happens before we teach (planning) and afterward (assessment) are equally as important.
- And, finally, thinking about *classroom environment* urges us to remember that teaching, learning, and subject matter all occur in a context and that context matters. Teachers send powerful messages to students through their decisions about curriculum, teaching methods, and assessment. They also send important messages through the kind of classroom discourse, organization, and dispositions they foster.

Using the Commonplaces to Analyze Classroom Situations

Each of the commonplace components is useful in its own right. As we have suggested, however, the real power of the commonplaces emerges when one views them in interaction, that is, seeing how each contributes to or detracts from a classroom situation.

To demonstrate this point, let's return to two teachers from Chapter 4, Sandra Prosy and Pam Derson. When we presented these teachers, we did so to illustrate issues around teachers and teaching. In what follows, we encourage you to expand your exploration of their teaching in light of what you now understand about the other commonplaces.

Sandra Prosy (Chapter 4) reminds us of many traditional elementary school teachers. We do not doubt her sincere intentions, but her instruction resembles the kind of teaching students regularly describe as boring. Considered from a commonplaces perspective, we can see how Prosy's teaching makes sense: Her views of learners and learning, subject matter, teachers and teaching, and classroom environment all support one another. But taken together, those views also support a thin approach to teaching social studies.

The fourth-grade teacher (on the left) and student teacher (in the middle) are listening as the leader of a small group explains how they want to work on their project. What commonplaces can you infer from this scene?

Consider how Prosy's view of *learners and learning* interacts with her view of *subject matter.* Her view of learners reflects the traditional notion that children learn best when ideas are broken down into the finest details. Learning, she believes, is a process of accumulating these details. The subject matter she chooses—the "facts" about the U.S. government—supports that view of learners. Prosy seems interested in learning what facts her children already know, but she pursues no questions and gives students no opportunities that would provide a deep connection to the students' lives. Instead, she assumes that fifth-graders should study government for its own sake, and that they will know about government when they know all the facts.

Prosy's views of *teaching* and *classroom environment* intersect with the commonplaces above. She sees teaching as the act of transmitting into her learners' heads the knowledge that she and the textbook hold. To that end, she uses traditional means of instruction such as worksheets, end-of-chapter reviews, and I-R-E questioning. Not surprisingly, then, Prosy's classroom environment is a traditional one: the discourse is primarily teacher-centered, classroom work is done individually, and the favored dispositions are those of obeying the teacher, working quietly and efficiently, and seeking external rewards such as high grades and teacher praise.

Pam Derson (Chapter 4) represents a different kind of teacher, which becomes clear as one analyzes her teaching through the commonplaces. Well versed in her *subject matter,* Derson understands that the question "how do we know what we know" represents a powerful idea in social studies. She knows that *learning* includes capturing factual knowledge, but she also knows that facts need to add up to something. In this unit, she believes that the question of how we know what we know is worth thinking hard about. She also believes that her students will struggle with this idea until they find a way to connect it to their own lives.

And that leads us to consider her approach to *teaching* and the kind of *classroom environment* she strives for. Derson uses a variety of instructional and organizational approaches: individual, small-group, and whole-class lessons; assignments that span reading, writing, and other school subjects; classroom materials that reflect multiple points of view; and activities, such as the map-making exercise, that put learners squarely in the middle of a problem-solving situation. In these several ways, Derson sends strong messages about the kind of classroom environment she supports. Derson still does most of the talking, but the kind of talk she uses and the opportunities she provides for student talk look more like a conversation than a recitation. Moreover, the dispositions evident hint at the kind of emphasis on inquiry, ideas, arguments, and evidence found in genuine classroom communities.

Commonplaces in the Classroom

Now it is your turn. Think back to any of the several teachers we have presented—Ramona Palmer (Chapter 3), Janice Mead (Chapter 4), Don Kite (Chapter 5), or Suzanne Wilson (Chapter 6) and ask yourself how the commonplaces play out in each teacher's classroom.

We expect two things become obvious as you consider the teachers we've discussed with a view to the commonplaces. One is that "seeing" the commonplaces, both individually and in interaction, is easier now than it was earlier in this book. The second is that discerning and understanding the differences between teachers is easier from a commonplaces perspective. Both realizations should be useful as you refine your own teaching practice.

Using the individual commonplaces to isolate issues of learning or teaching or subject matter or classroom environment is helpful. But, as the examples above suggest, you get even more leverage if you try to understand classroom situations by bringing all four commonplaces to bear.

Using the Commonplaces to Understand Typical Classroom Problems

Teaching offers no hard and fast prescriptions for success, and so analyzing the classroom situations and experiences of other teachers is an important part of learning this craft. It is also important to learn from your own teaching experiences and to use the commonplaces as a means of understanding them. We can't anticipate all the classroom problems you might encounter, but we can imagine some of them, so let's try to think our way through them using the commonplaces.

"These kids just don't pay attention!" One of the most commonly reported classroom problems is student inattention. Inattention may surface as daydreaming, talking with a neighbor, behavior unrelated to the current activity, or sticking pencils up one's nose. (Kids say *and* do the darnedest things!) Now, a whole raft of reasons unrelated to your teaching may be behind this behavior. Problems at home or on the playground, for example, can cause children's attention to wander. More likely, however, the cause lies closer to the classroom; if so, thinking through the commonplaces may prove helpful. For example:

- *Consider what the students already know about the topic.* Students may already know the material you are discussing, or they may be missing a critical piece that you assume they have. Bored or confused learners are likely to drift off.

- *Consider whether the material connects with students' lives and interests.* The topic may be part of your curriculum, and you may even believe it is important, but if the students fail to see any particular relevance between it and what they know and care about, their attention may stray.
- *Consider whether the students can see the big idea that is driving the lesson.* Most students will cooperate if they have faith that their teacher is leading them someplace worthwhile. But even the most patient students will fall off if they cannot figure out where your instruction is leading.
- *Consider how you are teaching the lesson.* Everyone likes a little variety. Although you may favor small- and whole-group discussions, using only those approaches (or any other) may frustrate and discourage some students.
- *Consider what the classroom environment is communicating.* Do the children believe that what they have to say is important? Do they have opportunities to work with a variety of their peers? Do they sense that they have a stake in what goes on in class? If not, they may believe that they are just going through the routine of "doing school." And if that is the case, they are far more likely to seek more engaging activities—such as putting pencils up their noses.

And don't forget the "first sunny day in spring" factor. Only the strongest-willed child (or teacher!) can give his or her full attention as the smell of spring wafts through the classroom windows. Of course, you can close the windows and pull the shades, but the point is that children, like adults, are distractible, and some distractions are powerful indeed. As the list above suggests, however, many distractions are well within your ability to contend with, and thinking through the commonplaces may help you identify where the *real* problem(s) lies.

TEACHER REFLECTION

Using the Commonplaces

The following is a list of common classroom situations, all designed to drive teachers a little nutty. Use the commonplaces to think through what might be going on when students:

- do not cooperate on group assignments
- fail to meet the high academic expectations you hold
- score poorly on standardized tests
- talk out of turn
- say the work assigned is too difficult

- fail to do their homework
- look only for right answers
- lack the requisite background knowledge

How did you do? The commonplaces provide a framework for reflecting on classroom situations in general and to think through classroom problems more specifically. Using the commonplaces won't resolve classroom problems, but they will provide an important and useful analytic and planning tool and we urge you to work with them.

SECTION SUMMARY Using the Commonplaces

- Using the commonplaces individually and in interaction is a good way to analyze general classroom situations.
- The commonplaces also provide a useful framework for understanding specific classroom problems.

Pulling It All Together: The Unit Plan

Another task where the commonplaces prove useful is construction of classroom units. Unit planning has a technical aspect in that you must craft a realistic teaching plan of action. As you do that, however, remember that the units you design send strong messages about your values for learning, teaching, subject matter, and classroom environment.

In the following sections, we describe unit planning from four angles:

1. What is a unit plan?
2. What does a unit plan look like?
3. How do I develop a unit plan?
4. What purpose does a unit plan serve?

What Is a Unit Plan?

Put simply, a unit plan is an attempt to work through the many ideas, materials, approaches, and assessments that represent your best thinking about a chunk of subject matter. Unit plans can take many forms, but at their core, each plan addresses four questions:

- What am I planning to teach, and why should learners care? (Introduction)
- How does my big idea look spread out across the thread categories? (Threads)
- How is my big idea represented in my sequence of lessons? (Lessons)
- How will I know if the students understand what I am trying to teach? (Assessment)

To illustrate these questions and the ideas behind them, we draw from two unit plans developed by former students. One is Katie Salisbury's first-grade unit *What Makes a Good Citizen?* The second is Kristen Stricker's fourth-grade unit *What Is Freedom?*

What Does a Unit Plan Look Like?

The heart of a unit plan is the big idea and the classroom lessons that represent it. A complete unit plan, however, addresses the four questions posed above.

The introduction: What am I planning to teach, and why should learners care? The introduction to a unit plan does more than say, "Here it is!" A good introduction addresses what you are planning to teach, and why students should care. In other words, a reader should clearly understand where your unit is going, and why you consider it important to go there.

CHOOSING GOALS

For example, Katie Salisbury's unit, *What Makes a Good Citizen?*, explores the complex issue of good citizenship. As she explains, "There is no one clear view or definition of good citizen, [so] the focus of this unit will be to study the idea of citizenship through example, debate, and discussion." As her introduction continues, she explains:

> Developing a sense of citizenship is named as one of the primary goals in social studies education. When looking through the New York State curriculum, one will find little instructional direction as to how to undertake such a large endeavor. I see our role as educators as not to impose upon children one particular view of the proper role as a citizen, but to foster citizens who think for themselves and look at every issue that affects them from a variety of views.

Katie goes on to explain that she thinks students will embrace this unit because it addresses issues that are important to them and it encourages them to express their ideas and, if appropriate, to take action:

> The main goal is to keep the dialogue of important issues going in our classroom. We are trying to help the children to become more involved in and aware of the events that are going on around them and have a direct

affect on our world. We feel that one of the most important characteristics of a good citizen is her or his ability to stay informed. We hope that these topics will bring about rich discussions and possible points of action that our students would like to take for or against the issues we discuss.

TEACHING RESOURCES

What Students Care About

Children care about many subjects; their worlds are often much richer and complex than we adults credit. Finding out what particular subjects intrigue your students will take some time. As you create your initial social studies units, one source of ideas children find interesting is R. Freeman Butts's *Decalogue of Democratic Values* (1980, p. 128).

Justice	Freedom
Equality	Diversity
Authority	Privacy
Participation	Due Process
Personal Obligation for the Greater Good	International Human Rights

Butts suggests that these concepts represent enduring ideas and ideals Americans of all ages should think about. We agree, and social studies units that attend to one or more of these values are likely to strike a chord with your students.

CHOOSING GOALS

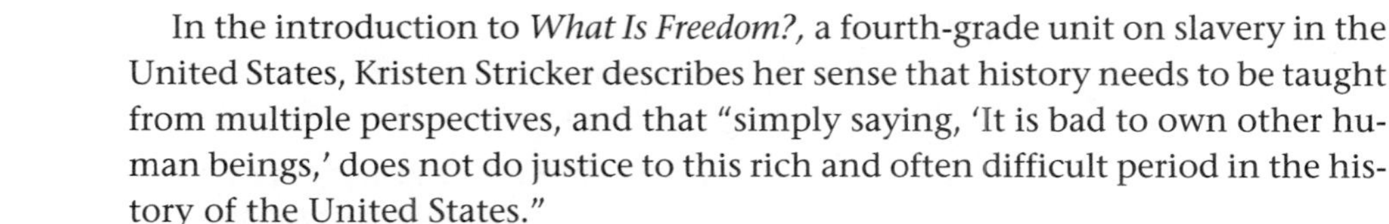

In the introduction to *What Is Freedom?,* a fourth-grade unit on slavery in the United States, Kristen Stricker describes her sense that history needs to be taught from multiple perspectives, and that "simply saying, 'It is bad to own other human beings,' does not do justice to this rich and often difficult period in the history of the United States."

Kristen puts forth a clear sense of why she chose to develop her unit. One driving impulse is her interest in integrating children's literature into social studies. Kristen knows that children respond particularly well to narrative text, and in the issue of slavery she sees ample opportunity to extend learners' knowledge and experiences through literature. A second impulse is to help her learners become "more understanding and empathic people." "Much of the heartbreak of the world," Kristen explains, "comes from people not listening to each other's views and realizing what another is feeling." She knows that her students are fascinated with their own lives and their own questions of what it means to be free. After all, Kristen asserts, "freedom is a central idea about what it means to be alive." She believes she can help her students understand themselves better by examining how others have dealt with questions of freedom and how they have lived their lives.

Your unit plan should center on the big idea and the learning activities that support it. A thoughtful introduction is useful, however, as a way to orient the reader to the unit and especially to provide a sense of how learners will benefit and why they should care about the subject matter at hand.

How does my big idea look spread out across the threads categories? A second useful piece in unit planning is a section where you demonstrate how your big idea maps onto the threads framework. We suggested in Chapter 3 that most any social studies topic can be better understood by exploring the geographic, political, economic, cultural, and global concept connections. Let's see how Katie and Kristen handle this part of their units.

Katie outlines the thread connections this way:

- GEOGRAPHIC: emphasizing the difference between nation, state, and community.
- POLITICAL: emphasizing the ideas of decision-making, laws, power, and the structure of government.
- ECONOMIC: emphasizing inequities in the distribution of resources throughout society.
- SOCIOCULTURAL: emphasizing the issues of race, ethnicity, gender, and education as well the differences among social classes.
- GLOBAL: emphasizing the notion of global citizenship.

In addition to this outline, Katie adds comments that illustrate her sense of how the thread in question made sense to her and to the unit. For example, under the political thread, she explains that, while she might find more opportunities to discuss political issues with older students, she'll use this unit to:

> . . . expose [my students] to the idea that real people can and have influenced the shaping of our government and its laws. I would like to illustrate for them that the government is a *body of people* that is changing all the time as decided by the people for whom they govern.

Katie concludes the threads section by returning to her main point, sparking in her students "the drive to develop in themselves the ability to question issues and become involved in the process of decision-making."

IN YOUR CLASSROOM: Interdisciplinary Teaching

Each of the thread categories represents a social science discipline (for example, geographic = geography). Using the threads to help organize the content you teach is an easy way of ensuring that your teaching is interdisciplinary. Good teachers like Katie and Kristen also incorporate other school subjects such as language arts, mathematics, and science when appropriate. As you are reading through these units, think about the many cross-subject connections these two teachers are making.

In her unit on slavery and freedom, Kristen also uses the threads to demonstrate the conceptual possibilities of her big idea. More specifically, Kristen notes that the threads "allow teachers to 'test' whether proposed topics are truly complex and generative." By "generative," Kristen means ideas that will encourage learners to see and think about new ideas. She adds that the threads can also be used as a graphic organizer for students.

An outline of the thread connections in Kristen's unit looks like this:

- GEOGRAPHIC: emphasizing the geography of slave-holding, the routes of the Atlantic slave trade and the Underground Railroad, and the demographics of free and enslaved Americans.
- POLITICAL: emphasizing laws related to slave-holding, the abolitionist movement, the legal end of slavery, and the status of African-Americans after the Civil War.
- ECONOMIC: emphasizing the origins of slavery, the notion of slaves as property, and the differences between free and slave labor.
- SOCIOCULTURAL: emphasizing the irony of slavery in the midst of an America cast as the "land of opportunity," the use of African folktales, spirituals, and quilts as means of outwitting their captors, and the changes in white and black relations.
- GLOBAL: emphasizing the African origins of American slavery, the Triangle Trade, and the international pressure on the U.S. to end slavery.

Kristen points out that even this abbreviated listing presents "much more information than I could ever hope my students could explore." She explains, however, that her big idea, *What Is Freedom?,* helps her and her learners keep track of the issues they consider important to examine.

How is my big idea represented in my sequence of lessons? Let's turn now to the sequences of lessons Katie and Kristen develop to support their big ideas. Katie constructs a series of eleven lessons aimed at helping her young learners work through a range of issues around citizenship. Some of those lessons ask students to think about themselves in relation to geographic and political borders—our planet, our continent, our nation, our state, our city, and our town. Other lessons encourage students to share their ideas about a "good citizen." Still others push students to consider issues of fairness, equality, and justice by using a piece of videotape from the PBS series, "Eyes on the Prize." One particularly interesting activity involves exploring whether or not Dr. Martin Luther King, Jr., was a "good" citizen. Here is how Katie explains that activity:

This teacher and her second-graders decided to make a large poster to display what they had learned about Martin Luther King, Jr. How else might students demonstrate their understandings? How might your decisions change if the students were fifth-graders?

> Without disclosing who the person is, discuss characteristics of Martin Luther King, Jr. Tell the students that this person broke some laws and that he encouraged other people to break them, too. He spoke to people in large groups and would get them all riled up to speak out against laws and to try to change them. He would appear at marches, and the police would come to keep the peace.
>
> Then ask the students what kind of citizen they think this would be: good or bad? Later, disclose to them that the person described as a lawbreaker was Martin Luther King, Jr., and ask what they think of that citizen. Follow up by asking the children if we may need to add some characteristics to our developing list of what a good citizen is.

Katie's unit ends with two activities that help pull it together. The first is an assessment in which students create a journal entry to describe their current thinking about what a good citizen is. To ensure that her students continue thinking about the ideas that emerge in the unit, Katie introduces a **discussion box** into which students (with their parents' assistance) can contribute pieces from newspapers and magazines that speak to issues students care about and want to know more about. These issues become the subject of weekly **circle meetings,** during which students and teacher gather in a circle for discussion. The specifics of Katie's sequence of lessons are represented in Figure 8.1.

Figure 8.1 • Katie's Sequence of Lessons

What Makes a Good Citizen?

Day 1: Read and discuss the book *Somewhere in the Universe*, which situates students in space, from our galaxy to our nation to our town.

Day 2: Use a variety of maps and globes to complete the teacher-made cloze book, *My Place in the World*, which asks students to fill in blanks related to their place in the world and to the leaders of various political entities (e.g., Nation—President Clinton).

Day 3: Make a student-written big book in which the children script their own story featuring what they have learned about the universe, nation, government, and the like. The book should end with a page that connects this activity with the next. For example, it might read, "And in that kind and quiet town there lived bright, beautiful children who care about the huge universe that we all share!"

Day 4: Without discussing the phrase first, ask students to define "good citizen" and script their current interpretations.

Day 5: Without disclosing who the person is, discuss characteristics and experiences of Dr. Martin Luther King, Jr., and ask students what kind of citizen they think he is. Then revise their previously made list of good citizen characteristics if necessary. (See the expanded version of this day's lesson on page 250.)

Day 6: Show a piece of the video *Eyes on the Prize*, around the issue of school desegregation, then hold an open discussion in the form of a circle meeting where only one person may speak at a time. Script students' comments and points of view on chart paper. After all students have had a chance to speak, ask if there are any group decisions that might be made.

Day 7: Do a "fairness" experiment in which, after discussing this activity ahead of time, students are divided into two groups, and one half is assigned blue stickers and the other half is assigned green stickers. The "blue" children will then have certain rights revoked (according to the previous decisions). Use the class reactions to this activity as a way of talking about the experiences of African-American children.

Day 8: Discuss further the previous day's activity and ask students to make a journal entry about a time when they felt they were treated unfairly. Discuss these experiences in a circle meeting in light of the concepts of fairness and justice. Conclude by writing a class definition of fairness to be used in the small group debate the next day.

Day 9: Divide the class into four heterogeneous groups and give each group one of the following topic cards:

- Should recycling be required and non-recyclers fined or imprisoned?
- Should the cafeteria rule about being allowed to purchase snacks only after eating the main portion of your meal be changed?
- Should students in our school have to wear uniforms?
- Should the rule about walking single file in the hallways be changed?

Ask students to think about why such rules might be made, whether they are fair, if they allow us to still be free and make choices, whether they might be necessary to help a larger cause. Allow groups 10–15 minutes to discuss their issues and script a response. Ask each group to share their issue and their ideas with the whole class and to answer questions. After the last group, pull the whole lesson together by charting those words that come up repeatedly (e.g., fairness, choice, laws) and point out that these words (and the concepts behind them) are often part of political discussions around new laws. Conclude by charting "What have we learned?"

Day 10: Ask students to make a journal entry describing their definition of a good citizen.

Day 11: Introduce the discussion box into which students (with their parents' help) can insert issues that would make for fruitful discussions during weekly circle meetings.

Now let's turn to Kristen's three-week, integrated social studies and language arts unit. Kristen begins by role-playing Harriet Tubman for her students. She creates a K-W-L chart with which students can talk about what they know and what they would like to learn about slavery. From there, Kristen's students begin a range of reading, writing, and interactive experiences. For example, Kristen allows students to choose independent-reading books and to participate in a whole-class reading of *The Captive* (Hansen, 1994), the fictional account of a twelve-year-old boy kidnapped into slavery in post-Revolutionary Massachusetts. To extend the students' writing, Kristen requires that they keep a **literature log,** a notebook where they record their thoughts and ideas about the books they read, and a **learning log,** a folder where they record their thoughts and ideas related to the social studies centers she creates.

IN YOUR CLASSROOM: Using Learning Logs

A *log* is a generic term for any collection of regularly recorded ideas and experiences. As the example above suggests, a student's log may take the form of a notebook or folder and may serve different purposes. Key to successful use of student logs are the following:

- Use them regularly enough so that children can see their progress.
- Keep them sufficiently organized so that each child can find the right one.

One other point is worth raising. Some teachers argue that informal writing, such as journals and logs, should not be marked up and graded because doing so tends to inhibit less confident writers. Others believe that bad habits develop when errors are not pointed out in all the writing they do. We understand the latter argument, but are more persuaded by the first. Developing good writing skills is important, but so too is the writing act itself. If your students write little and reluctantly because they are afraid of making errors, writing exercises like log-keeping will be of limited value.

Centers are one opportunity for students to interact with Kristen and their peers. In the corners of the room, Kristen places materials designed to pique students' interest in slavery. One center, for example, is devoted to the slave trade. The materials include information displays about African societies, maps of Africa and the U.S., pictures and drawings of the interior of slave ships, and personal accounts of kidnapped Africans. Other opportunities for students to interact include circle meetings, listening activities (including a guest speaker), and reenactment presentations.

Kristen also sprinkles a set of **mini-lessons** throughout her unit. Mini-lessons are brief, teacher-led presentations that emphasize key ideas a teacher wants all students to grasp. Kristen's unit calls for mini-lessons on the geographies and economies of northern and southern states, the Underground Railroad, and the Emancipation Proclamation.

The unit concludes with two distinct but related activities. The first is a small-group discussion around the question "Does the end of slavery mean freedom?" After sharing their ideas in small groups, Kristen encourages students to contribute to a whole-class debate about whether or not emancipation truly made slaves free. The second activity is a **mind-extender project.** Here, Kristen pushes her students to reflect on the various individual and class activities and to synthesize them into a new form. Kristen describes the activity this way:

> Students will be encouraged to create their own projects, pursuing a unit-related idea or topic that has captured their interest and imagination. Students will have their proposal approved by the teacher before starting the work. Together, they will decide what will be included in the project. An example of an acceptable mind extender would be for the student to consult the social studies textbook to see what information it presents about slavery in America. The student would add or delete information and provide her or his reasoning for doing so.
>
> Students should keep in mind the following goals as they work on these projects:
>
> 1. Show me that you understand the concepts discussed in class.
> 2. Show me that you have gone beyond class discussions and have done research and thinking of your own.
> 3. Use creativity in your project—let me see how you think through the issues and ideas of this project.
> 4. Use good work habits.

Kristen uses the mind-extender project as the unit's final assessment, but she builds in assessment opportunities throughout. She informally assesses students' understanding through class discussions, learning and literature logs, and circle shares. More formal assessments occur after the independent reading assignment, the reenactment of a scene from *The Captive,* and a spiritual/folktale activity. Figure 8.2 represents the specific sequence of lessons Kristen planned.

Both Katie's and Kristen's big ideas are illustrated and extended through the range of learning activities they selected. We particularly like the variety of these lessons, and the way they push students to think hard about issues. We do have questions about each set of lessons, however. For example, we wonder about Katie's list of issues (see Day 9). Are these all questions students care about?

Figure 8.2 • Kristen's Sequence of Lessons

What Is Freedom?

Day 1: Introduce *Harriet Tubman* to the class and answer student questions. Introduce books related to slavery and do the first two steps of a KWL activity (i.e., what students know and what they would like to learn). Post this list on a classroom wall.

Day 2: Ask students to select an independent reading book from those introduced. Describe the literature log they are to keep. Begin reading the class book, *The Captive*.

Days 3–5: Continue reading from *The Captive*. Direct students to the first Social Studies Center, which is related to the African slave trade. Introduce the learning log students will keep as they engage with Center materials. On Day 4, organize small groups to discuss what students like to do now and whether or not they would have been able to do these things as slaves. Share responses with class. Ask one group to pretend to be white slaveowners. Ask them to brainstorm why slaves were generally not allowed to learn how to read and write.

Days 6–7: Continue reading from *The Captive*, the action of which will be taking place in New England. Present a mini-lesson on differences between northern and southern states (e.g., geographies, climates, economies). Direct students to the second Social Studies Center, which features life for slaves in America. On Day 7, ask students to brainstorm response activities to their self-selected readings. Organize small groups to discuss the quote, "To maintain injustice requires that it be rationalized," and how slaveholders and others chose to view slaves as less than human. Share small-group discussions in whole-class setting.

Day 8: Last day of *The Captive*. Form small groups and ask them to choose a favorite scene from the book and to plan to reenact it the next day.

Day 9: Stage reenactment presentations. Groups should also field questions about why they chose the scene they did and if they made any historically accurate changes.

Day 10: Present a mini-lesson on slave efforts to resist and escape slavery. Discuss the risks slaves took. Direct students to the final Social Studies Center, which focuses on slaves' quest for freedom.

Day 11: Discuss secret codes students may have developed and used. Brainstorm how slaves might have used codes to communicate information about freedom. Listen to African-American spirituals and read from the picture book *Follow the Drinking Gourd*. Brainstorm what code words are evident. In pairs, develop encoded spirituals.

Day 12: Read aloud and discuss African-American folktales. Encourage students to begin thinking about the mind-extender project (see page 253).

Day 13: Guest storyteller from the African Cultural Center. Continue work on Mind Extender project.

Day 14: Discuss the question "Does the end of slavery mean freedom?" in small groups. Share ideas in whole class. Present a mini-lesson on the Emancipation Proclamation and the creation of the Jim Crow laws. Decide on activity for tomorrow's final day of the unit.

Day 15: Student choice activity—perhaps musical, dramatic, artistic, or literary—combined with a food activity (e.g., making roasted peanuts in the traditional African way).

What other possibilities might exist? We also wonder what happens to the entries students make in the learning log Kristen assigns. These questions aside, however, we think these lesson sequences work well.

Preservice teachers often struggle with assessing how much time an activity will take. This is a difficult issue, even for veteran teachers, largely because it is difficult to know with any precision how learners will interact with new ideas. Teachers will give you countless examples of situations where a lesson they thought would take half an hour spread out over two days. Conversely, they will describe the quick thinking they had to do when a lesson they thought the children would struggle with ended after fifteen minutes.

We raise the issue of time for two reasons. One is to explain that Katie and Kristen planned each of their activities to last approximately thirty minutes. Each knows, however, that she cannot always find that amount of time for social studies alone. Consequently, each tries to incorporate elements of her lessons into other parts of the day in order to squeeze out more time. For example, Katie uses some of the fifteen to twenty minutes regularly allotted for circle time to discuss aspects of good citizenship. Kristen creates time by designing a unit that integrates social studies and language arts.

CHOOSING GOALS

The second reason we raise the issue of time is to urge you to think flexibly about your unit planning and your teaching. Planning ahead is crucial, but so too is being able to revise your planned activities as situations change. Good teachers keep their eyes on their ultimate objectives and adapt their planned lessons to meet the variable needs of their students (McCutcheon, 1981).

One last point: Katie and Kristen both opt to present their sequence of lessons in a narrative list. We think this is particularly useful because it makes the skeleton of the lessons immediately visible. The point is to communicate your ideas as clearly as possible, and to use a format you think best serves that purpose.

IN YOUR CLASSROOM: Teaching Strategies

Review the lists of individual, small-group, and whole-group teaching strategies described in Chapter 5. Supplement those lists with strategies Katie and Kristen use above. Keep these master lists close to you for easy reference as you plan your units.

In both Katie's and Kristen's units we see two key pieces of a unit plan—a big idea and a series of activities that support and extend that idea. We also see that these units send strong messages about how these teachers view the interaction of learning, teaching, subject matter, and classroom environment. For example, although neither Katie nor Kristen seem to expect their learners to know everything about the topics in these units, they both emphasize multiple opportunities to read, write, and think about important ideas. These messages stand in stark contrast to those sent by the more traditional teachers we have considered.

Assessment: How will I know if the students understand? One last piece of a successful unit plan is assessment. The key here is to address as clearly as possible the question "How will I know if the students understand?" Assessing students' understanding is not easy, but if you have thought through the other pieces of your plan, you'll have less difficulty choosing an appropriate assessment.

In her plan, Katie chooses to weave the assessments into her sequence of lessons. These are not big, time-consuming tests and reports, but rather subtle, age-appropriate tasks that she integrates into her instruction. Katie's assessments function just as they are supposed to—they help her understand what her students know and can do. An outline of the assessments in Katie's unit include

- cloze-book assignment (day 2)
- big-book project (day 3)
- initial and revised listing of the characteristics of a good citizen (days 4 and 5)
- class discussions (days 6 and 7)
- class definition of fairness (day 8)
- "What have we learned?" chart (day 9)
- journal entry (day 10)

CLASSROOM MANAGEMENT

Two points are obvious here. First, Katie plans some form of assessment during most class periods. This is important because it shows a seamlessness between her teaching and her assessment; one works in support of the other. Second, Katie uses a wide range of assessment approaches. She does not use end-of-unit exams (although we know of primary teachers who do). Instead, she employs various means to understand what her students know and can do.

One last point is worth noting. In Chapter 5, we suggested that assessment is valuable, in part, because it can help a teacher modify her or his practice along the way. We don't see this key feature of assessment at work here because this is an *outline* of Katie's plan, not a description of her actual teaching practice.

Like Katie, Kristen uses an array of assessments and merges them into her teaching lessons. See if you can identify them. Go back to the listing of Kristen's lesson sequence and underline those activities that might function as assessments of student understanding.

How did you do? Were some forms of assessment more obvious than others? Did the assessment activities you underlined make sense, given the topic? What modifications would you make?

IN YOUR CLASSROOM: Assessment

After reviewing the range of assessment methods described in Chapter 5, supplement that list with assessment approaches Katie and Kristen use in their units. Keep this list close to you for easy reference as you plan your units.

If you were to plan a unit similar to Kristen's (or Katie's), you can expect to make a range of changes. You'll come to work with different knowledge and experiences. You'll have different students in your class. You may work from different goals, as we pointed out in Chapter 7. Even if you were to try to follow another teacher's plan, you would make modifications along the way.

The point is this: Unit plans are never set in stone. Instead, they should represent your best thinking at the time you create them with the full understanding that they may change either in the course of teaching them, or in a subsequent use, or both. In any event, the questions that frame the unit—What am I planning to teach and why should kids care? How does my big idea look spread out across the thread categories? What does my sequence of lessons look like? And how will I know if the students understand?—remain good ones to consider.

How Do I Develop a Unit Plan?

We addressed this question in Chapter 5. Nevertheless, two points are worth echoing:

- No single path leads to big-idealand.
- A unit plan is more than a list of lessons.

No single path leads to big idealand. Conversations with Katie and Kristen reveal the different routes they took in conceiving of and developing their unit ideas. In fact, the differences surface immediately as each teacher gives us a hint into the origins of her plan.

CHOOSING GOALS

Katie reports that her interest in citizenship began with a personal frustration about the lack of specifics in the state curriculum guide. She said, "When I started thinking about this concept as a unit of study, I began to consider the more obvious aspects of citizenship: voting, abiding by the laws, and serving others who are less fortunate." As she thought more about the nature of citizenship and particularly what makes a "good" citizen, Katie came to an astounding conclusion: There is no single clear view or definition of a good citizen. Now, many teachers would cut and run at this point. Not Katie. She thought about a big idea: What makes a good citizen? "With that statement as

The Internet provides access to literally millions of opportunities for constructing and developing big idea–based teaching units. Be careful, though: the quality of lessons and units on the Internet can vary widely. Be sure to think through the goals, activities, materials, and assessments of any teaching resource you plan to use.

a jumping off point, I could guide the students through much the same process I myself went through in going from the obvious aspects of citizenship to the less obvious characteristics of a good citizen."

CHOOSING GOALS

Kristen's foray into slavery had a different genesis, although she too drew from a personal experience. Early in her thinking about her unit, she had a conversation with a colleague. After outlining her ideas, this person said, half-jokingly, "Well, you're going to teach that slavery is a good thing aren't you?" Although Kristen's jaw dropped, this fellow continued, "Think about it. With slavery, there's no welfare system. Slaves had shelter, clothing, food, and something to do all day. Now, people like me are becoming slaves to support welfare." Kristen declares that right then any doubts that she had about doing this unit evaporated. That attitudes like this fellow's exist, Kristen believes, is a powerful reason to push her students to avoid such facile thinking.

You can come to the idea behind your plan by a variety of paths. Likewise, the means by which you develop the plan can take many forms. Some of our students begin by working on a big idea. Others start with activities. Still others explore libraries and curriculum centers for resources. It really doesn't matter where you start as long as you eventually work through all the necessary issues.

TEACHING RESOURCES

Unit Plans

The following site, the Learning Exchange for Teachers and Students Through the Internet (LetsNet), is a good source of ideas for unit plans.

- http://commtechlab.msu.edu/sites/letsnet/index.html

A unit plan is more than a list of lessons. One of the most common shortcomings we see in unit plans is that they begin and end with a set of lessons. Two problems follow from this approach. One problem is that the other elements of a unit—introduction, threads, and assessment—are either underdeveloped or absent. A sequence of lessons "works" only when it is well-integrated into a comprehensive plan of instruction. And that point suggests a second problem with the list-of-lessons approach: It sends mixed messages about the commonplaces of education. A unit that consists solely of teaching activities suggests little consideration of the learners, subject matter, or classroom environment. For example, if the plan fails to address assessment, it is difficult to know what subject matter ideas are valuable and how learners are to respond to those ideas. Similarly, if the teacher offers no rationale for learning about the topic, it is difficult to understand the classroom environment that teacher hopes to foster.

We are not implying that your unit plans must explicitly address each and every commonplace connection. We are suggesting, however, that you think about how the elements of your plan work individually and together and about the messages these elements send about each commonplace. To do any less is to invite needless confusion and frustration.

What Purpose Does a Unit Plan Serve?

We think the case is clear—unit planning will help you become a more thoughtful, focused, and resourceful teacher. It's not as easy as teaching out of a textbook or from worksheets, but we think you will find it more rewarding, and we know your learners will find it more engaging.

That said, let's discuss two last issues related to unit planning:

- Unit plans for daily practice
- Unit plans over a career

Unit plans for daily classroom practice Reality check: The type of unit plans you produce for a social studies methods course will differ from those you develop for use in your daily classroom practice. It would be terrific if you had the time to construct the kind of full-scale units we describe here for each area of your social studies curriculum. The realities of classroom life, however, mean that time will be your most precious commodity, and that the luxury of spending several weeks planning one unit as we outline in this book is just that—a luxury. This is not to say that over the course of your teaching career you won't have given as much thought to the units you teach. It simply means that your classroom units will likely take a sketchier form. For example, the time spent writing out an extensive introduction and threads section for a university course unit plan may be a luxury you cannot afford as a school teacher.

And we see no particular problem with this. The unit you develop for a social studies methods course should be useful as a teaching unit. Because it is also a university course, however, much of what you will leave unsaid in a classroom unit will need to be spelled out in a unit-as-course-project.

Whether or not you write out your actual classroom units in the same detail as your course unit, the *thinking* you do around the four questions we pose above should not vary. In short, plan to write less, but to think just as hard.

IN YOUR CLASSROOM: Unit Plans for Daily Practice

As soon as you feel comfortable writing unit plans that address the four questions we list above, you are ready to develop a shorthand approach to unit planning. Consider this approach:

A. Synthesize your introduction into a sentence or two that expresses the topic you have chosen in terms of a big idea and one reason why it should matter to your students. For example:

Big idea: The big idea for this third-grade unit on the rain forest is *The Endangered Rain Forest: What's So Dangerous?* It will appeal to students' sense that they are connected to the rest of the world and can make a difference.

B. List the sequence of lessons you have planned. **Highlight** the terms that suggest thread connections, adding an abbreviation in parentheses (for example, GEO, POL, ECO, SOC, GLO). Underline the activities that will function as assessments.

Lesson 1: (One day) Divide the class into two groups. Give one group the "rain forest grab bag" (a paper bag filled with rubber erasers and other rain forest–related products); give the other group the "smell the rain forest" containers (individual film canisters filled with samples of rain forest woods or other materials). Students examine objects and brainstorm ways they might be related. Switch items and repeat. Share results of brainstorming. Talk about relation of all objects to rain forest (GEO). Journal entry: Brainstorm a recipe using only rain forest items.

Lesson 2: (Two days) Read *Rain Forest Secrets* (Dorros, 1990) this day and next. Discuss characteristics of rain forest (GEO), such as location, animals, why it is becoming endangered (GLO). Next day, display world map (GEO) and point out location of rain forests in relation to school. Journal entry: Begin designing a brochure for the rain forest.

Lesson 3: (Two days) Students use reference materials to choose and research an endangered rain forest animal (GEO), including location and range, habitat, living habits, endangered status, and a drawing of the animal. Share findings with class. Bind reports into class book. Journal entry: Students write a letter to an imaginary child in the Amazon rain forest and describe their daily routine.

Lesson 4: (One day) Teacher-led discussion of Yanomami culture (CUL). In small groups, students complete Venn diagram comparing their culture with Yanomami's. Share diagrams with class.

Lesson 5: (Two days) On day one, read *The Great Kapok Tree* (Cherry, 1990), the story of a man who falls asleep after beginning to chop down a tree and dreams that animals take turns offering reasons why he should not continue. Discuss why the man was chopping down the tree (ECO) and the pros and cons of doing so. Students draw pictures of the book from the animals' point of view and share with class.

On day two, discuss slash and burn deforestation (GEO/ECO). Divide class into groups, assign roles (for example, logger, environmentalist, poor farmer, rain forest native, and timber company owner), and role play the situation where the company owner has gained rights to forest lands and plans to begin cutting trees. Share experiences with class.

Lesson 6: (Two-three days) Ask students how they might share what they've learned with schoolmates and others, such as creating brochures that encourage recycling (GEO), planting trees (GEO), creating bulletin boards that describe the economic and cultural impact of deforestation (ECO/CUL), writing letters to political leaders (POL) and organizations in support of environmental causes (GLO). Form groups around actions and monitor their efforts. Invite parents and community members to view the results of the students' efforts.[1]

Unit planning for a career We have hinted at this, but let's make it clear: The thinking you do around one classroom unit is the same kind of thinking you should do for your whole social studies curriculum. This takes time, especially if you are a rookie teacher. Building a repertoire of solid big-idea units is a career-long enterprise. You might find it best to work on a couple of new big ideas and units a year as you continue to refine those you started with. In a few years you will have built a rich social studies program of which you can be proud and through which your learners will become powerful thinkers, knowers, and social actors.

Conclusion

We billed this as a chapter designed to pull together ideas developed over the course of the book. As you begin your teaching career, you may find it helpful to return to this chapter and review our discussion of the commonplaces, especially if you are stuck with a tough classroom problem. We also hope you'll come back to the discussion of unit planning if you need to rework one or more elements of your plan, or if you are having trouble thinking about how those elements should work together to support one another and to send coherent and consistent messages about the commonplaces.

CHAPTER SUMMARY

1. How do the commonplaces help teachers understand and analyze classroom situations and problems?

Considered individually and in interaction, the commonplaces—learners and learning, teachers and teaching, subject matter, and classroom environment—can help teachers isolate, analyze, and respond to classroom situations and problems.

2. What are the components of a unit plan?

The primary components of a unit plan are responses to the following questions:

- What am I planning to teach, and why should learners care? (Introduction)
- How does my big idea look spread out across the thread categories? (Threads)
- How is my big idea represented in my sequence of lessons? (Lessons)
- How will I know if the students understand what I am trying to teach? (Assessment)

3. What purposes does unit planning serve?

Unit planning is a means to becoming a more thoughtful, focused, and resourceful teacher. Because the form a unit plan takes is less important than the thinking behind it, it's beneficial to experiment with plan structures while developing units for daily practice.

TEACHING RESOURCES

Print Resources

Brophy, J., & VanSledright, B. (1997). *Teaching and learning history in elementary schools.* New York: Teachers College Press. This volume offers deep and thoughtful case studies of three elementary school teachers and their students as they negotiate issues of teaching, learning, subject matter, and environment.

Jorgensen, K. (1993). *History workshop.* Portsmouth, NH: Heinemann. This book nicely describes some of the teaching strategies Katie and Kristen use in their unit plans, as well as many others.

Onosko, J., & Swenson, L. (1996). Designing issue-based unit plans. In R. Evans & D. Saxe (Eds.), *Handbook on teaching social issues* (pp. 89–98). Washington, DC: National Council for the Social Studies. This short chapter well describes the principal features of unit planning around big ideas.

Schwab, J. (1978). The practical: Translation into curriculum. In I. Westbury & I. Wilkof (Eds.), *Science, curriculum, and liberal education* (pp. 365–383). Chicago: University of Chicago Press. The source of the commonplaces framework we use in this book, this chapter is no easy read. Schwab's insightful and articulate presentation of the commonplaces, however, is worth the effort.

Two other sources of good ideas for lessons and units are *Social Studies and the Young Learner* and *Social Education,* both publications of the National Council for the Social Studies. Both journals feature classroom-ready materials in each issue.

Technology Resources

The Internet is proving a boon to teachers looking for interesting classroom materials. You must, however, be a critical reader—just because information is posted on the Web does not mean that it is accurate! Nevertheless, a little searching can yield a wealth of neat ideas, resources, and activities. We like the following sites because of the breadth of topics they cover:

- **http://www.ed.gov.free**

This is the all-purpose site for any resources available from the U.S. government.

- **http://edsitement.neh.gov**

This site comes from the National Endowment for the Humanities and offers a wealth of resources, including unit and lesson plans, for social and cultural studies.

- **http://www.ukans.edu/carrie/docs/amdocs_index.html**

The AMDOCS site offers an incredible array of primary source documents geared to the study of American history.

- **http://www.nationalgeographic.com/education/index/html**

The National Geographic Society has made a major investment in public education. This site features both school- and classroom-based K-12 projects.

NOTE

1. Our thanks to Darlene Swannie for this activity.

Chapter 9

Becoming a Reflective Social Studies Teacher

In the preceding chapters we have examined from a variety of angles how clear, powerful, ambitious social studies teaching in elementary school requires careful attention to the four commonplaces. Such teaching also requires **reflective practice:** regular examinations of and introspection into what, who, and how you're teaching, and why you choose to do what you do. The decisions you make should be based on a sound goal framework. Being reflective and thoughtful about your teaching practice is essential to becoming an effective elementary social studies teacher; in fact, some argue that it is *the* key to becoming a great teacher in any subject matter. Reflective teachers think hard about their teaching practices, the learners in front of them, the social studies subject matter they teach, and the learning community they build in their classrooms. They also consider the larger school community context within which their reflective practice occurs and is shaped. Given its centrality to all that is good teaching, we close this book with a discussion of teacher reflection.

When you have completed this chapter, you should be able to answer these questions:

1. ***What does it mean to be reflective?***
2. ***What does reflection entail?***
3. ***What are the different types of reflection?***

Defining Reflective Practice

When we talk about being reflective, we mean—to paraphrase John Dewey (1933)—conscious, repeated, and careful thought about your beliefs and teaching practices with respect to the reasons that you claim support for them, and with regard to how they influence what you might believe and do in the future. In part, this definition is particularly personal. It points inward toward an analysis of what you believe and do and the reasons you hold for thinking and acting in these ways. It also points outward toward a consideration of how your beliefs and actions will influence your students, the subject matter you teach, and the classroom learning opportunities and structures you create. Let's consider first the inward view and look at it in relationship to how, as Dewey indicates, it inevitably points outward.

Becoming a Reflective Teacher: Personal Growth

Continual inward self-assessment is essential to growth as a teacher; without it, you atrophy. You simply lose your interest in teaching, and then you ill serve your students. Learning to teach is something we never quite master; it's an ongoing, lifelong pursuit. The best social studies teachers we know are those who are quickest to say that they have much to learn, even though they may have been teaching for twenty years or more.

The key for these teachers, if you ask them, is their ability to constantly challenge themselves through the reflective self-assessment process. They know they have chosen no easy path, but they live for the journey and they love the opportunity for continued development as teachers and human beings. Sometimes it's difficult and downright intimidating to question and assess what you do and believe. Even so, we can't stress enough the important connection between looking inward at your beliefs and actions and as an ambitious social studies teacher.

It is essential to keep asking, for example, whether or not you know enough about the social studies subject matter you are teaching. If you think not, you embark on a journey to learn more by reading and taking classes and by borrowing thoughts and ideas from your colleagues. This is what we mean by personal growth: Using the self-reflection, question-asking process to

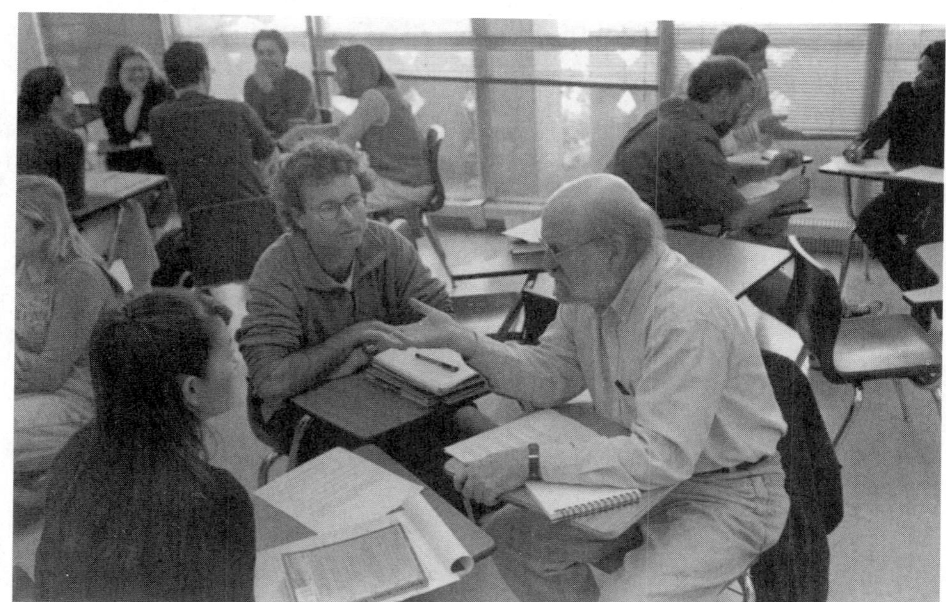

Personal growth can take many forms—quiet reflection, journal writing, reading, and the like. But there is much to be said for reflection growing out of interactions with other adults, in which we try out our ideas on others, listen to their responses, reform our ideas, and then try them out again.

change and expand as a social studies teacher. The teachers who regularly engage in this process continue to love teaching. Through the growth process of self-reflection they continually remake themselves as thoughtful and caring teachers.

Becoming a Reflective Teacher: Professional Responsibility

As Dewey intimates, however, there is more to being reflective than your personal growth. Reflective practice has an outward, public dimension as well. In the end, teaching is essentially a moral endeavor, for the many teaching decisions you make affect the lives of children, often in quite profound ways. You have a moral obligation and professional responsibility to do the best you can by them, to make the best choices on their behalf. Although making choices may often feel like a solitary effort teachers perform on the drive to school in the morning or during a planning period, decision-making does happen within a broader context. Here's how.

As a teacher, you are a professional educator, part of the larger teaching profession comprised of many who, like you, pride themselves on being up to date about what they know and do. Therefore, you have to pay attention to teachers' **craft knowledge,** those practices teachers regularly use in the classroom. As our profession's understanding of that craft develops, you must stay abreast of it by continued reading, conversation with colleagues, course work, and other professional development activities.

The commonplaces are a useful way to check your understandings. You need to stay in close touch with your students, learning about them individually and as an age-related group. The first you accomplish through regular attention to the many ways your individual students think about and express their ideas, hopes, and ambitions. The latter you develop by interacting with your colleagues and through reading and studying research on how children learn and grow. You must attend to the social studies subject matter through what you know and continue to learn, and by understanding the curricular demands within your school district and state. And finally, you will monitor your classroom community and attempt to keep your goals and aims there aligned with your practices.

TEACHING RESOURCES

Professional Resources

The following site provides a wide range of materials on which teachers can draw for professional growth.

- http://matrix.crosswinds.net/~dboals/gen.html

Just as we want students to become lifelong learners, important too is the notion that teachers see themselves as learners. To that end, continuing professional development is an increasingly vital part of teachers' lives.

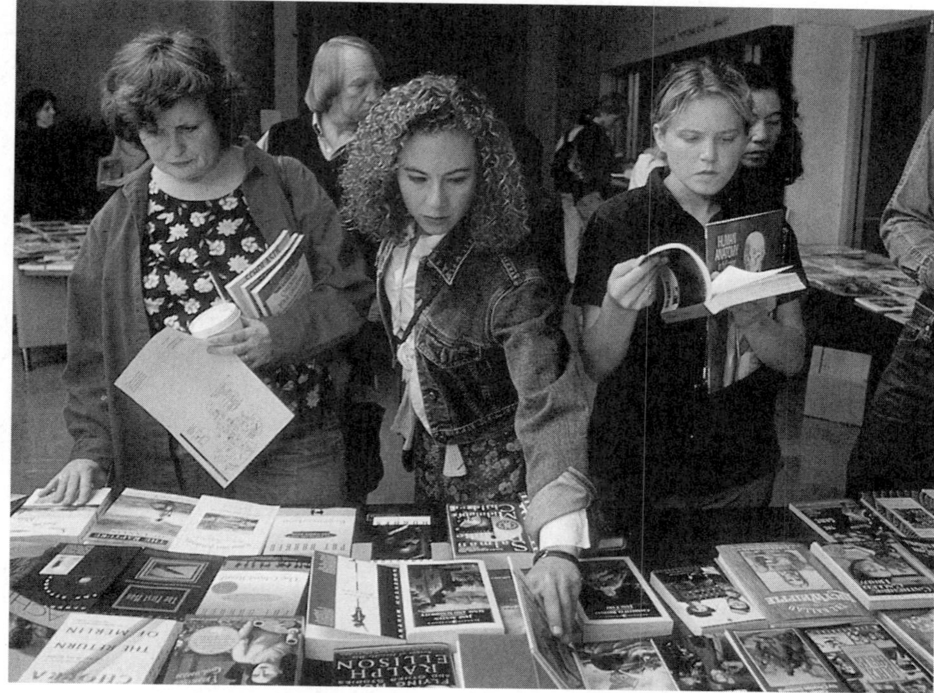

A good source of teacher learning opportunities are professional organizations such as National Council for the Social Studies. A big part of NCSS-sponsored conferences held at the national, state, and local levels are book exhibits where publishers present their wares for teachers' perusal.

Having as much knowledge as possible about the commonplaces, and continuing to seek more, can enhance the quality of your teaching choices. Reflection is the vehicle by which enhancing this knowledge and understanding can take place, for it helps frame good questions that will enable you to maximize your personal and professional growth.

TEACHER REFLECTION

What Is Reflective Practice?

What do you think of when you hear someone talk about reflective teaching practice? How does this compare or contrast with our discussion of reflection as defined by John Dewey? Do you agree or disagree with Dewey?

SECTION SUMMARY Defining Reflective Practice

- Reflection involves the conscious, repeated, and careful thought about your beliefs and teaching practices with respect to the reasons that you claim support for them, and with regard to how they influence what you might believe and do in the future.
- Reflection moves in two directions at the same time. Looking inward, teachers' reflections contribute to their personal growth. Looking outward, teachers' reflections contribute to their growth as professionals.

Reflectiveness in Teaching: An Illustration

We realize that what we describe above is a tall order. This view of reflection, although complete with wonderful personal opportunities, also means powerful obligations and responsibilities, especially to the children who are your students. To put some substance around these ideas and to further depict various aspects of reflection, let's consider how we, Bruce and S. G., discussed one aspect of how Bruce taught a piece of his elementary school social studies course. This illustration of reflective practice, although not comprehensive, allows us to show you how it works, how it can be a natural, regular outgrowth of the interactions you have with your students and other professionals.

The Context of the Exchange

Bruce teaches a course to prospective teachers on learning to become an elementary school social studies teacher. Each time he teaches this course he modifies the syllabus as a result of what he's done in the past, how well he thinks the course succeeded in fostering learning among his students, and questions he has about how to enhance the experience for the prospective teachers. The path down this road has been bumpy and criss-crossed. No big surprise there: Teaching is a never-ending quest to reflect and improve on practice, regardless of the level.

In the course, Bruce uses a book titled *Teaching and Learning History in Elementary Schools* (Brophy & VanSledright, 1997), which includes detailed case studies of three fifth-grade teachers teaching American history: Mary Lake, Ramona Palmer, and Sara Atkinson (we've discussed some of these teachers in earlier chapters). After assigning readings related to these teachers, Bruce encourages his students to focus on trying to understand the teachers and make sense of their social studies teaching practices and decision making.

The three teachers present significantly different cases, from which Bruce hopes his students will learn much about teaching social studies. Mary Lake's version of teaching history hinges on her storytelling approach. She conveys the American past by engaging her students in detailed, sometimes mesmerizing accounts of the historical actors' activities. Lake searches out dramatic and human-interest elements of the historical record that she can narrate to her students to provoke their curiosity and encourage their understanding. She typically follows the scripts provided by her textbook—the common celebrations of American nation-building and achievement told through the perspectives of European Americans—and reconstructs them using her own dramatic flourishes.

Ramona Palmer sees American history as a story of cause-and-effect relationships that plays out over and over again. In her view, for example, the American Revolution is the *effect* caused by economic and political differences between the colonists and England. Some of these differences were *caused* by the French and Indian War, which was settled only a few years before the Revolution. The *effect* of the war was to leave the English saddled with significant debt, which they tried to collect in part from the colonists. Unlike Lake, Palmer isn't interested in telling dramatic stories per se. She wants to help her students understand historical cause-and-effect relationships.

Sara Atkinson views American history as a story about choices in which Americans made mistakes, acknowledged them, and made other choices to correct those mistakes. For example, she sees the amendments to the Constitution as clear illustrations of this effort to use history to learn from errors in judgment. She teaches the chronology of American history to help her students understand the importance of decision-making reform, how it plays out over time, and how they can play a role in changing society.

Each teacher approaches teaching American history differently and therefore displays goals that vary from the others. Likewise, each teacher's teaching practices vary as do the learning communities each strives to create. No teacher can do it all. Therefore, choosing an approach to teaching history influences student learning in particular ways and produces trade-offs in the classroom. For example, Atkinson is critical of choices that American leaders have made (for example, she noted the weaknesses of the Articles of Confederation, the fact that women and blacks were deprived from voting, and the like) and she shows her students how remedies for these choices were conceived. Unlike Lake, she engages in no storytelling practices. On the other hand, Lake motivates and engages her students in a subject that many find lifeless. However, she seldom if ever asks her students to develop a critical, questioning attitude or approach to the study of history.

Bruce wants his prospective teachers to understand the differences among the three teachers and the trade-offs embedded in their practices. He expects his students to use the cases to analyze and reflect on their own thinking about teaching, learning, subject matter, and classroom environment. After three weeks of studying each case, Bruce asks his students a seemingly simple question: Of the three teachers, who do you approve of and why?

This question provokes a flurry of in-class commentary. Some students choose Lake, others choose Palmer, and still others choose Atkinson. Vigorous defenses support each choice. The prospective teachers often put themselves in the places of their favorite teachers as they argue on their behalf and supply reasons for the trade-offs made by their choice teacher. A bit of a fevered pitch builds right up until the third class ends.

After the first time this discussion took place, Bruce immediately e-mailed S. G., who teaches a similar class at his institution. Bruce explained what had happened, much as it is conveyed here. S. G. responded within a few hours, and the ensuing exchange lasted about a week. In effect, Bruce asked S. G. to help him reflect on what occurred, to assist him in sorting out the many details, and to help him find ways to enhance this learning experience for students the next time around.

A Reflective Conversation

CHOOSING GOALS

After giving S. G. the details of the experience from his perspective, Bruce raved about how intense the in-class discussion had become, to the point where the class took over the direction of the conversation and he became only a relatively passive participant. Bruce rejoiced in the idea that students could become this animated and personally involved, but, like many teachers, he worried about what understanding students were developing. Are these three teachers truly such model teachers that any one of them is fine to emulate? None of his students suggested that they wouldn't endorse any of the three because they had a different, more exemplary teacher in mind. Was this a problem? How could he encourage his students to become yet more critically thoughtful about these teachers and therefore about the teachers they would become?

The usefulness of informal conversations among teachers cannot be overestimated. Face-to-face interactions such as the one among the teachers in this photograph are valuable, but so too are the teacher chat lines that abound on the Internet.

Based on these questions, S. G. and Bruce had the following exchange:

SG: The notion of a "teaching model" seems both helpful and problematic. Did both ideas surface in the class discussion? What sense, if any, did your students make of this?

BV: Actually, *model* is my word. None of the students used that term. I think the term *cases* is probably a better way to think about this. But I did use the word *model,* didn't I? I think I was getting at this idea of helping them build a mental structure around particular ways of teaching history at fifth grade—different ways of thinking about history subject matter, kids, and learning communities. My students often tell me that they never see social studies taught. With these three cases, I was hoping to give them examples, ones that they don't see in the field. I think I need to go back and point out how the term *model* is both useful and problematic. How do *you* think it's both?

SG: Your note makes me think of two things. One is this conundrum of social studies being left out of the elementary school day. I just don't get it. Given that social studies is about how and why people do the things they do *and* that we all seem to be innately interested in this stuff, how can teachers just leave it out? My guess is that what teachers see in their textbooks looks only remotely interesting and so, when pressed for time, it becomes easier to put social studies off.

It doesn't have to be that way, and that's why I like the idea of using cases of teachers like the ones you describe (I like *cases* better than *models,* but more on that in a minute). The Palmer and Atkinson cases show me that elementary teachers and kids can engage in real and thoughtful discussions. The Lake case shows me that one way to make more time for social studies stuff is by forging a strong connection to one's literacy instruction—historical fiction is a way to teach *both* history and reading.

In these ways, the cases of these teachers serve as models, that is, instances of wise practice that are worth emulating. What seems especially important about these teachers is that none does her work flawlessly. Looking at the successes these teachers have is made even more instructive and important when we consider the challenges they face. None of us (least of all you and me!) do things perfectly, and so presenting the full scope of these teachers' efforts seems critical.

Now, maybe I'm just being too particular, but *model* implies a focus on only the good stuff, a "here's what I did and you should do the same" kind of thing. A *case,* on the other hand, implies a fuller consideration of a teacher's actions, the good parts as well as the problems. Moreover, a case usually suggests the importance of the context in which the teacher works. Models are supposed to work regardless of the context. Cases are context-specific; the implication being that another teacher in another context can expect differences to surface. And that seems like an important thing to remember.

I'm probably rambling, but the point I want to make is that if your students see these three teachers as one-dimensional success stories or models, rather than as full, rich, complex cases, I think they're only getting half the value of them. But all this makes me think about another question: How do you know what sense your students are making of all this? I really struggle with this question in my own classes.

BV: I, too, am troubled by how little social studies appears in the elementary school curriculum. Science suffers the same fate. I wonder if it has something to do with the heavy subject matter demands these topics make on teachers. When I see reading and math taught, it's largely skills-based. On the surface, I think teachers might think math and reading are easier because you can teach these distinct skills in a particular order. Progress seems equally easy to measure. Social studies, on the other hand, requires a large pool of conceptual understandings to teach it well. That may scare teachers away. These three cases, I think, are encouraging because they show teachers diving into the history subject matter and bringing their kids along. Some students liked Lake because they could see how she integrated reading and history, but they weren't especially quick to notice (judging by classroom comments) that her approach was rather narrow and didn't allow her students to see history from perspectives other than the celebration stories she told and had them read.

Your thoughts about cases are almost exactly what I thought about the three teachers. They're hardly perfect. In fact, after the discussion I worried a great deal about my students picking one of them as their model social studies teacher. So perhaps asking them to pick a teacher they approved of was not such a good idea, despite all the great discussion that followed. That "model" idea is so tempting for me, though, and I suspect for my students. Teachers want magic bullets, the way that will work, regardless of context and setting. I need to do a better job of helping them to see how learning varies by class and students, how the learning community must shift accordingly, and how subject matter representations and content need adjusting also. I must stress the moral dimension of teaching, how teachers constantly choose different courses of action based on their assumptions and understandings of the context. Using these three teachers as different cases of decision making is probably a better approach.

As to the question you asked at the end, I, too, wonder how to get a grip on what my students understand from these cases. I listen to them very carefully in class. I puzzle aloud with them. I ask them more questions and listen again carefully, but how can I know what sense they make? How long do their understandings last before they are changed, say, by a school practicum setting where they see a teacher teach social studies in yet another way? I think this discussion is helping me see that I need to develop some form of assessment (an essay they write analyzing the cases?) that can help me get a better idea about their thinking. Any thoughts on this?

At this point, the conversation begins to broaden out into the larger terrain of teaching. As reflective talk goes, this is pretty common. One set of ideas can lead to a wide scope of practice-related concerns. Because teaching results often are uncertain, you shouldn't be surprised that S. G. and Bruce end up reflecting considerably on their anxieties concerning this uncertainty.

SG: As usual, you make some nice points that help me think harder about what I do and why. But those points also raise more anxieties about whether or not I'm being as helpful as I can. I suppose you can't have one without the other, so let me try out a little more of my thinking on you.

First, I suspect you're right about the discomfort elementary school teachers seem to feel about teaching social studies. I wonder how much teachers' knowledge of social studies plays into their reluctance. I survey my class as to their undergraduate majors (remember that our teacher preparation program is largely at the post-B.A. level) on the first night of class. Few come with anything like a social studies major (for example, history, political science, sociology). Not only that, but most come with a pervading sense that social studies, and history in particular, is just one long and dull list of people, places, and dates. There's a double whammy: Not only do my students come with little content knowledge, they also come with few positive experiences as social studies learners. If that generalization holds for the wider population, no wonder many practicing elementary school teachers avoid social studies instruction if they can.

Second, on your point about your students wanting magic bullets, who doesn't? Even though we say several times in our book that there is no such thing, that doesn't stop me from wanting a plain and simple answer to the complicated messiness of teaching and learning. That messiness is truly why I love this field, but sometimes it's a big pain in the butt!

And that brings me to your last point about how to know what our students know. Sometimes, I think this is the most difficult job teachers face. Planning lessons and units is hard, but truly understanding what sense one's students make of those activities is a daunting task. And what makes it especially problematic is that, as you point out, teaching social studies offers no simple progression of ideas and skills. For example, I teach my students the commonplaces on the first night of class. At that point, I'm fairly confident that if I gave them a multiple-choice test (for example, The ___ commonplace deals primarily with students: a) learners and learning; b) teachers and teaching; c) subject matter; or, d) classroom environment), most would do pretty well. It's hardly enough, however, to be able to identify differences between subject matter and classroom environment. So, we keep coming back to these constructs in different contexts throughout the semester, each time (hopefully) stretching and deepening our understanding of them. That recursiveness—the idea of continually coming back to an idea—makes a lot of sense to me, but it also means that what my students know at any one time is likely to be different from what they know at another time. Determining if and when they finally get it is terribly difficult.

Like you, I raise a lot of questions in class and listen as hard as I can. I'd be interested in your thoughts about a couple other things that I also do. One is that I put my students in a lot of different situations, hoping that the more they talk about ideas, the more sense those ideas will make. For example, I like to use flexible grouping—partners and small groups—as well as whole-class settings to talk about ideas. My thought here is that those students who are reluctant to try out their thinking in the large group may be more likely to do so in more intimate settings. I also have students write about their ideas. Sometimes that takes the form of in-class fastwrites, but I also require that students keep a class journal. I like this because it's a good place for students to write about the readings and class discussions. I especially like it because students (and I) can look back and see how their ideas mature as the semester unfolds. Journals are a great source of insight into students' thinking, especially those students who may not say a lot in class. In addition, I require a reflective narrative as part of the course unit plan assignment. I like this because it provides a place for students to think back on what they've learned and to pull together some of the themes that stand out.

I like all these efforts, but to tell the truth, I still can't shake the feeling that I really don't understand what my students know, and maybe more importantly, what they will do with all this stuff once they begin teaching. What do you think?

Let's stop here and take a closer look at several features of reflection in general and this reflective conversation in specific. But first, take a moment to reflect on this e-mail conversation yourself.

TEACHER REFLECTION

What Should Reflection Consist Of?

What do you think of the exchange between Bruce and S. G.? Does it meet your expectations for productive reflection? How does it stack up against Dewey's ideas about reflection? Does it contain both the inward-looking and outward-looking elements?

Analyzing the Conversation: Five Types of Reflection

RELEVANT RESEARCH

In the section that follows, we reconsider our exchange above in light of Linda Valli's (1997) framework for understanding teacher reflection. Valli identifies five types of reflection which are: **technical reflection, reflection-in-action, deliberative reflection, personalistic reflection,** and **critical reflection** (see Figure 9.1 for summary definitions).

Technical reflection One common type of reflection, perhaps the most frequent in teacher talk about their practice, involves what Valli calls technical reflection. In this form, teachers try to answer the question "Did I use the right teaching method?" Bruce's concern over how he used the cases of the three teachers to spur discussion is, in some ways, an example of technical reflection.

Figure 9.1 • **Types of Reflection in Teaching**
(Adapted from Valli, 1997)

Type of reflection	Description
Technical reflection	Trying to answer the question "Did I use the right teaching technique?"
Reflection-in-action	Thinking about, assessing, and adjusting your practice as you teach
Deliberative reflection	Concerning yourself with a variety of issues involved in teaching, from subject matter and learners' understanding of it, to teaching method and its relationship to classroom milieu
Personalistic reflection	Using and expanding your personal knowledge and that of others to enhance growth as a teaching professional
Critical reflection	Focusing on the social, moral, and political dimensions of teaching and schooling

Bruce wonders if his method or technique—asking his students to grapple with issues related to which teacher's style they preferred and why—is the most effective in helping them think about the teachers they are and wish to become. S. G. subsequently presses Bruce to think more deeply about his practice.

Reflection-in-action Technical reflection is important, but it can be rather narrowly conceived. As we have noted throughout this book, and as our reflective conversation suggests, no method or technique really achieves magic-bullet status. Methods are context specific: You have to know your students. You have to adjust your methods as you go, sometimes in the thick of the action of actual teaching, or on the fly.

Valli describes this process as reflection-in-action. Teachers do this all the time, often without being entirely aware of it. Good teachers, we think, consciously and deliberately adjust their teaching methods, or pedagogy as class circumstances and learners' reactions dictate. Our reflective conversation above cannot provide examples of this because the discussion occurred in the week after the teaching episode. But good cases that describe in detail teaching as it proceeds (such as those of Lake, Palmer, and Atkinson) illustrate how this reflection-in-action occurs.

Deliberative reflection The conversation about Bruce's teaching episode contains considerable talk about what Valli refers to as deliberative reflection. This type of reflection covers a variety of issues involved in teaching, from concerns over subject matter and learners' understanding of it, to teaching method and its relationship to classroom environment. S. G. and Bruce reflect on the limited role social studies appears to play in the elementary school curriculum, on teachers' knowledge of social studies, and on their experiences of learning social studies. They also discuss various strategies for helping students to connect their prior knowledge to what goes on in class (for example, S. G.'s fast-writes, journals, and group work). Finally, they talk of assessing student knowledge and how difficult it is to construct good assessment tools to help teachers understand what sense students make of things. Each of these types of talk suggests a deliberative form of reflection. Deliberative reflection often arises from technical reflection if both are done intentionally. Technical reflection, as we noted, can be limited. Deliberative reflection opens up the terrain and serves to enhance what we learn from being reflective by encouraging talk about alternative teaching approaches and competing viewpoints. As a result, it can't help but improve practice.

Personalistic reflection A fourth type of reflective talk is what Valli calls personalistic reflection. Much of Bruce and S. G.'s conversation brings their own understandings into play. We referred to this earlier as looking inward. Both want to improve what they do. They talk about their personal understandings of what happens in their classrooms with their students in an effort to sort out the complexities of teaching. Each tries to use his own knowledge and that of the other to enhance his personal growth as professionals. This is a fundamental aspect of teaching. The practice of teaching is something we never quite master. We are always learners, seeking to become more capable educators. Personalistic reflection is crucial to this process.

Critical reflection Finally, S. G. and Bruce reflect on several dimensions of their teaching experience that have ethical repercussions. They both worry about the reduced role of social studies in elementary school and the possible impact that role may have on the intellectual and personal growth of youngsters. They express concern that the emphasis on other subjects such as reading and mathematics and the choices school districts make to put more resources into those subjects could effectively eliminate key social studies learning opportunities for students. They worry about how teachers may contribute to those losses if they value social studies less than other subjects because of their poor experiences with social studies. Valli calls to this type of exchange critical reflection because it focuses on the social, moral, and political dimensions of teaching and schooling. It centers on the goals and purposes of what teachers and schools do (or fail to do) that contribute to providing students with equal (or unequal) opportunities to learn.

These five different types of reflection—technical, in-action, deliberative, personalistic, and critical—all are important to the growth of professional teachers. None is really more important than the others. One focuses on looking inward (personalistic); the other four focus on looking outward. This probably reflects the right balance; teaching should be more about serving others—students, students' parents, communities, culture—than serving one's self.

Nevertheless, all five are fundamental. They simply serve different purposes and focus reflection on different aspects of teaching. We only tease them apart here to call your attention to their different features and goals, and to persuade you to engage all of them frequently and deliberatively.

TEACHER REFLECTION

Evolution of Reflection

Here again, take a moment to stop and think: What do you think about the ratio of reflectivity being one part inward looking to four parts outward looking? Do you agree with our claim here? Why or why not?

Consider this also: Some studies on how teachers learn to teach across their careers indicate that, for the first two to three years, new teachers focus almost exclusively on forms of personalistic reflection and only later aim their reflections on the other four types. What do you think of this? Granting the research point for a moment, why do you think reflection in learning to teach evolves this way, from inward-looking, personal forms to outward-looking ones? What might this mean for you as a new teacher?

SECTION SUMMARY Types of Reflection

- Reflection, both self-reflection and reflection with others, is a powerful means of improving one's teaching practice.
- Reflection takes many forms. *Technical reflection* focuses on whether or not the right teaching strategies were used; *reflection-in-action* emphasizes thinking about, assessing, and adjusting one's practice during the teaching act; *deliberative reflection* is concerned with issues such as teaching, subject matter, learners, and environment; *personalistic reflection* emphasizes the growth of personal knowledge; and *critical reflection* focuses on the social, moral, and political dimensions of teaching and schooling.

Reflection and the Social Context of Teaching

The most common approach in our culture to organizing schools is to build large buildings and to divide them up into smaller egg-crate-like units. We typically see lone teachers in classrooms with twenty to thirty students. This makes teaching a mighty solitary affair. On the one hand, many teachers enjoy the feel of greater personal autonomy over their practice. They can teach about the geography of the Great Plains, or the causes of the American Revolution, or the unique roles of people in our local communities whichever way they choose. On the other hand, some teachers feel quite isolated from professional camaraderie and collective knowledge sharing and thus remain fairly silent about what they do. We believe that few teachers want to be silent about their practices; we think those silences spring from how schools are organized and the teacher isolation that often results.

Breaking the Silences Around Teaching Practice

Our exchange regarding Bruce's teaching demonstrates the potential benefits of breaking through professional silence. Teachers are social creatures, and their professional growth and understanding is enhanced considerably when they talk with others who share in their commitments. In fact, some research suggests that the most powerful learning occurs in social contexts such as group discussions, small and large, and in one-on-one reflection exercises where the participants are knowledgeable and the focus of the talk is considered mutually shared and important by the discussants (Johnson & Johnson, 1987; Johnson, Johnson, & Holubec, 1993).

RELEVANT RESEARCH

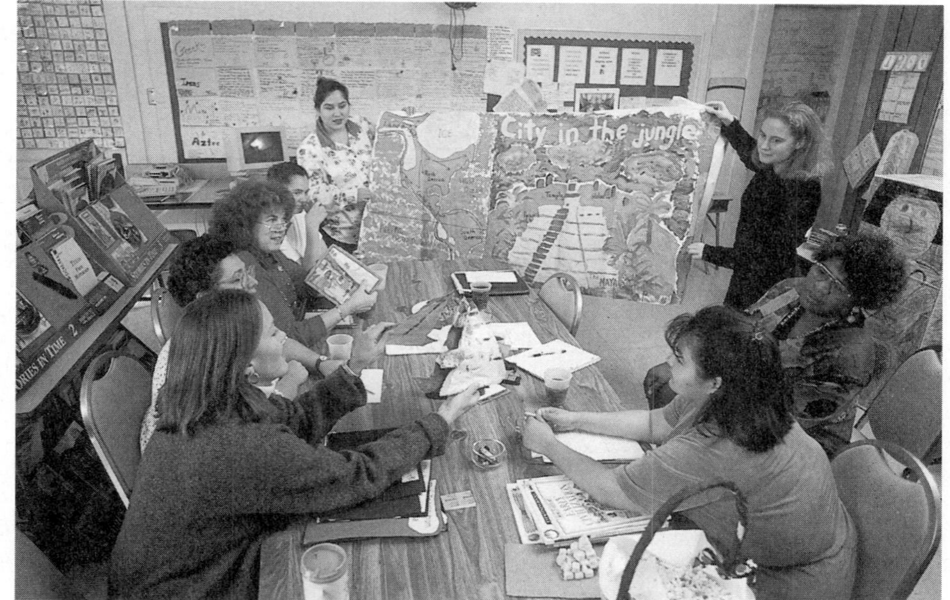

The power of teachers talking with one another is becoming recognized to the point where forward-thinking school administrators are encouraging and facilitating the development of teacher teams. The schedules of this group of second-grade teachers have been arranged such that they have two periods each week to meet together. During that time, they share new ideas and practices, review curriculum materials, discuss classroom problems, brainstorm solutions, and provide support to one another.

We encourage you to avoid the tendency toward professional isolation and the resulting silence about teaching practice. Engage in these various forms of reflection not only in your own thoughts, but *with others*—teachers, administrators, parents, and university professors—professional communities that strive to assist participants in enhancing their professional growth. We hope that you can locate such a reflective, conversational community.[1] If you find none readily available, create one with those who share your passions about teaching and learning.

TEACHING RESOURCES

Using Discussion Boards

To help break some of the silences around teaching, the National Council for the Social Studies has created an on-line discussion board where teachers can raise and conduct on-going discussions of an unlimited range of issues. You can find the discussion at the following web site.

- http://www.ncss.org/wwwboard1/wwwboard.shtml

TEACHER REFLECTION

Isolation Versus Collaboration

In your experiences observing teachers in school, do you see the isolation we discussed? Or do you see more collaboration between and among teachers, more sharing of ideas about teaching practice? If you have seen much more of the latter, what do you think accounts for the more collaborative processes you have witnessed? Do these more collaborative environments among teachers attract you or are they intimidating?

Reviewing Our Key Themes: Some Parting Thoughts

With all this talk of reflection, this is a good place to review some of the themes percolating throughout the preceding chapters.

The Commonplaces of Education

The first theme is the power of the *commonplaces of education*—learners and learning, subject matter, teachers and teaching, and classroom environment. Taken individually, each of the commonplaces provides a useful lens focused on a central dimension of your teaching practice. Taken together, however, they are even more powerful for they provide a wide-angle lens that is especially useful when tackling classroom problems, constructing teaching unit plans, and as we have seen above, reflecting on what one knows.

Constructivist Learning Theory

We introduced and explained a *constructivist theory of learning* social studies subject matter. We think this theory best explains how your students learn. Children are active, meaning-making human beings who are eager to make sense of the interesting ideas and topics you teach them. They come to you with already developing ideas about these topics based on their out-of-school life experiences. In the classroom, you will interact with the understandings they already possess as you help them construct and shape new ideas. Paying attention to children's prior knowledge by asking questions and listening carefully is crucial to knowledge construction and to your students' success as they make new meaning from the learning opportunities they encounter.

Big Ideas and the Subject Matter Threads

Third, we believe that working with *big ideas* in social studies is pivotal to powerful teaching. Social studies is a broad area filled with myriad facts and concepts and people and events. It's easy to get lost in a rather mindless effort to feed these into students as though all of them were equally important. The rub is that, even if they were indeed equally important (needless to say, we don't think they are), you would never find the time to teach all them well. Instead, you must pick and choose. We encourage you to focus on the big, rich social studies ideas that will lead to the most powerful learning experiences for your children.

This raises the important question about where to find the big ideas. You can find the beginnings of many such ideas among the *threads* of social studies, which draw on the disciplines of history and the social sciences. Not only do the threads offer potential big ideas, but the greater the number of thread linkages you make, the more powerful your social studies ideas will be.

Ambitious Teaching

A focus on *ambitious teaching* also plays a central role in what we have been advocating. As we have noted many times, much of what passes for social studies teaching and learning in public schools is vapid and lifeless. You can change that. We encourage you to pull out the stops, grab on to big, powerful social studies ideas, and invite and challenge your students to make sense of them. Social studies is a rich, fascinating, and mind-expanding subject matter, one that when taught well is deeply stimulating and wholly engaging to elementary school children.

Genuine Classroom Communities

We have suggested the importance of building a *genuine classroom community* with your students. Such a community is marked by the presence of big ideas and the discourse, classroom organization, and dispositions to pursue knowledge construction via individual and collective meaning-making. By the latter, we mean a community characterized by powerful learning opportunities, wherein children wrestle with the ideas, ask many questions and inquire into the subject matter, talk a lot to you and to each other about their emerging understandings, listen respectfully to new approaches and thoughts, and demonstrate deep interest and engagement in what you ask of them and what they in turn ask of each other.

Goal-Mindedness and Reflection

Finally, we believe that thoughtful teachers display two additional characteristics. One is that they are *goal-minded.* By this, we mean teachers who, despite competing views of what constitutes good citizenship and what it means to teach children about it, push themselves to construct a coherent and workable perspective that frames their social studies practice. We recognize that this is no easy task and that teachers' perspectives on such goal-oriented matters may well change over time and with experience. With that in mind, we offer the second characteristic of good teaching, namely, *reflection.* Reflective teachers do not know everything about teaching, learning, subject matter, and classroom environment. Who could? They do, however, know that their effectiveness as a teacher is rooted in their willingness to think hard, listen hard, and try hard to be the best teacher they can be. These are the teachers who most often experience the greatest compliment, the student who says, "Thanks. You really helped me learn." We hope you will strive to be that kind of teacher.

CHAPTER SUMMARY

1. What does it mean to be reflective?

To paraphrase John Dewey, reflection means the conscious, careful, and repeated thought about your beliefs and teaching practices with respect to the reasons that you claim support for them and with regard to how they influence what you might believe and do in the future.

2. What does reflection entail?

Reflection generally points in two directions. Personal growth generally develops as teachers look inward. Professional growth develops as teachers cast their gaze outward toward the people with whom and the contexts in which they work. Reflection can take many forms. It can be in a subvocal conversation you have with yourself in the mirror before school in the morning, or it can be in a conversation with another teacher who values open reflection on teaching practice.

3. What are the different types of reflection?

Linda Valli (1997) outlines five types of reflection: technical reflection, reflection-in-action, deliberative reflection, personalistic reflection, and critical reflection.

TEACHING RESOURCES

Print Resources

Fraenkel, J. (1973). *Helping students think and value: Strategies for teaching the social studies*. Englewood Cliffs, NJ: Prentice-Hall. An older, but still valuable discussion of approaches to teaching social studies.

Jackson, P., Boostrom, R., & Hansen, D. (1993). *The moral life of schools*. San Francisco: Jossey-Bass.

Tom, A. (1984). *Teaching as a moral craft*. New York: Longman.

These two books, both classics, explore the notion of teaching and schooling as moral endeavors.

Technology Resources

- **http://www.21ct.org/sit08_pub/owa/main**
- **http://www.k12connection.org**

These two sites, the 21st Century Teachers Network and the K-12 Collaborative, feature a wide range of materials, suggestions, and opportunities for teachers interested in advancing their professional growth.

NOTES

1. To read more on the power of conversational community, see Grant and VanSledright (1992).

Appendix

Children's Literature: Choosing Content Resources

In Chapter 5, we discussed the use of literature in the context of social studies units to help children develop a richer understanding of ideas than can be found routinely in textbooks. What follows is a listing of recent children's book titles, both fiction and nonfiction. We organized these books to correspond with the unit ideas we have described throughout the book.

The list that follows comes with two caveats. First, with so many children's titles available, this list is meant to be illustrative rather than exhaustive. And second, a list like this one soon becomes outdated as new titles are added each year. One good source of new books is *Social Education,* which publishes an annual review of children's titles.

American Revolution

Bober, N. (1995). *Abigail Adams: Witness to a revolution.* New York: Atheneum.

Cox, C. (1998). *Come all you brave soldiers: Blacks in the Revolutionary War.* New York: Scholastic.

Davis, B. (1992). *Black heroes of the American Revolution.* San Diego: Harcourt Brace.

Dolan, E. (1995). *The American Revolution: How we fought the war of independence.* Brookfield, CT: Millbrook.

Forbes, E. (1999). *Johnny Tremain.* New York: Bantam.

McGovern, A. (1975). *Secret soldier: The story of Deborah Sampson.* New York: Scholastic.

Bill of Rights/Citizenship

Fritz, J. (1987). *Shh! We're writing the Constitution.* New York: Putnam.

Johnson, L. (1992). *Our Constitution.* Brookfield, CT: Millbrook.

Levy, E. (1987). *If you were there when they signed the Constitution.* New York: Scholastic.

Quinn, C. (1987). *The signers of the Constitution of the United States.* New York: Bronx County Historical Society.

Quiri, P. (1998). *The Bill of Rights.* New York: Children's Press.

Swanson, J. (1990). *I pledge allegiance.* Minneapolis: Carolrhoda Books.

Canada

Aska, W. (1986). *Who hides in the park?* Toronto: Tundra Books.
Cohlene, T. (1990). *Little firefly: An Algonquian legend.* Mahwah, NJ: Watermill Press.
Garrigue, S. (1994). *Eternal spring of Mr. Ito.* New York: Aladdin.
Schwartz, N. (1997). *Crazy for Canada.* Downsview, ON: Tumbleweed Press.
Sorensen, L. (1995). *Visiting Canada.* Vero Beach, FL: Rourke.

Civil War

Beatty, P. (1989). *Charley Skedaddle.* New York: Troll.
Hansen, J. (1986). *Which way freedom?* New York: Walker.
Haskins, T. (1998). *Black, blue, and gray.* New York: Simon & Schuster.
Lincoln, A. (1995). *The Gettysburg Address.* Boston: Houghton Mifflin.
Lyon, G. (1991). *Cecil's story.* New York: Orchard.
Reeder, C. (1997). *Across the lines.* New York: Atheneum.
Reit, S. (1991). *Behind rebel lines: The incredible story of Emma Edmonds, Civil War spy.* San Diego: Harcourt Brace.

Colonization/Colonial America

Hall, D. (1983). *Ox-cart man.* New York: Viking.
Keehn, S. (1991). *I am Regina.* New York: Philomel.
Penner, L. (1991). *Eating the plates: A Pilgrim book of food and manners.* New York: Simon & Schuster.
Roop, C., & Roop, P. (Eds.). (1995). *Pilgrim voices: Our first year in the new world.* New York: Walker.
Sanford, P., & Ribblett, D. (1995). *Archaeology for young explorers: Uncovering history at colonial Williamsburg.* Williamsburg, VA: Colonial Williamsburg Foundation.
Speare, E. (1999). *Sign of the beaver.* New York: Bantam.
Turkle, B. (1969). *Thy friend, Obediah.* New York: Viking.

Family History

Adoff, A. (1973). *Black is brown is tan.* New York: Harper & Row.
Hazen, B. (1985). *Why are people different?* New York: Golden Books.
Floury, V. (1989). *The patchwork quilt.* New York: Dial Press.
Meyer, C. (1997). *Jubilee journey.* San Diego: Harcourt Brace.
Tax, M. (1981). *Families.* Boston: Little, Brown.

Immigration

Knight, M. (1993). *Who belongs here? An American story.* Gardiner, ME: Tilbury House.
Kuklin, S. (1992). *How my family lives in America.* New York: Simon & Schuster.
Lawlor, V. (Ed.). (1995). *I was dreaming to come to America: Memories of the Ellis Island oral history project.* New York: Viking.
Levine, E. (1994). *If your name was changed at Ellis Island.* New York: Scholastic.
Minh-Hoa, H., & Minh-Hoa, N. (1987). *The little weaver of Thai-yen village.* San Francisco, CA: Children's Book Press.
Mohr, N. (1999). *Felita.* New York: Puffin.
Paek, M. (1988). *Aekyung's dream.* San Francisco: Children's Book Press.
Sandler, M. (1995). *Immigrants.* New York: Harper Collins.
Surat, M. (1983). *Angel child, dragon child.* New York: Scholastic.

Maps and Map-Making

Barnes, B. (1998). *Which way to the revolution? A book about maps.* New York: Holiday House.
Gackenbach, D. (1989). *With love from Gran.* New York: Clarion.
Gershator, D., & Gershator, P. (1995). *Bread is for eating.* New York: Holt.

Hartman, G. (1993). *As the crow flies: A first book of maps.* New York: Aladdin.
Holling, H. (1984). *Paddle-to-the-sea.* Boston: Houghton Mifflin.
Taylor, B. (1993). *Maps and mapping: Geography facts and experiments.* New York: Kingfisher.
Tivers, J., & Day, M. (1994). *The new Viking children's world atlas.* New York: Viking.

Native Americans

Bruhac, J. (1993). *First strawberries.* New York: Dial.
Bruhac, J. (1999). *Eagle song.* New York: Dial.
DePaola, T. (1986). *The legend of the bluebonnet.* New York: Putnam.
French, F. (1997). *Lord of the animals: A Miwok Indian creation myth.* Brookfield, CT: Millbrook Press.
Goble, P. (1991). *Star boy.* New York: Aladdin.
Harjo, J. (1996). *The woman who fell from the sky: Poems.* New York: Norton.
Jeffers, S. (1991). *Brother eagle, sister sky.* New York: Dial.
Neihardt, J. (1992). *Black Elk speaks.* Lincoln, NE: University of Nebraska Press.
Ortiz, S. (1977). *The people shall come.* San Francisco: Children's Book Press.
Shermie, B. (1993). *Houses of bark.* Toronto: Tundra.
White Deer of Autumn. (1992). *The great change.* Hillsboro, OR: Beyond Words.
White Deer of Autumn. (1992). *Native American book of knowledge.* Hillsboro, OR: Beyond Words.

Rain Forest

Baker, L. (1993). *Life in the rain forest.* New York: Scholastic.
Cherry, L. (1990). *The great kapok tree.* San Diego: Harcourt Brace.
Cherry, L., & Plotkin, M. (1998). *The shaman's apprentice: A tale of the Amazon rain forest.* San Diego: Harcourt Brace.
Erbacher, J., & Erbacher, S. (1993). *Life in the rain forest.* New York: Cambridge University Press.

Slavery/Underground Railroad

Bial, R. (1995). *The underground railroad.* Boston: Houghton Mifflin.
Fleischner, J. (1997). *I was born a slave: The story of Harriet Jacobs.* Brookfield, CT: Millbrook.
Fox, P. (1973). *Slave dancer.* New York: Yearling.
Gorrell, G. (1997). *North star to freedom: The story of the underground railroad.* New York: Delacorte.
Johnson, D. (1997). *Now let me fly: The story of a slave family.* New York: Aladdin.
Lester, J. (1998). *From slave ship to freedom road.* New York: Dial.
Meltzer, M. (Ed.). (1995). *Frederick Douglass: In his own words.* San Diego: Harcourt Brace.
Wesley, V. (1997). *Freedom's gifts: A Juneteenth story.* New York: Simon & Schuster.
Winter, J. (1988). *Follow the drinking gourd.* New York: Knopf.
Yates, E. (1950). *Amos Fortune, free man.* New York: Viking.

Glossary

affective outcome—a desired goal that emphasizes students' personal development.

argument—the ability to make a series of points that build to a reasonable conclusion.

assessment—a general term used to describe approaches to understanding what students know and can do.

authentic assessment—activities designed to allow students to demonstrate their understanding in real and genuine ways.

autonomy—the relative freedom of teachers to make content, instructional, and assessment decisions in their classrooms.

B. F. Skinner—a psychologist who developed a range of theories in support of a behavioral view of psychology.

behaviorism—a psychological theory that explains behavior in terms of stimulus–response interactions.

big book—an oversized text, usually written by students.

big idea—a question or generalization that helps a teacher decide what to teach and how to teach it.

blank slate—the idea that children's minds are empty until someone inscribes something on them.

book talk—a brief presentation in which a student provides a synopsis of a whole book or a key element or concept.

brainstorming—a teaching strategy designed to elicit the widest array of ideas students can generate around a topic, question, or issue.

circle meeting—an activity where children and their teacher meet in a circle to discuss issues.

classroom management—the range of approaches teachers take to monitor and control children's classroom behavior.

classroom organization—the ways in which learning activities are structured.

cloze book—an activity where the teacher writes out the material she or he wants students to understand leaving spaces or blanks for key words and phrases that the children are to supply.

cognitive outcome—a desired goal that emphasizes students' academic or knowledge growth.

commonplaces of education—a conceptual framework consisting of *learners and learning, teachers and teaching, subject matter,* and *classroom environment* designed to help educators analyze classroom situations and understand classroom problems.

concept—a term for expressing a complex set of ideas, such as "change" or "justice."

conflation—the idea that children will mix historical details from one event with another.

constructivism—a psychological theory that asserts that people actively construct their understandings based on a wide range of internal and external influences.

cooperative learning—an approach to group learning that emphasizes specific roles and responsibilities for group members.

craft knowledge—those practices in which teachers regularly engage in the classroom.

critical reflection—a form of reflection that focuses on the social, moral, and political dimensions of teaching and schooling.

cultural toolkit—the knowledge that individuals and societies hold that enables them to function.

curriculum framework—see "curriculum guide."

curriculum guide—a generic term for a document that expresses a set of subject matter goals and objectives.

curriculum materials—a general term for a range of instructional resources, such as textbooks, trade books, maps, globes, and computer programs.

curriculum standards—documents produced by state and national entities that specify a course of study.

deliberative reflection—a form of reflection where one examines a variety of issues involved in teaching, from subject matter and learners' understanding of it, to teaching method and its relationship to classroom environment.

developmental stages—the idea that children progress through a series of clearly identifiable and mutually exclusive levels of intellectual growth.

dilemma—a classroom situation for which there is no one right or best solution.

discourse—the nature of the talk that occurs in a classroom.

discussion box—a receptacle located in a classroom into which children and their parents can deposit suggestions for class conversations.

Disney effect—the idea that children may take what they see in various media presentations as authoritative.

dispositions—the values and attitudes teachers and their learners create and practice during classroom activity.

empathy—the attempt to perceive a situation through the perspective of another.

evaluation—a particular form of assessment that emphasizes the judgment of students' efforts.

evidence—the support one marshals in defense of an argument.

expanding communities—a curriculum scope and sequence developed by Paul Hanna that grows outward from the student to the world.

fact—a means of expressing ideas that are provable and accepted by most people, such as "George Washington was the first president of the United States."

factory model of schooling—a conception of schooling in which teachers push students to accumulate as much knowledge as possible and then test them to see if they have succeeded.

genuine classroom community—a classroom environment where ambitious teaching is sensitive to the needs of learners and the subject matter and where discourse, classroom organization, and dispositions encourage the development of thoughtful, caring, active human beings.

goal—a specific aim that teachers hold.

goal framework—a cluster of aims that help teachers decide how to design learning opportunities, what the opportunities should consist of, when to put them in place and in what order, and how to explain why engaging these opportunities is important. In social studies, goal frameworks typically express a view of good citizenship.

good citizenship—although subject to many different definitions, this aim is a fundamental part of social studies education.

grading—the assignment of a number or letter evaluation to a piece of student work or a performance.

heterogeneous group—arrangement of students of mixed achievement.

historical fiction—a form of narrative that employs fictional and real characters to dramatize a historical event.

IRE—a form of classroom recitation that represents: teacher *I*nitiation—student *R*esponse—teacher *E*valuation.

individual assignment—an instructional activity designed to be done by each student independently.

informal assessment—the information collected in order to understand what sense learners are making of the material to date and to make instructional adjustments.

inquiry—the act of pulling ideas apart and putting them back together.

instructional strategies—the range of approaches teachers consider and use in planning and enacting their lesson and unit plans.

interdisciplinary—refers to the practice of linking ideas across subject matter and/or disciplinary boundaries.

issues-centered social studies—an approach to defining good citizenship that focuses on the need to address public issues.

jigsaw activity—an instructional activity in which each member of a small group becomes an "expert" on one idea, which she or he shares with other group members.

John Dewey—a philosopher who promoted, among other things, ideas about the linkages between learning and culture, and between children and subject matter.

journal—a notebook in which students make regular entries either based on a prompt offered by a teacher or on a personal reflection.

K-W-L—a teaching strategy that highlights what students *K*now, what they *W*ant to know, and what they have *L*earned.

learning center—an area designated within a classroom where teachers place a range of instructional materials and activities.

learning log—a folder where students can record their thoughts and ideas.

literature log—a notebook where students record their thoughts and ideas about the books they read.

Mercator projection—the representation of the world on a flat surface that is accurate only along the equator.

mini-lesson—a brief, teacher-led presentation that emphasizes a key idea that a teacher wants all students to attend to.

mind-extender project—an activity designed to push students' thinking beyond an in-class task.

multicultural education—an approach to defining good citizenship that focuses on creating a greater awareness of the ethnic and racial diversity of our culture.

narrative—a form of story that usually features a chronological and causal retelling of an event.

objective-type test—an assessment that emphasizes factual recall, such as multiple-choice, fill-in-the-blank, and matching questions.

open-ended task—an assessment that asks students to consider broader questions and to respond in more complete expressions, such as essays and journal entries.

organizational influences—factors such as roles and responsibilities, norms and expectations, and resources that can shape teachers' pedagogical thinking and actions.

pedagogical plan—a term that represents attention to instructional strategies, curriculum materials, and assessment.

pedagogical reasoning—the approach teachers take in transforming the curriculum into instructional representations that reflect attention both to the subject matter and the learners at hand.

performance-based assessment—activities designed to allow students the opportunities to demonstrate what they know and can do.

personal influences—factors such as teachers' knowledge, beliefs, and experiences that represent their lived experience.

personalistic reflection—a form of reflection that emphasizes using and expanding one's personal knowledge and that of the others to enhance growth as a teaching professional.

Piagetian theory—refers to the work of Swiss psychologist Jean Piaget, who argued that children pass through identifiable and age-dependent stages of intellectual development.

policy—documents such as curriculum frameworks, tests, and policy statements that can shape teachers' thinking and actions.

portfolio—a collection of student work used to demonstrate learning over time.

positive reinforcement—a reward for expected behavior.

posttest—an examination given at the end of an instructional unit to assess students' learning.

pretest—an examination given before any instruction to assess students' prior knowledge.

prior knowledge—the ideas, beliefs, and experiences that one brings to a new learning situation.

procedural knowledge—see "syntactic knowledge."

propositional knowledge—the accumulative ideas, concepts, and theories in an academic discipline.

psychic reward—the gratification teachers experience when they believe they have positively influenced learners.

recitation—a form of classroom discourse that emphasizes fact-based questions and answers.

reflection-in-action—a form of reflection that emphasizes thinking about, assessing, and adjusting your practice as you teach.

reflective practice—making decisions about the who, what, how, and why of teaching based on purposeful, ongoing introspection into alternative beliefs and choices available and with reference to future possibilities.

repair strategies—approaches researchers take in order to make text more comprehensible to students.

response—a reaction to a stimulus.

role-play—a teacher-created situation in which students assume roles different from those they normally play.

scaffold—a conceptual framework for understanding an idea, issue, or topic.

scope and sequence—see "curriculum guide."

Sigmund Freud—a psychiatrist who specialized in trying to understand the inner forces that shape people's behavior.

simulation—a teacher-created situation in which students are confronted with a series of problems and decisions.

small-group activity—an instructional activity in which children work together, usually in groups of two to five students.

social outcome—a desired goal that focuses on how students interact with one another.

social science disciplines—the formal study of subjects such as anthropology, geography, economics, political science, psychology, sociology, and international relations.

standardized test—an assessment of student learning developed by either state departments of education or by commercial test publishing companies that is given to large numbers of students.

stimulus—any catalyst for behavior.

story grammar—the elements of a narrative account.

structural factor—see "organizational influences."

substantive knowledge—see "propositional knowledge."

syntactic knowledge—the ideas people within academic disciplines hold about developing new understandings.

T-chart—an instructional activity in which students record their ideas, usually in a comparative sense, on a divided chart.

teaching strategy—see "instructional strategies."

technical reflection—a form of reflection that tries to answer the question "Did I use the right teaching technique?"

test-based assessment—see "evaluation."

think-aloud protocol—an approach to research where students are asked to talk about the sense they are making as they read a piece of text.

threads of social studies—a conceptual framework consisting of *geographic, political, economic, sociocultural,* and *global* concepts designed to help teachers think about and organize the content they teach.

topic—a means of labeling a large amount of information, such as "American Revolution."

trade books—a generic term for commercially published books, fiction or nonfiction, that are geared toward children.

traditional assessment—see "evaluation."

traditional classroom setting—a classroom environment where teacher-centered instruction focuses on the quiet, orderly, and individual acquisition of knowledge.

unit plan—a teaching plan of action.

whole-group activity—an instructional activity in which the entire class participates.

References

Adelson, J., & O'Neil, R. (1966). Growth of political ideas in adolescence: The sense of community. *Journal of Personality and Social Psychology, 4,* 295–306.

Afflerbach, P., & VanSledright, B. A. (1998, December). *The challenge of understanding the past: How do fifth-grade readers construct meaning from diverse history texts?* Paper presented at the annual meeting of the National Reading Conference, Austin, TX.

Angell, A. (1991). Democratic climates in elementary classrooms: A review of theory and research. *Theory and Research in Social Education, 19*(3), 241–266.

Ankeney, K., Del Rio, R., Nash, G., & Vigilante, D. (1996). *Bring history alive! A sourcebook for teaching United States history.* Los Angeles: UCLA.

Anyon, J. (1981). Social class and school knowledge. *Curriculum Inquiry, 11*(1), 3–42.

Banks, J. (1994). *An introduction to multicultural education.* Boston: Allyn & Bacon.

Barton, K., & Levstik, L. (1996). "Back when God was around and everything": Elementary students' understanding of historical time. *American Educational Research Journal, 33,* 419–454.

Beck, I., McKeown, M., & Gromoll, E. (1989). Learning from social studies texts. *Cognition and Instruction, 6,* 99–158.

Berti, A., & Bombi, A. (1988). *The child's construction of economics.* Cambridge, MA: Cambridge University Press.

Bluestein, N., & Acredolo, L. (1979). Developmental changes in map-reading skills. *Child Development, 50,* 691–697.

Brophy, J., & VanSledright, B. A. (1997). *Teaching and learning history in elementary schools.* New York: Teachers College Press.

Brophy, J., McMahon, S., & Prawat, R. (1991). Elementary social studies series: Critique of a representative example by six experts. *Social Education, 55*(3), 155–160.

Brophy, J., VanSledright, B. A., & Bredin, N. (1993). What do entering fifth-graders know about American history? *Journal of Social Studies Research, 16/17,* 2–22.

Bruner, J. (1996). *The culture of education.* Cambridge, MA: Harvard University Press.

Butts, R. F. (1980). *The revival of civic learning.* Washington, DC: Phi Delta Kappa Educational Foundation.

California Board of Education. (1988). *History-social science framework for the California public schools.* Sacramento: California Department of Education.

Center for Civic Education. (1994). *National standards for civics and government.* Calabasas, CA: Author.

Cherry, L. (1990). *The great kapok tree.* New York: Gloucester Press.

Clark, C., & Peterson, P. (1986). Teachers' thought processes. In M. C. Whitrock (Ed.), *Handbook of research on teaching* (3rd ed., pp. 255–296). New York: Macmillan.

Cohen, D. (1989). Teaching practice: Plus ça change . . . In P. Jackson (Ed.), *Contributing to educational change: Perspectives on research and practice* (pp. 27–84). Berkeley, CA: McCutchan.

Cohen, D., & Barnes, C. (1993). Pedagogy and policy. In D. Cohen, M. McLaughlin, & J. Talbert (Eds.), *Teaching for understanding: Challenges for policy and practice* (pp. 207–239). San Francisco: Jossey-Bass.

Coles, R. (1986). *The political lives of children.* Boston: Houghton Mifflin.

Connell, R. (1971). *The child's construction of politics.* Carlton, Australia: Melbourne University Press.

Cuban, L. (1984). *How teachers taught: Constancy and change in American classrooms, 1890–1980.* New York: Longman.

Delpit, L. (1988). The silenced dialogue: Power and pedagogy in educating other people's children. *Harvard Educational Review, 58*(3), 280–298.

Dewey, J. (1902/1969). *The child and the curriculum*. Chicago: University of Chicago Press.

Dewey, J. (1933). *How we think*. Chicago: Henry Regnery.

Dorros, A. (1990). *Rain forest secrets*. New York: Scholastic.

Dreikurs, R., Grunwald, B., & Pepper, F. (1971). *Maintaining sanity in the classroom: Illustrated teaching techniques*. New York: Harper & Row.

Edwards, A., & Westgage, D. (1987). *Investigating classroom talk*. Philadelphia: Falmer.

Ehman, L. H., & Hahn, C. L. (1981). Contributions of research to social studies education. *Eightieth yearbook of the National Society for the Study of Education*, (pp. 60–81). Chicago, IL: University of Chicago Press.

Eisenhart, M., Shrum, J., Harding, J., & Cuthbert, A. (1988). Teacher beliefs: Definitions, findings, and directions. *Educational Policy, 2*, 51–70.

Engle, S., & Ochoa, A. (1988). *Education for democratic citizenship: Decision making in the social studies*. New York: Teachers College Press.

Evans, R., & Saxe, D. W. (1996). *Handbook on teaching social issues*. Washington, D. C.: National Council for the Social Studies.

Farquhar, M. (1962). *Colonial life in America*. New York: Holt.

Fell, B. (1976). *America B.C.: Ancient settlers in the new world*. New York: Quadrangle/New York Times Book.

Finch, F. (1991). The blue and the gray. In D. Ravitch (Ed.), *The American reader: Words that moved a nation* (p. 159). New York: Harper Perennial.

Fitzgerald, F. (1980). *America revised*. New York: Vintage.

Fritz, J. (1977). *Can't you make them behave, King George?* New York: Coward-McCann.

Furth, H. (1980). *The world of grown-ups*. New York: Elsevier.

Gall, M. (1984). Synthesis of research on teachers' questioning. *Educational Leadership, 41*, 40–47.

Geography Education Standards Project. (1994) *Geography for Life: National Geography Standards*. Washington, DC: National Geographic Society.

Goodlad, J. (1984). *A place called school*. New York: McGraw-Hill.

Goodman, J. (1992). *Elementary schooling for critical democracy*. Albany, NY: SUNY Press.

Grant, S. G. (1996). Locating authority over content and pedagogy: Cross-current influences on teachers' thinking and practice. *Theory and Research in Social Education, 24*(3), 237–272.

Grant, S. G. (in press). An uncertain lever: The influence of state-level testing in New York State on teaching social studies. *Teachers College Record*.

Grant, S. G. (1998). *Reforming reading, writing, and mathematics: Teachers' responses and the prospects for systemic reform*. Mahwah, NJ: Lawrence Erlbaum.

Grant, S. G., & Tzetzo, K. (1997). Mixed messages and unanswered questions. *Theory and Research in Social Education, 25*(4), 521–531.

Grant, S. G., & VanSledright, B. A. (1992). The first questions of social studies: Initiating a conversation. *Social Education, 56*, 141–143.

Greene, B. (1995). *From forge to fast food: A history of child labor in New York State*. Troy, NY: Council for Citizenship Education.

Gregg, M., & Leinhardt, G. (1994). Mapping out geography: An example of epistemology and education. *Review of Educational Research, 64*, 311–361.

Haladyna, T., & Shaughnessy, J. (1985). Research on student attitudes toward social studies. *Social Education, 49*(8), 692–695.

Hanna, P. (1963). Revising the social studies: What is needed. *Social Education, 27*(4), 190–196.

Hansen, J. (1994). *The captive*. New York: Scholastic.

Hawkins, D. (1974). I, thou, and it. In *The informed vision: Essays on learning and human nature* (pp. 48–62). New York: Agathon Press.

Holt, T. (1990). *Thinking historically: Narrative, imagination, and understanding*. New York: College Entrance Examination Board.

Hirsch, E. D. (1987). *Cultural literacy: What every American needs to know*. Boston: Houghton Mifflin.

Hirsch, E. D. (1999). *The schools we need and why we don't have them*. Lake Forest, CA: Anchor Books.

Jahoda, G. (1984). The development of thinking about socioeconomic systems. In H. Tajfal (Ed.), *The social dimension* (Vol. 1, pp. 69–88). Cambridge, MA: Cambridge University Press.

Johnson, D., & Johnson, R. (1987). *Learning together and alone: Cooperative, competitive, and individualistic learning*. Englewood Cliffs, NJ: Prentice-Hall.

Johnson, D., Johnson, R., & Holubec, E. (1993). *Circles of learning: Cooperation in the classroom* (4th ed.). Edina, MN: Interaction Books.

Kalman, B. (1992). *A colonial town, Williamsburg*. New York: Crabtree.

Kozol, J. (1991). *Savage inequalities: Children in America's schools.* New York: Crown.

Kubelick, C. (1982). Building a just community in the elementary school. In L. W. Rosenzweig (Ed.), *Developmental perspectives on the social studies* (pp. 15–29). National Council for the Social Studies.

Ladson-Billings, G. (1994). *The dreamkeepers: Successful teachers of African American children.* San Francisco: Jossey-Bass.

Larkins, A., Hawkins, M., & Gilmore, A. (1987). Trivial and noninformative content of elementary social studies: A review of primary texts in four series. *Theory and Research in Social Education, 15,* 299–311.

Levine, E., & Johnson, L. (1993). *If you traveled on the underground railroad.* Washington, DC: Scholastic.

Levstik, L. S. (1989). Historical narrative and the young reader. *Theory into Practice, 28,* 114–119.

Levstik, L. (1993). Building a sense of history in a first-grade classroom. In J. Brophy (Ed.), *Advances in research on teaching* (Vol. 4, pp. 1–31). Greenwich, CT: JAI.

Levstik, L., & Barton, K. (1997). *Doing history: Investigating with children in elementary and middle schools.* Mahway, NJ: Lawrence Erlbaum.

Levstik L. S., & Pappas, C. C. (1987). Exploring the development of historical understanding. *Journal of Research and Development in Education, 21,* 1–15.

Liben, L., & Downs, R. (1989). Understanding maps as symbols: The development of map concepts in children. In H. Reese (Ed.), *Advances in child development* (pp. 145–201). New York: Academic.

Lickona, T. (1977). Creating the just community with children. *Theory into Practice, 16*(2), 97–104.

Loewen, J. (1995). *Lies my teacher told me: Everything your American history textbook got wrong.* New York: New Press.

Lortie, D. (1975). *Schoolteacher.* Chicago: University of Chicago Press.

Marshall, H. (1990). Beyond the workplace metaphor: The classroom in a learning setting. *Theory Into Practice, 29,* 94–107.

McCabe, P. (1993). Considerateness of fifth-grade social studies texts. *Theory and Research in Social Education, 21,* 128–142.

McCutcheon, G. (1981). Elementary school teachers' planning for social studies and other subjects. *Theory and Research in Social Education, 9*(1), 45–66.

McGowan, T., Sutton, A., & Smith, P. (1990). Instructional elements influencing student attitudes toward social studies. *Theory and Research in Social Education, 18,* 37–52.

McKeown, M. G., & Beck, I. L. (1990). The assessment and characterization of young learners' knowledge of a topic in history. *American Educational Research Journal, 27,* 688–726.

McKeown, M., & Beck, I. (1994). Making sense of accounts of history: Why young students don't and how they might. In G. Leinhardt, I. Beck, & C. Stainton (Eds.), *Teaching and learning in history* (pp. 1–26). Hillsdale, NJ: Erlbaum.

Moore, S., Lare, L., & Wagner, K. (1985). *The child's political world: A longitudinal perspective.* New York: Praeger.

Morgan, T. (1993). *Wilderness at dawn.* New York: Simon & Schuster.

National Board for Professional Teaching Standards. (1994). *Social studies-history: Draft standards for National Board certification.* Detroit, MI: Author.

National Center for History in the Schools. (1994). *National standards for world history: Exploring paths to the present.* Los Angeles: Author.

National Center for History in the Schools. (1996). *National standards for history, basic edition.* Los Angeles: Author.

National Council for the Social Studies. (1993). Definition of the social studies. *The Social Studies Professional, 114,* 7.

National Council for the Social Studies. (1994). *Curriculum standards for social studies: Expectations of excellence.* Washington, DC: Author.

National Council on Economic Education. (1997). *Voluntary national content standards in economics.* New York: Author.

National Geographic Society. (1994). *Geography for life: National geography standards.*Washington, DC: Author.

Naylor, D., & Diem, R. (1987). *Elementary and middle school social studies.* New York: Random House.

New York State Education Department. (1998). *Social studies resource guide.* Albany, NY: Author.

Nickell, P. (1992). "Doing the stuff of social studies": A conversation with Grant Wiggins. *Social Education, 56*(2), 91–94.

Ogle, D. (1986). K-W-L: A teaching model that develops active reading of expository text. *Reading Teacher, 39,* 564–570.

Parker, W., & Jarolimek, J. (1984). *Citizenship and the critical role of the social studies.* Washington, DC: National Council for the Social Studies.

Ravitch, D., & Finn, C., Jr. (1987). *What do our 17-year-olds know? A report on the first National Assessment of History and Literature.* New York: Harper and Row.

Schwab, J. (1978). The practical: Translation into curriculum. In I. Westbury & N. Wilkop (Eds.), *Science, curriculum, and liberal education: Selected essays* (pp. 365–383). Chicago: University of Chicago Press.

Shaver, J., Davis, O. L., & Helburn, S. W. (1980). An interpretive report on the status of precollege social studies education based on three NSF-funded studies. In National Science Foundation (Ed.), *What are the needs in precollege science, mathematics, and social science education? Views from the field* (pp. 3–18). Washington, DC: Author.

Shulman, L. (1987). Knowledge and teaching: Foundations of the new reform. *Harvard Educational Review, 57*(1), 1–22.

Silver Burdett. (1984). *The United States and its neighbors.* Morristown, NJ: Author.

Sleeter, C., & Grant, C. (1994). *Making choices for multicultural education. Five approaches to race, class, and gender,* 2nd ed. New York: Macmillan.

Speare, E. (1983). *Sign of the beaver.* Boston: Houghton Mifflin.

Taylor, M. (1976). *Roll of thunder, hear my cry.* New York: Penguin.

Turiel, E. (1983). *The development of social knowledge.* Cambridge, MA: Cambridge University Press.

Valli, L. (1997). Listening to other voices: A description of teacher reflection in the United States. *Peabody Journal of Education, 72,* 67–88.

Van Sertima, I. (1976). *They came before Columbus: The African presence in ancient America.* New York: Random House.

VanSledright, B. A. (1995). 'I don't remember—the ideas are all jumbled in my head': Eighth-graders' reconstructions of colonial American history. *Journal of Curriculum & Supervision, 10,* 317–345.

VanSledright, B. A. (1997). And Santayana lives on: Students' views on the purposes for studying American history. *Journal of Curriculum Studies, 29,* 529–557.

VanSledright, B. A., & Brophy, J. (1992). Storytelling, imagination, and fanciful elaboration in children's reconstructions of history. *American Educational Research Journal, 29,* 837–859.

VanSledright, B. A., & Grant, S. G. (1994). Citizenship education and the persistence of classroom dilemmas. *Theory and Research in Social Education, 22*(3), 305–339.

VanSledright, B. A., & Kelly, C. (1998). Reading American history: The influence of using multiple sources on six fifth-graders. *The Elementary School Journal, 98,* 239–265.

Wahlgren, E. (1986). *The Vikings and America.* New York: Thames and Hudson.

Wiggins, G. (1989). The futility of trying to teach everything of importance. *Educational Leadership, 47,* 44–59.

Wiggins, G. (1993). *Assessing student performance: Exploring the purpose and limits of testing.* San Francisco: Jossey-Bass.

Wilen, W., & White, J. (1991). Interaction and discourse in social studies classrooms. In J. Shaver (Ed.), *Handbook of research on social studies teaching and learning* (pp. 483–495). New York: Macmillan.

Wilson, S. M. (1990). *Mastodons, maps, and Michigan: Exploring uncharted territory while teaching elementary school social studies.* (Elementary Subjects Center Paper No. 24). East Lansing, MI: Michigan State University, Institute for Research on Teaching, Center for the Learning and Teaching of Elementary Subjects.

Wood, G. (1990). Teaching for democracy. *Educational Leadership, 48*(3), 32–37.

Index

Guide to the Special Features in This Book

CLASSROOM EXAMPLE

Real-life illustrations of powerful teaching will encourage you to incorporate similar strategies in your classroom.

RELEVANT RESEARCH

Knowledge of current research findings can help you make more effective decisions in the classroom.

TEACHING RESOURCES

An array of resources, including multimedia and Internet sites, are presented as potential tools to use when teaching social studies.

CLASSROOM MANAGEMENT

Learn tips on building a classroom learning community that supports thoughtful social studies teaching.

TEACHER REFLECTION

A range of questions, issues, ideas, and situations stimulate reflection upon and encourage your thinking as a teacher.

CHOOSING GOALS

Discover ways to create and follow up on teaching goals, within the context of the social studies classroom.